CATCH AND RELEASE

Catch and Release

The Enduring yet Vulnerable Horseshoe Crab

Lisa Jean Moore

NEW YORK UNIVERSITY PRESS

New York

NEW YORK UNIVERSITY PRESS
New York
www.nyupress.org

References to Internet websites (URLs) were accurate at the time of writing. Neither the author nor New York University Press is responsible for URLs that may have expired or changed since the manuscript was prepared.

Library of Congress Cataloging-in-Publication Data
Names: Moore, Lisa Jean, 1967– author.
Title: Catch and release : the enduring yet vulnerable horseshoe crab / Lisa Jean Moore.
Description: New York : New York University Press, [2017] | Includes bibliographical references and index.
Identifiers: LCCN 2017010865 | ISBN 9781479876303 (cl : alk. paper) | ISBN 9781479848478 (pb : alk. paper)
Subjects: LCSH: Merostomata.
Classification: LCC QL447.7 .M66 2017 | DDC 595.4/9—dc23
LC record available at https://lccn.loc.gov/2017010865

New York University Press books are printed on acid-free paper, and their binding materials are chosen for strength and durability. We strive to use environmentally responsible suppliers and materials to the greatest extent possible in publishing our books.

Manufactured in the United States of America

10 9 8 7 6 5 4 3 2 1

Also available as an ebook

This book is dedicated to my two inspirational friends,

Patricia Jeanne Wieger Curtis and

Patricia Marie Howells.

CONTENTS

Preface   ix

Acknowledgments   xvii

1. Fieldwork in the Mudflats   1

2. Endangered   31

3. Amplexed   68

4. Bled   94

5. Enmeshed   126

   Conclusion: From the Sea   155

   Notes   165

   References   175

   Index   187

   About the Author   197

PREFACE

I get irritated by a certain type of academic voice. I react at times with both envy and incredulity at the ability to make sweeping declarations about large-scale interconnected phenomena spanning time, space, and economies. These statements resound with a manly, assured forcefulness of Truth, and I nod along in supportive feminine pantomime. I secretly think: "How does he know that?" and "How can he say it so definitely?" Everyone else seems to buy it, so I shrug and go along.

The contemporary cultural meme of how men explain things, or mansplaining,[1] so diverges somewhat from my own reaction to this kind of academic voice. It is as if I hold out hope that I can do womansplaining, my own way of claiming a valued and respected voice, without having to be an annoying know-it-all. I want to be able to break out of the standard performance of scholar and be valued as a significant contributor, even if I am less declarative and more circumspect. And yet I certainly don't want my methodological rigor and status as a reliable narrator to be dismissed because I openly voice these internal dialogues. Instead of being seen as someone who produces knowledge in spite of this internal struggle, I want to deploy this struggle as an integral strength of my method and my scholarship.

Even as an undergraduate sociology student, I was drawn to symbolic interactionism, a theoretical and methodological perspective that examines the creation of social meaning. This sociological paradigm nourishes me at my intellectual core. I enjoy reveling in the creativity of meaning-making humans, learning and relearning the concept of the *definition of the situation*, and examining the unfolding human conflict inherent in wrestling with normative expectations. When making claims about my own research, I've always been more comfortable keeping my analysis on the level of the microsociological—symbolic interactionism's bailiwick.

My brand of qualitative research—immersion in a field site, long unstructured interviews with humans, learning new skill sets from indigenous knowledge producers—serves as the basis for my interpretations about social life. So, for example, being on a blistering hot urban rooftop with a beekeeper as she carefully explains how to do a hive check becomes the basis for my grounded theories about the social world of urban beekeeping and its cultural significance. And watching a lab technician observing sperm through a microscope and using a hand tally counter, I can understand how *sperm count* comes to be pragmatically and discursively quantified as a measure of a man. As in all my empirical work, rarely do I stray too far from my data to make grand claims, relying instead on informants' quotes for "evidence" of the claims I make. Deploying their words allows me to make larger observations—about human reproduction, the spread of disease, the world, or the climate—as a safeguard against my own grand theorizing or deploying my intellect.

When I signed the contract for this book, my lifeline and editor Ilene Kalish said, "Well, we don't think this book will have a very large profile. Especially if you don't answer any questions, just raise them." Ouch. She referred to my previous books and my ambivalence in adding my voice to large-scale sweeping claims. Am I an academic wimp imprisoned by my femininity? Do I hedge my bets rather than stake my place as a knowledge producer? A dear friend encouraged me, after reviewing multiple drafts of my work, to liberate myself from my tendency to quote or genuflect textually to others. Why do I feel so uncertain about "proving something," having a conclusion, or making a point? I do understand the critique, yet I can't manage to wholeheartedly embrace the epistemic authority of making definitive statements rather than raising important questions.

Perhaps I am a day late (2 decades?) and a dollar short in trying to amplify my voice as a "knowledge producer"—someone who makes definitive statements about FINDINGS. During my graduate school years

in the 1990s, the swirling debates about human subjectivity and epistemology generated lively discussions of who has the permission to access and create knowledge. In particular, we examined what qualifies a
scholar as "legitimate," especially one from an "othered" position. We
analyzed the feminist philosopher Nancy Hartsock's now oft-quoted la-
ment about the plight of so many of us: "Why is it that just at the moment when so many of us who have been silenced begin to demand the
right to name ourselves, to act as subjects rather than objects of history,
that just then the concept of subjecthood becomes problematic?"[2] We
were attempting to come to terms with the opportunity to contribute to
epistemology from our situated perspectives while simultaneously acknowledging that subjectivity itself was being dismantled.

As much as I want to join the club of those who can make larger
pronouncements with the heft to back them up, to add to epistemology,
there is always a tacit asking of permission, a split-second hesitation, or
an implied qualification. The pleasures and dangers of reflexivity, adding the anecdotal reflection, can break up my inner tension. Instead of
just saying something specific and firm, I opt to reveal some internal
ambivalence couched in a humorous story. Writing from my own voice,
grounded in my painstaking qualitative immersion, seems both self-
indulgent and elusive in its legitimacy. This hand-wringing does feel
particularly human, probably bourgeois, and most definitely feminine—
similar to the ubiquitous apologizing of my sex. Perhaps this is what
womansplaining looks like?

Thinking with Tenderness

While I am tentatively taking steps to move into, if not grand theorizing,
at least less molecular theorizing, the clear waters of epistemological authority have been muddied by urgent calls to acknowledge our
"becoming with nonhuman animals."[3] Just as Harstock called to inter-
rogate the politics of the "death of the subject," I now must confront
my humanness as yet another position of superiority in knowledge

projection. Getting a handle on my humanness and my ability to speak from my standpoint has been a grind.[4] Ever so slowly, I've grown to proffer contingent feminist epistemological and empirically grounded claims. But this is further complicated by my recent turn toward non-human animal ethnography—multispecies ethnography. No longer is it simply a matter of contributing to knowledge—if creating epistemology is level 1, the academic field is now at level 2: the re-emergence of, and reckoning with, ontology. The travails of knowledge production have in some ways become subordinated to matters of ontology. I believe it is only through these interactional, entangled, minute observations and speculations that I can begin to contribute to the literature on climate change, geologic time, conservation ecology, and biopharmaceutical industry. I do this through my examination and movement toward an engaged becoming with horseshoe crabs.

At first the idea of having to take in more subject positions and ontologies while simultaneously re-evaluating my own position in a system of stratification (this time with animal others) became almost too much to handle. But ultimately, horseshoe crabs have offered me another fascinating and very personal opportunity. Through knowing and being with horseshoe crabs I have discovered again my voice as one co-produced through polyphonic contributions of willing, unwilling, and unknowing others, animal and human.

In what follows, I explore the entanglements of horseshoe crabs and humans—how these becomings, these assemblages, these social worlds of intraactions between crabs and people enable us to understand the world in a fresh way. *Catch and Release* is a book that has allowed me to take more risks with making claims and thinking beyond the microsociological. At the same time it has forced me to pay very close attention to the micro-intraactions between crabs, the sand, the water, humans, time, tides, and biomedicine. I am using the term "intraactions" from my reading of the feminist science studies scholar Karen Barad.[5] Intraactions are a "mutual constitution of entangled agencies"—that is, the horseshoe crabs and humans materialize from within their relationship with one another. Moving from interaction, whereby humans and horse-shoe crabs exist independent from one another, my analysis attempts to show how they become co-constitutive of one another.

This work is also decidedly political. Perhaps because of my training in feminist and queer studies, I am struck by the ways in which we humans perceive ourselves as other in relation to nature. This is a thoroughly constructed concept in which we separate ourselves from non-human animals in order to systematically exploit them (as well as the environment). Even when we express a desire to protect nonhuman animals or ecosystems, it is commonly in the service of human interests—they are extrinsically but not intrinsically valuable. In previous work on bees, sperm, and clitorises, I have investigated the narratives about the interrelationships between humans and body parts, and humans and animals, to generate ideas about the narrators and their relationships to animals/nature. I believe it is possible to shift our ingrained hierarchical way of understanding and relating to nature/nonhuman animals by engaging in intraspecies mindfulness. This practice of intraspecies mindfulness, the constant situating of ourselves in a mesh instead of a hierarchy, allows for a natural empathy to unfold between humans and nonhuman animals (and the greater environment).[6]

I've slowly and sometimes painfully come to understand that my feminine socialization, an insecure femininity, is in many ways an asset. Wrestling with my own positionality as a knowledge producer has meant that I privilege the process of knowing versus the final product of what is known—once and for all. I work to understand how historical and contingent findings are actually powerful, more so perhaps than grand pronouncements. I am a tender thinker who doesn't always think I know what's right, and I use this reflexive tentativeness to create a more textured and nuanced interpretation of the social and natural world and how we come to know it.

Encountering Horseshoe Crabs

After completing *Buzz* with Mary Kosut, a book that explored urban beekeeping,[7] I was excited to continue examining the ideas that emerged from that project. Specifically, I wanted to explore intraactions between humans and animals in urban settings. Horseshoe crabs emerged as a possible species since they are available to me in Brooklyn, and they have so many applications in human worlds. The fact that I had been encountering horseshoe crabs since I was a child bolstered my intellectual interest.

Becoming with horseshoe crabs has truly been a constant thread running through the course my life. I grew up sharing the ecological habitats of the horseshoe crab as I recklessly "played" with them on the beach as a child. As an adolescent, I feigned marine expertise and showed off my fearlessness to my shrieking peers who were unfamiliar with the burrowing prehistoric crab. As a new parent, I introduced the crabs to each of my daughters in turn, living out maternal dreams of instilling courageousness, intelligence, and reverence. Raising three girls in Brooklyn, I want them to have some sense of Donna Haraway's naturecultures, within which we co-exist.[8] In other words, I want us (the girls, myself, other people) to figure out how to be better neighbors with all of Earth's inhabitants. I've used the crabs as a conduit to do that work by making the kids aware of the crabs' existence and how to momentarily ease their suffering. For example, the girls know to flip over the crabs when they are on their backs so they don't dry out.

As a sociologist, during the fieldwork and writing of this book, I've mined these memories, and in bringing them out into the light of day, I've realized that horseshoe crabs have always been a part of who I am. This book is an articulation of that understanding, one in which I explore how I've come to know myself and the crabs—and a speculation on what this becoming with means to me and to broader interspecies relationships.

My early investigations to determine the feasibility of this project led me to some truly serendipitous connections with expert scientists.

Mark Botton, the marine biologist I follow most closely in this project, is on the faculty of Fordham University and conducts much of his field-work at Plumb Beach in Brooklyn, where I live. Because I met Mark and Christina Colon of Kingsborough Community College, my project was able to pick up steam, enabling me to gain entrée and rapport with Jennifer Mattei of Sacred Heart University (Connecticut). I especially admire Jennifer's brilliance at making her intellectual and scientific work part of larger projects of ecological restoration. These scientists invited me to attend international meetings of horseshoe crab experts in Japan. At these meetings, I met even more individuals who became informants for my project. Later, during another field visit, I traveled to Cedar Key, Florida, and interviewed Jane Brockmann and Mary Hart while I participated in a 3-day horseshoe crab–tagging workshop. To understand the invaluable role of conservation and population dynam-ics, I interviewed Gary Kreamer, aquatic resources educator for Dela-ware Fish and Wildlife, and Dave Smith of the Leetown Science Center, U.S. Geological Survey, who offered astute expertise. While attending a celebration of Carl Shuster's instrumental work in horseshoe crab sci-ence and conservation, I met Ron Berzofsky, who provided background on the pharmaceutical industry. Tom Novitsky has been an invaluable and patient contact for me, in particular for helping me understand horseshoe crab blood.

Beyond attending these professional and scientific events, I also spent a lot of time in the field—on the beaches of Brooklyn and Long Island's South Shore. I learned to find and identify juvenile crabs during my time with Mark, and I discovered how easily these fieldwork skills be-came part of my own leisurely walks on the beaches with my daughters. Reaching down and finding juvenile horseshoe crabs the size of small pebbles or stones, nestled in the sand, is an immediate and visceral re-minder that we share space with ecological others. Far more than just a clever environmental parlor trick, demonstrating the variable meanings of habitat—to and for whom—literally means to tread lightly: It matters where we step.

Horseshoe crab on Plumb Beach, 2014. Photo by Lisa Jean Moore.

ACKNOWLEDGMENTS

This research has been supported through the generosity of grants from Purchase College through a Doris and Carl Kempner Award and State University of New York Faculty Support Awards. Additionally, the Third International Workshop on the Science and Conservation of Horseshoe Crabs provided supplemental funding to attend the meetings in Sasebo, Japan, in June 2015. My union, the United University Professors, also supported my fieldwork through Joint Labor-Management Committee grants. Suzanne Kessler, dean of Natural and Social Sciences; Linda Bastone, chair of Natural and Social Sciences; and Chrys Ingraham, coordinator of Sociology, made my scholarly endeavors more achievable.

This work could not have happened without the patience, brilliance, and dedication of several environmental and natural scientists. One of the most rewarding benefits of extended fieldwork is getting to know people I would not ordinarily meet. Mark Botton has been a thoughtful, generous, and compassionate teacher and guide through the global horseshoe crab universe. He has also read every word of this book and greatly improved it. Smart, innovative, and committed scientists constantly inspire me; the immense wisdom they have imparted to me to me is deeply appreciated—most especially from Jennifer Mattei, Christina Colon, Jane Brockmann, Mary Hart, Ron Berzofsky, Dave Smith, Tom Novitsky, and Yumiko Iwasaki. John Tanacredi and Sixto Portillo welcomed me for a visit to their Center for Environmental Research and Coastal Oceans Monitoring at Molloy College in Long Island. Special thanks to Jane Brockmann and Tom Novitsky for offering close readings of chapters and their scientific expertise.

I am most grateful to my intrepid writing group. Jill Weiss, Megan Davidson, Andrea Long Chu, and C. Ray Borck have each contributed to my confidence as a writer and my ability to make my ideas meaningful across disciplinary divides. A lawyer, a doula, a feminist philosopher, and a sociologist make a good team. I am so lucky to have been able to work with this group of humans, and I look forward to continuing sharing of our very different but intertwined projects every other week. Extra gratitude goes to C. Ray for the beautiful hand-drawn and painted illustrations.

I am also fortunate to have many magnificent colleagues at Purchase College and beyond. Jason Pine has never failed to talk me off the ledge and remind me why this work is important; he makes me a better thinker. I'm so glad to continue conversations beyond our intellectual collaborations with the whip-smart Mary Kosut. Shaka McGlotten has an uncanny ability to say precisely the right thing at the right time. Jan Factor and George Kraemer both provided introductions and access to their scientific colleagues and vouched for me as I entered the field. Matthew Immergut, Alexis Silver, Liza Steele, Chrys Ingraham, and Kristen Karlberg make me happy to be a sociologist at Purchase College. Each has added to the strength of my analysis. In particular, Alexis Silver gave cogent feedback at a critical juncture. For skillful library magic and speedy responses, I thank the invaluable Darcy Gervasio. Monica Casper, my longtime collaborator and dear friend, enriches my life—both professionally and personally. My critical animal studies colleagues and students John Hartigan, Eben Kirksey, Liz Cherry, Anna Krol, Kyle Moran, and Jeffrey Mathias help me work through the pesky persistence of humanism. Mal Blum and Leah Wellbaum provided musical assistance. The Animals and Society Section of the American Sociological Association has been an intellectual home to me for the last few years, and I am grateful for the connections I have made.

I am blessed to have the most remarkable network of human friends, in particular Patty Howells, who originally suggested this project and has lovingly read every word, and Patti Curtis, my dearest friend and soulmate. I've dedicated this book to these two Patricias. I've also been blessed with Mira Handman, my pillow-talk companion; Pat Evans, who cheered me on at a particularly tricky spot; and Robyn Mierzwa, who collaborates on two very special lifelong projects. Sally Rappeport, Tine Pahl, and Shari Colburn have all offered perfectly timed support to me throughout this project. In a moment of anxiety during revisions, Laura Brahm generously read sections of the work.

I have worked for over a decade with New York University Press, publishing several books under the intelligence and grace of Ilene Kalish. Again and again I return to Ilene's advice, "Good writing is rewriting." Special thanks to Caelyn Cobb for editorial assistance.

Finally, I'd like to thank my family. When I fell down the stairs with an open computer, my brother-in-law Kel Currah didn't judge me; he just went out and bought me a new one. My aunt, Joan Pendergast, is my fairy godmother with no compare. My parents, Linda and Richard Moore, are responsible for introducing me to horseshoe crabs and making sure I had access to them every single summer of my childhood and beyond. My daughters are my unqualified joy: Grace helped me think through some of the more scientific complexities of this book, Georgia enthusiastically participated in muddy fieldwork, and Greta cheerfully pointed out horseshoe crabs in any possible location. My husband, Paisley Currah, understands me like no other. Once, during a particularly difficult moment of self-recrimination, Paisley reassured me, "No, you aren't terrible, you're just human." Like a mantra, I return to that phrase over and over again. It reassures me, makes me remember my own species being and my connection to all flawed others. It is important to remember I am just human, and it is amazing to remember I am a human being connected to his human being.

1

Fieldwork in the Mudflats

Balancing six baby horseshoe crabs in my hand, I rotate my wrist to keep them all in my palm. They are wriggling and jostling one another, trying to get some traction on my skin. Taken from their nestled watery mound into my clammy human hands, being held above their home in the dusky sea breeze must be strange. My feet are deep in the muck of the tidal flat, squishing sandy silt between my toes. The late summer sun fades behind me. I feel alive and excited by my fieldwork site. The thrill of being outside with the crabs is invigorating, different from the usual anxiety I feel before an interview with a merely human informant, anxious that any misstep could jeopardize my rapport or entrée. These horseshoe crabs are my reason for being here, I tell myself, but is it just an excuse to enjoy another day at the beach, filthy as this urban shoreline is? I think, feel, and become with the vibrant matter around me—the bubbling of my sinking feet, the tickling of the tiny crab legs, the burn of the sun on my back. I revel in the odors and sounds, the smell of the sulfury tidal flats, the calls of the shore birds, the hum of the Belt Parkway.

* * *

What has drawn me to this beach, month after month, year after year? I have shifted my focus from all things human—body fluids, anatomies, sexuality, interpersonal relationships—to insects and animals—bees, horseshoe crabs. Many friends, colleagues, and family members have asked me why I am researching horseshoe crabs since I am a sociologist, not an ecologist or marine biologist. Sometimes my answers betray my exasperation, and I stumble over my words. I recount the greatest hits of horseshoe crab talents, their capacities, their use in human applications, their exploitation. Yet, over time, I have come to resent the question.

Holding baby horseshoe crabs in the palm of my hand. Photo by Lisa Jean Moore.

I feel as if I am being asked to convince humans that another species can matter and be worthy of concern as either a surrogate or a product for humans. The arrogance of the sentiment "Tell me why you care so I can decide if I care" frustrates me. I want to protest that the foundational "What's in it for me?" query is the basis for the very human exceptionalism and capitalist consciousness that has gotten us into this environmental mess: global warming, massive species extinction, estrangement, disenchantment, alienation. And then I come back to relative calm, realizing that I must gradually build a case for the horseshoe crab. Just as it was a process for me to understand how an ontologically based interpretation of things can have its own intrinsic value, I must now translate that process for others. Generally, the way to garner that interest, concern, or empathy is to bring it back to the human, the self.

I have been handling horseshoe crabs since I was a child on the beaches of Long Island, New York. Running down the shore, telson— the tail—in hand, I terrorized my little brother. No compassion toward the crab as it bucked back and forth gesticulating its legs in a desperate attempt to defend itself. Separating amplexed—attached—crabs was also a favorite early summertime activity, and in my youthful stupidity and human hubris I asserted how I was helping the crabs to "stop fighting." Through endless summer days, we'd have contests to see who could throw the crab further into the sea, our own version of playing horseshoes. Torture of animals is a sign of certain psychopathologies in children, and if it had been kittens we tossed into the sea by their tail, my parents would have certainly intervened—but the horseshoe crab raised not an eyebrow. My re-introduction to the crab, many years later, makes me shudder at my callous girlhood antics. When I began this research project in 2013, perhaps it was some sort of psychic penance for the sins of my former self.

Beyond a sentimental attachment to crabs, much later in life I become aware of horseshoe crabs' vast contributions to human life through their sacrifice for biomedicine, fishing, and evolutionary theories. As I have written this book, horseshoe crabs have transformed my awareness of the world. They are both materially wondrous as well as symbolically generous. Observing the crabs, their habits, movements, growth, I've come to appreciate the shoreline in a new way. Like honeybees, horseshoe crabs are designated an *indicator species*, a biological species that provides useful data to scientists monitoring the health of the environment. Through associations and extrapolations, scientists are able to track the migration, health, and fertility of other species and can infer the sustainability of habitats. Indicator species, also known as sentinel species, are useful for biomonitoring ecological health, and horseshoe crabs can serve as a proxy for the health of shorelines. If the horseshoe crabs leave, migrate, or die, that indicates that the environment is degraded. I, too, have come to see the horseshoe crab as signifying larger ecological and sociological trends—rising seas, biological interdependence, geologic time.

My study centers on interviews with over 30 conservationists, field biologists, ecologists, and paleontologists and over 4 years of fieldwork (2012–2016) at urban beaches in the New York City area; natural preserves in Nagasaki Prefecture, Japan; and marine research sites in Cedar Key, Florida.[1] In *Catch and Release*, I explore the interspecies relationships between humans and horseshoe crabs—our multiple sites of entanglement and enmeshment as we both come to matter. As I show, crabs and humans are meaningful to one another in particular ways. Humans have literally harvested the life out of horseshoe crabs for multiple purposes; we interpret them for understanding geologic time, we bleed them for biomedical applications, we collect them for agricultural fertilizer, we eat them as delicacies, we capture them as bait. Once cognizant of the consequences of harvesting, we rescue them for conservation, and we categorize them as endangered. In contrast, the crabs make humans matter by revealing our species vulnerability to endotoxins,[2] a process that offers career opportunities and profiteering from crab bodies, and fertilizing the soil of agricultural harvest for human food. In these acts of harvesting, horseshoe crabs and humans can apprehend important ecological events: geological time shifts, global warming, and biomedical innovation. My work situates the crabs within my own intellectual grounding in sociology; however, this sociological perspective is not seamless, it is rife with debate.

A major contribution of sociologists to contemporary thought is our production of theories and methods to determine, measure, and interpret social stratification and human inequity. Any introductory sociology course worth its weight provides students with critical thinking tools to examine race, class, gender, sexuality, age, and ability as social constructs that constrain our lived experiences. Armed with sociological insights to understand racism, classism, sexism, heterosexism, ageism, and ableism, the student explores how personal feelings are entangled with structural location. As a sociologist, I've made my living analyzing, teaching, and investigating aspects of human inequity, but I've recently come to consider the ways we determine the relative status, rights, or power of nonhuman animals. For instance, how do we explain how our companion animals—any cohabiting dog, cat, fish, or hamster—rank more highly than those pesky pigeons, rats, or roaches? What are the mechanisms we use to justify the relative worth of animals "scientifically proven" to be "closer" to us—such as gorillas, chimps, and other primates—versus those deemed more strange and distant—such as crickets, rattlesnakes, or frogs? The domination of humans over all other beings has created an assumption that our species has more value and, thus, has the right to act upon other species in our own interest. *Speciesism*, the belief in the inherent superiority of one species over others, was coined by the British psychologist Richard Ryder in *Victims of Science: The Use of Animals in Research* and popularized by the Australian philosopher Peter Singer.[3]

Speciesism is not just a ranking system of humans over all animals. Rather, humans create an even more specialized way of determining the worthiness of an animal—worthy of our care, our protection, our attention, and our love. How much we care seems to be very closely associated with how we regulate our scientific research and handling of animals. During an all-day visit to several shoreline field sites in Connecticut, the conservation ecologist Jennifer Mattei and I engaged in a philosophical discussion about the relative compassion for shorebirds compared to horseshoe crabs. I asked why so many seem to rank birds above the horseshoe crab. "It's because it doesn't have a backbone," she instantly replied. I laughed, thinking she was joking and that the answer had to be more complicated than that. Although she was driving, she turned to make eye contact, and said, "I could crush a horseshoe crab, and no one would care, but if I did it to a bird, I would be arrested. Any research with animals with a backbone has all these protections. It's total human bias that things more like us [require] more protection than things not like us." I nodded, coming to terms with the fact that maybe it was as simple as that. She continued, "Who cares about a spider when they don't have as many neurons as us and can't feel what we feel? It's the whole vertebrate-invertebrate divide."[4] Jennifer is right in the fact that the lack of a spine has had serious implications for the social status of the horseshoe crab and other invertebrates. Insisting that a backbone is required to feel pain creates a definitional absolute that leaves horseshoe crabs and other animals in an impossible position. Their responses to injurious stimuli are interpreted as something other than affect—a reflex—and as such, compassionate care does not need to be rendered. Despite mounting evidence,[5] this popular and intransigent belief among many humans that animals without backbones do not feel pain influences our dismissive treatment of 95% of the total number of species on earth.[6] But returning to horseshoe crabs specifically, what are the other distinguishing characteristics of this species?

Horseshoe Crab Biology and Anatomy

The ocean-dwelling horseshoe crab of North America, *Limulus polyphemus*, is a strange-looking animal. It crawls along the ocean floor with its maroon helmet-like hard-shelled top, the *carapace*, made of chitin and proteins. It has 10 "eyes" and six pairs of legs and claws underneath. In addition to its two compound lateral eyes, its other eyes are light-sensing organs located on different parts of its body—the top of the shell, the tail, and near the mouth. These eyes assist the crab in adjusting to visible and ultraviolet light and enhance adaptation to darkness in various environments, aquatic and terrestrial.[7] A crab uses a nonpoisonous 4–5 inch hard tail, called a *telson*, to steer or right itself when it is overturned.[8] The telson is dragged in the sand as the horseshoe crab lumbers along the shoreline. Adult crabs weigh 3–5 pounds and are 18–19 inches in length from head to tail for females (males are a few inches shorter). They can live for about 20 years. During spawning, they are either on the beach around high tide or swimming in 2–3 feet of water. When not spawning, they crawl along the bottom of the ocean at depths of 20–400 feet.[9] On the shore, they are "slow and easy to catch" making them an ideal species for field biologists to study and to engage students.

Despite their spiny and spiky exterior, they are also comical to human eyes. As described by the biologist Rebecca Anderson, the first time she worked with horseshoe crabs she "pretty much fell in love with them because they look like these fearsome creatures with armored bodies and all their legs, but they are ineffectual as defenders. And they look so adorable when they walk on land." It is difficult for most humans to observe horseshoe crabs in the water, but they have been described as "rather graceful compared to their tank-like appearance when they come to the shore."[10] Omnivorous creatures, they eat mostly clams and worms. They do so by crushing and grinding their food with their legs—or, more accurately, their knees—and shoveling the food into their stomach.

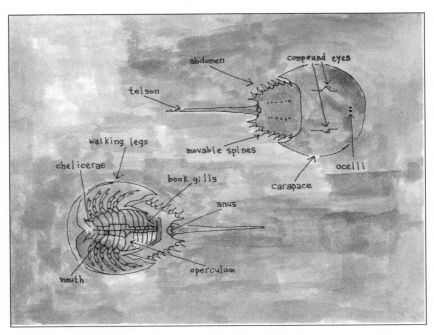

Anatomical illustration of the horseshoe crab. Illustration by C. Ray Borck.

Globally, there are four species of horseshoe crabs living on the continental shelf—one in North America, *Limulus polyphemus*, and three in Southeast and East Asia. The three species of horseshoe crab in Asia are *Tachypleus gigas*, *Tachypleus tridentatus*, and *Carcinoscorpius rotundicauda*.

Some humans have been drawn to the horseshoe crab because it unlocks secrets about the "sea of life." With a fossil record to verify its ancient lineage, the horseshoe crab is among the oldest old. According to geologist Blazej Blazejowski, when traced by looking at modification by descent, crabs haven't changed morphologically over tens of millions of years and as such are *stabilomorphs*, organisms that are morphologically stable through time and space. Their closest relatives are trilobites, which lived from 510 millions years ago. Amazingly, the horseshoe crab has survived longer than 99% of all animals that have ever lived.[11] One of the reasons the species have survived for so long is because of the composition of horseshoe crab blood cells called *amoebocytes*. The blood is copper based, and when it hits the air it turns blue. Because of the chemicals in the ameoboyctes, the horseshoe crab's blue blood coagulates when it detects contamination. This instantaneous reaction to threat through clotting protects the animal from harm. It is this very quality of their blood, the ability to transform into a biopharmaceutical gel, that has been used to insure the safety of all injectables and insertables in human and veterinary applications.[12]

These ancient species are also remarkable because they are primarily aquatic, coming onto the shore for spawning and nesting for brief periods every year. Indeed, if we accept the anthropologist Stefan Helmreich's definition—"the alien inhabits perceptions of the sea as a domain inaccessible to direct, unmediated human encounter"—then horseshoe crabs are aliens.[13] Unlike many domesticated animals or pets, these aliens are not intimately knowable since their primary place of residence is uninhabitable by humans. Adding to their alien-ness, horseshoe crabs are not easy for the layperson to categorize. They live in the sea, but some suggest they look like spiders. They are sometimes attached—"amplexed"—to one another. (You find yourself asking, *Is one of them a baby? Is it catching a ride? Are they fighting? Are they mating?*) They are prehistoric, and yet they seem so vulnerable. On land, they are practically defenseless, writhing helplessly when upside down with their fragile bits exposed to hungry birds.

Contrary to their name, horseshoe crabs are not true crabs. They are not even crustaceans. Taxonomically they belong to the same broad category that crustaceans do, the phylum Arthropoda—meaning that as invertebrates they have no backbone or inner skeleton; they have jointed legs and a hard outer shell, an exoskeleton, which protects a soft body. Horseshoe crabs are chelicerates, belonging to the same group that includes ticks, spiders, and scorpions.

After spawning during high tides in March through July, the North American species buries its eggs, which develop within the beach sediments after a couple of weeks to reach the trilobite (first instar) larval stage.[14] They become reproductive adults after 16–17 molts or 8–10 years—which is slow growing for a marine invertebrate. Molting is the process of shedding the old shell and emerging from it with a new body. At first this body is soft and small, but it will swell with water and increase in size as the shell hardens.

Significantly, humans have been able to breed crabs in captivity, but they cannot get them to live beyond their tenth molt—at that time the crabs die instead of surviving through the remaining 6–8 molts and becoming reproductive adults. Scientists do not understand why this might be so.[15] Our inability to replicate "natural conditions" for horseshoe crabs means that their reproduction must be primarily studied in the wild. In my experience studying horseshoe crabs when they spawn, there is a great deal of physical contact between humans and crabs. Picking up crabs is relatively simple since they do not pinch, bite, or sting. And they are not too fragile to be handled. As the biologist Mark Botton, one of my key informants, describes them, "They are tough, and ancient, and in many ways indestructible. They are the perfect species to teach undergrads about field biology since they are so easy to catch."

A female horseshoe crab returning to the water at high tide on Plumb Beach, Brooklyn. Photo by Lisa Jean Moore.

Another of my informants, the esteemed horseshoe crab scientist Jane Brockmann, adds, "What I like about them is that they are predictable. Breeding on the new and full moon high tides makes it pretty predictable. So you can take a class out there and expect to find something."

My Intellectual Path to Horseshoe Crabs

Sociology, as a discipline, is historically indebted to humanism. In the Western tradition, the human is viewed as the ultimate social/rational/political being: one that is able to perceive the world, think about it, and communicate about that world back to others. The doctrine of humanism affirms the existence of a thinking ego, a self, or an I—the fact that we all share the ability to conceptualize our own respective selves demonstrates a sort of harmonious connection among us, which in turn demonstrates our superiority over all other entities, living and nonliving. For centuries, scholars have explored the role of consciousness and reason as the foundation of our autonomy. We are the only beings who are capable of giving anything meaning or of exerting our influence within the world. Humanism is a vexing philosophy because it is both liberating—freeing us from supernatural explanations over which we have little control—and damning—bogging us down in endless debates about who gets to count as "human." Sociology has made its business studying (un)harmonious connections, investigating the dynamics of social order, social problems, social organization, social control, conflict, and cooperation. But in the process, sociologists have overwhelmingly privileged humans in their analyses and interpretations.

As I was trained in the humanist traditions of sociology's sub-field of symbolic interactionism, my original research studies took the human as the starting point of all methods of inquiry. I am a feminist medical sociologist who was educated in grounded theory in the early 1990s by Adele Clarke, and I have occupied this strange position of not really fitting in as a legitimate member of either the sociological or cultural studies worlds. "She's not sociological enough," I've overheard more than a few times—particularly because my work resists quantification toward overarching meta claims, rules, or laws about "society." And at the same time, my use of methods is often suspicious to cultural studies folks who fear it is a form of nonreflexive data generation and Truth (with a capital T) claims. Since my methods act toward the world as if it exists, no matter how it is constructed, I start my projects with what I consider to be material realities. These are contested, politically, and heterogeneously represented realities, and yet they are still material realities. I have shown that honeybees die, clitorises disappear in genital anatomy textbooks, and sperm counts decline. Understanding how we co-produce the conditions of these material realities and then work to interpret them is, in part, my job.[16]

I came of age intellectually at the time of what some academics called the "Science Wars," which were characterized by fervent debates about scientific truth claims and social constructionism—as well as the rise of queer theory and the influence of interdisciplinarity and, more specifically, cultural studies in social science. I learned how to become a qualitative sociologist through methodological training that rejected strict adherence to positivism or the creation of singular and universal social facts. At the same time, my empirical training demanded that I measure things by relying on vaguely positivist tools to categorize and apprehend the social world. For example, establishing categories for sexual identity for an interview questionnaire required lengthy in-class debates about the formation and rejection of certain static, singular categories or statuses—endless debates about "What is a lesbian? What is bisexual?" The solution was "self-identification," a sort of work-around to avoid a priori categories. Yet still, when conducting the interview, the informant was asked, "What is your sexual orientation?" And when writing up the analysis of the data, informants were neatly placed in categories as if they were self-evident and transparent—measurable, real, and singular. In other words, the category of "lesbian" always became reified or real in the process of trying to make it emergent through informants' own words.

Over the last several years, my work has shifted toward a decidedly posthumanist frame where I feel the work resonates with the intellectual project of new materialism that considers all matter (human and nonhuman, objects, nature, technologies) as having agency or the ability or potential to make action happen. The move from humanism and speciesism means that relationality is not just between human beings but between humans and animals or between horseshoe crabs with one another, the sand, the sun, the tides. In particular, I frame this book as part of the new materialist writings exemplified by the work of feminist scholars such as Karen Barad, Mel Chen, and Jane Bennett.[17] These scholars' work demonstrates the active participation of the nonhuman and human, the animate and inanimate in social life and social order. Posthumanism de-centers the human being as the foundation of all ontological inquiry, challenges the self-anointed autonomy of the human species as rational selves, and seeks to construct a multifaceted idea of what it means to become human. Feminist new materialism, a form of posthumanism, engages with the relationship of matter to social and cultural interpretations. Matter is commonly understood as something distinct from our thoughts and sacred meanings; it is commonly defined as something that occupies space and has mass. Theorists in this area explore the ontology, or essence of being, of matter as deeply consequential for how the world comes to be known and enacted.

Horseshoe crabs and I are entangled in a world of becoming; as we intraact, we make each other up. As *Catch and Release* argues, human and horseshoe crab bodies materialize based on our interdependent relationships—polluting resources, generating commerce, exploiting medical capacities. We are enmeshed in heterogeneous worlds of the local, urban, global, ecologic, and geologic. In my earlier book, *Buzz*, Mary Kosut and I discuss how honeybees and humans are entangled in a world of pesticides, global food production, urban renewal, and species disintegration.[18] The human/honeybee nexus also reveals our entanglement in a toxified world of interdependence. The cultural theorist Cary Wolfe, borrowing from Haraway's cyborgs, argues that we have become fundamentally "prosthetic creatures" with an ontology that has "coevolved with various forms of technicity and materiality, forms that are radically 'not-human' and yet have nevertheless made the human what it is."[19] For example, I come to matter in collaboration with the honeybees that pollinated my food and worked to shape the industrial food supply. And even if I had never apprehended a horseshoe crab, they have fertilized the land before me and changed biomedical production, just as I have circumscribed the bees and crabs lives and bodies through my enactments of being human and using resources.

The animal familiars, including horseshoe crabs, who make us what we are, companion species who have helped stabilize our bodies, and our selves, remain entangled in complex multispecies worlds.[20] For those of us whose health is fostered by government and corporate apparatuses, we exist in our current form as human because horseshoe crab blood has deemed our biomedicalization safe. Quite literally, our inoculated, pharmacologically enhanced, vaccinated bodies exist in their current status through a collaborated becoming with horseshoe crabs.

Anthropologist Claude Lévi-Strauss is often paraphrased as stating that "animals are good to think with." Here he means that human's interpretations of animals can offer very fruitful structures and frameworks for generating concepts and establishing larger connections between ways of thinking. Humans use animals to think with when we create metaphors and similes—"she's as busy as a bee," or "he's as brave as a lion"—or when we manufacture sports mascots. More specifically, academics use animals to think with as a means of understanding sociality. In my own collaborative work with bees and even in some ways with my research on sperm, I have used these nonhuman entities to reveal meta-level analysis about contemporary masculinity and types of endangerment.[21]

Social theorists are not the only ones, or the first, to see the wisdom in deep engagement with animals. While attending the celebration of the work of the 96-year-old Carl N. Shuster, Jr., the world's leading authority on North Atlantic horseshoe crabs, in June 2016, I was struck by his captivating combination of philosophical, naturalist, and artistic sensibilities while speaking about horseshoe crabs. "You want to know what's going on with the crab, you ask it. Heck, you want to know what's going on with the ocean, you ask a crab, too. You have to get down there with them, and just watch them and for a long time. Over a long time, you will start to know things."[22]

Horseshoe crabs *are* good to think with. In *Catch and Release* I make many connections among our contemporary biomedical, geopolitical, and ecological environments while also pushing my analysis and method to show we must move beyond seeing the bee, or the sperm cell, or in this case, the horseshoe crab as merely a lens that reflects and refracts human life. *Rather I argue that, not only are the crabs among us, but they are also in us (through their blood), and they are in many ways becoming us as we are becoming them.* I rely on meditations on my methodological choices and fieldwork notes to illustrate this enmeshment.

From both a scholarly and personal position, I muse about the ways our fates are in some ways deeply entangled, and yet the crabs reveal deep human vulnerabilities—to toxins, the climate, the ocean, and time.

Human Exploitation of Crabs

Catch and Release investigates and grapples with these questions: How do humans exploit the crabs, come to depend on them, and fret about their welfare? How is it that humans are simultaneously saviors and villains in stories about the crabs? Have the crabs met their match in humans after 480 million years, or are humans, in their speciesist ignorance, insignificant to the crabs' geologic legacy?

As a qualitative sociologist, my method of investigating these questions is to be with the crabs and the people who work with them. In the summer of 2015, I attended the Third International Workshop on the Conservation of the Horseshoe Crab in Sasebo, Japan. I share my field notes from the first day:

Fighting my bleary-eyed jet lag and fitful sleep on a tatami mat, I finger through my registration packet for the Third International Workshop on the Science and Conservation of the Horseshoe Crab. I am sitting on a generic conference chair in a hotel ballroom in Sasebo, Japan, scoping out the fellow humans. Attending mostly sociology and gender studies academic meetings in my professional life, where colleagues routinely complain about the lack of heterogeneous representation, it is interesting to see such a diverse audience of humans. I'm not sure there is any one dominant ethnic group in this crowd of natural scientists, conservationists, ecologists, and wildlife educators. I smile at the man next to me, looking down at his name tag—Jaime Zaldívar-Rae, Anahuac Mayab University, Merida, Yucatan, Mexico. He nods to the stage, as opening remarks are just beginning. A slightly hunched Japanese man in a loose-fitting suit is helped up the steps. The 87-year-old Mr. Keiji Tsuchiya is a former middle school teacher who dedicated his life, in part, to horseshoe crab conservation. He is a founding member of the Nippon Kabutogani wo Mamoru Kai (Japanese Society for the Preservation of the Horseshoe Crab). During his presentation, Mr. Tsuchiya speaks about the origin of his "love" for horseshoe crabs. As a 17-year-old drafted soldier, working off the shore of Hiroshima, he recounts through a female translator, "I saw a flash, heard loud sounds, and saw a mushroom cloud, and then all the sudden it was very dark and I could only smell burning." Once he arrived on the shoreline, Tsuchiya navigated through the burning structures to help line up victims side by side and vividly recalls the cries of "Give me water, sir." Pausing dramatically to choke back tears, Tsuchiya shares, "I can still hear the words of victims in their last moments begging for water."

After the recovery efforts, he continued his career training to be a middle school teacher.

Then in 1961, he witnessed 10,000 crabs dying on the beach because they missed the tides to return to the sea. This experience made a serious and lasting impression on Tsuchiya. He joined the Kasaoka-shi Kabutonagi Conservation Center, where he worked for many years. Although I speak no Japanese, his passion is obvious as he grips the podium: "This mass horseshoe crabs death occurred because they were drying out and asking for water." Raising his finger, he continues, "This memory of the atomic bomb where people were asking for water sounded just like the horseshoe crabs to me. 'Water, water, please give me water, sir.' It is the same. And since I have dedicated my life to love and conserve horseshoe crabs and to being a nuclear-free peace activist." He then steps aside from the podium and says in English, "I love horseshoe crabs." Two hundred international horseshoe crab experts jump to their feet and applaud.

* * *

The purpose of *Catch and Release* is to examine the myriad ways horseshoe crabs dramatically merge with human lives and how these intersections steer the trajectory of both species' lives and futures. Again and again, I illustrate how we are enmeshed. Sometimes, as in the experience of Mr. Tsuchiya, intraactions are framed in the spirit of a companion species—but overwhelmingly, as explored throughout the book, horse-shoe crabs are constructed and used as an exploitable resource. And still horseshoe crabs have a mighty past, suggesting a certain invulnerability, whereas comparatively humans are temporary. More on this later.

I detail Mr. Tsuchiya's story because I was and continue to be struck by how he puts horseshoe crabs on the same ontological plane as humans—both are worthy of similar grief. I could imagine some people finding this strange. To many, the comparison between human victims of a notorious nuclear bomb with beached, drying out horseshoe crabs can seem outrageous or callous. Standing in the ballroom, I did find myself looking around at those applauding and wondering if any of them thought it a strange opening to the meeting. These were mostly scientists, after all—pragmatic, humanist, positivist. Most of them were accustomed to using horseshoe crabs as research objects where pain and death were possible outcomes. And yet it was clear the audience was touched—emotionally in sync with Mr. Tsuchiya's story and able to tap into a sense of compassion for the crabs and their struggles.

One of the humans in that audience was the biologist Bob Loveland. During a smaller meeting in New York City, Bob explained the modern periodization of the horseshoe crab. The first threat to the horseshoe crabs occurred at the beginning of the last century, when the local populations of crabs began to decline precipitously. In the United States, horseshoe crabs were hand harvested and ground up for agricultural use until being replaced by chemical fertilizers in the 1950s.[23] After a measurable dip in their numbers, the population bounced back in the 1970s. Today, harvesting horseshoe crabs for use in agricultural fertilizer industry is no longer practiced in the United States.

The second threat began in the 1990s and is ongoing. Crabs are caught by fishermen to use as bait for eels (*Anguilla rostrata*) and whelks (*Busycon carica* and *Busycotypus canaliculatum*) and are worth an impressive 5 dollars each.[24] In the United States, the harvesting of crabs is supposedly controlled, limited and managed through a patchwork of intra- and interstate regulations including those by the Atlantic States Marine

Fisheries Commission and the Gulf States Marine Fisheries Commission. Despite these regulatory apparatuses, many of my informants believe there is great variability in enforcement, and as a result, there are several reports of a black market in horseshoe crabs.

The third and not insignificant threat to horseshoe crabs is their harvest for biomedical use. The crab's blood is used to create *Limulus* amoebocyte lysate (LAL). Since the 1970s, in order to get approval from the Food and Drug Administration (FDA) for any pharmaceutical product such as injectable, implantable, or biological/medical devices, there must be an LAL test conducted to detect any possible bacterial contamination.[25] These tests have become biomedical standards in mandated pharmaceutical testing protocols. There are fears of international poaching of North Atlantic horseshoe crabs as Asian species dwindle and biomedical demand grows. Currently in the United States, for biomedical purposes, horseshoe crabs are caught, bled, and released. As discussed at the meetings in Japan, since there is no catch-and-release practice in China, crabs are caught and bled to death. I call this *catch and kill*. Once the Asian horseshoe crabs are extinct, some researchers worry, there is potential for a black market in North American horseshoe crab blood and international poaching.[26] (This use of horseshoe crabs is explored in chapter 4.)

The fourth threat to crabs is the loss of habitat occurring through what Loveland identifies as the "ongoing sea level rise and our response to it." Horseshoe crabs are a type of sentinel species signaling the strain of environmental stressors, the rapidity of ecological degradation, and how human engineering might exacerbate downward trends.

Intraspecies Mindfulness with Horseshoe Crabs

A large part of my qualitative research over 4 years has been working at Plumb Beach as a research assistant to Mark Botton, a marine biologist at Fordham University, and Christina Colon, a conservation biologist at Kingsborough Community College. They have taught me how to do

On the tidal flats at Plumb Beach, collecting juvenile horseshoe crabs in a plastic take-out container as part of a timed count. Photo by Lisa Jean Moore.

census counts of horseshoe crabs. Additionally, they trained me how to assess the quality of a horseshoe crab carapace and how to identify the fouling organisms, or animals, that attach to carapaces. Over the years, I have become friendly with Mark and Christina, and I hope my participation in the fieldwork adds an additional intellectual aspect to their biological and ecological interventions. Over the years, I think I have also developed a skill for quickly finding juvenile horseshoe crabs in the sandy and muddy estuaries, which I describe below.

* * *

From my field notes representing a typical day of horseshoe crab field biology:

It's August 13, 2015. We are doing a juvenile count in the mud flats at Plumb Beach. I'm dressed in rubber boots, waterproof shorts, a tank top, and a floppy hat. Feeling cocky, I tell Christina that I will collect more crabs in our timed task, placing juveniles into a plastic take-out container for subsequent measurement. The four of us—Mark, Christina, a graduate student, and I—separate. Mark says "go" and I crouch down in the muddy sand, distinguishing between the mud snail and baby horseshoe crab trails. It takes me several times to tell the difference between these tracks in the sand, but now I am becoming more skilled. I sift quarter- to dime-sized mounds of sand under inch-deep water to find the babies. I plop them in the container and crawl down to the next area. With little regard to the crabs' experience, I feel happy. I am doing my job well, urged on by the side challenge to move quickly. Looking down, my container is full of crabs upside down, sideways, bending to and fro.

Taken from their wet, gritty, dark, and solitary self-fashioned mound, the crabs jostle against one another and the plastic slippery container walls. I

Mark Botton using calipers to measure juvenile crabs as I record their size on a data sheet. Photo by Lisa Jean Moore.

scurry about feeling a tiny bit of accomplishment at each crab I identify and capture. "Time," Mark shouts, and I run over to see who has more. Christina's container is definitely more full than mine, and I concede. We then measure each crab with calipers. Afterwards I put each individual crab back to the water, away from one another but several feet from where they originally were lodged.

After a few hours, I leave the beach. Driving home through Brooklyn, I think about whether or not I really connected with the crabs. The audacity of this thought process makes me laugh—who am I kidding? As if those crabs and I had any communion? I had no conscious thought about them other than as numbers to be added to my pile, then numbers to be written on a chart, later to be added to a spreadsheet, and finally quantified to some sign of health of the species on this spit of land in Brooklyn. Is that really going to make a difference to any individual crab? To the species? Probably not, I think. And yet, it could.

* * *

Animal studies scholars address the role of interactions and intersubjective exchanges between human and animals in social worlds and within their research processes.[27] This scholarship and research in critical animal studies wrestles with the human tendency toward anthropocentrism in our thinking about and acting toward the world. Anthropocentrism is a belief system or way of thinking that regards humans as the center to all existence above all other living things. This perspective slips into thinking of nonhuman beings as inferior to humans, and as such, anthropocentrism is akin to racism, sexism, and classism. In other words, anthropocentric thinking requires the same stratified value judgments as when we see certain types of people (men, white people, able-bodied people) as more worthy than other people (women, people of color, or people with disabilities). Critical animal studies implores us to challenge our anthropocentric worldviews through our scholarship and practices.

Much of the important work in this focuses on pets like dogs and cats, the mammalian domestic companion animals with which we have intimate encounters.[28] Moving from mammals, the anthropologist Hugh Raffles's *Insectopedia* explores our close encounters with insects and uncovers the vast continuum of insect/human entanglements—from being assaulted by malarial mosquitoes in the Amazon to betting on Chinese cricket fights.[29] In *Catch and Release*, I am a sociologist seeking to understand the experiences of horseshoe crabs. Even though I can't completely set aside my human standpoint, I can attempt to engage with "crabness" and to dwell in the strangeness of the ontology of another species. And while my attempts ultimately don't result in my being a crab, the work of trying does shift my consciousness, fostering a more attentive collaborator. At the same time, I reckon with my own and others' epistemological productions—the suppositions of what we know about the crab. Through this I try to begin to move further away from the socially constructed distinctions between human and animal, knowing and being, and the nature/culture binary. In many ways the title of this book, *Catch and Release*, refers to this larger project of simultaneously catching and releasing actual crabs and also the feeling of being always on the cusp of apprehension of another species. I am continuously cycling through catching, apprehending or knowing certain facts about horseshoe crabs, and then releasing, letting go, or refining those facts through the ontological experience of being with the crabs.

Engaging in the intersections between humans and crabs and entertaining the possibility of an ontology of other objects—sand, beaches, gravel, water, surgical tubing—enables us to reposition them through de-centering ourselves. This multispecies ethnography expands upon the methodology I developed with Mary Kosut in *Buzz: Urban Beekeeping and the Power of the Bee*. Multispecies ethnography is a new genre and mode of anthropological research seeking to bring "organisms whose lives and deaths are linked to human social worlds" closer into focus as living beings, rather than simply relegating them to "part of the landscape, as food for humans, (or) as symbols."[30]

Elsewhere Kosut and I have proposed an ethics of intraspecies mindfulness, a concept that was further developed in our shared scholarship.[31] Intraspecies mindfulness is a practice of speculation about nonhuman species that strives to resist anthropomorphic reflections or at least be aware of them as a means of empathetic understanding. It is an attempt at getting at, and with, another species from inside the relationship with that species instead of from a top-down relationship of difference. In our practices with bees, Kosut and I used our own sensory tools of seeing, hearing, touching, tasting, and smelling bees—their bodies, their habitats, and their products. Getting with the bee meant acquiring new modes of embodied attention and awareness. Getting at the bee has also meant that we must confront the reality that the human species is always and everywhere enmeshed with the bees—they pollinate our food, changing our agricultural landscape, and we transform their habitats (and our own).

Our creation of the term and practice of *intraspecies mindfulness* is drawn from the work of Karen Barad.[32] Again key to my work is also the term *intraaction*, in which materials come into being through the mutual constitution of entangled agencies. This approach requires that as fieldworkers we interrupt our tendency to think of animals as the object of study and that we resist thinking of ourselves, or the animal handlers (in this case, scientists and conservationists) as static, bounded, and permanently fixed entities. Instead, we need to see all—ourselves, crabs, scientists, and other objects—as bodies that are in the world and whose boundaries are created but also porous. These boundaries are managed through entanglements and conflicts. In fieldwork, I worked to treat each experience as an opportunity to witness this emergence of intraaction. Each moment was a chance to see the crabs and humans in intraaction, constituting each other in their own humanness and crabness.

In this research project, I not only perform a study of how scientists and crabs make each other but also a study of how I, as an examiner of scientists, make something of this studying of crabs. It is recursive in that I am reflecting on my own knowledge production as different from, and yet entangled in, the production practices of the scientists whom I accompany. *Catch and Release* is complexly layered in interpretation—my particular involvement in multispecies ethnography (in which I practice science very much like a scientist proper) gives me a unique advantage, perspective, distance. and proximity. I am an ethnographer sociologist apprehending and communing with crabs, and I am a scientific practitioner investigating how scientists work with crabs. Simultaneously, as each chapter reveals, I am an urban commuter adding emissions to the earth with a scandalous diesel Volkswagen automobile. I'm a mother bringing my sometimes-reluctant daughters on several fieldwork trips, cajoling them with promises of ice cream after swimming with crabs on hot Brooklyn days (in dubious urban waters).[33] There are many layers to the research project: research on human-and-crab, and on scientist-and-crab, and on sociologist-scientist-crab, and on driver-human-sociologist-scientists-crab-water-innertube-children.

My 4 years of fieldwork with horseshoe crabs and the community of humans they attract gives me the foundation for engagement in understanding the ways humans and crabs interact, intraact, and intersect. Through interviews with an international array of scientists, conservationists, pharmaceutical executives, fishermen, students, and beachcombers, I examine the ways humans come to use and know crabs. Also balancing intraspecies mindfulness with scientific data collection, I have spent hours and hours on beaches (primarily in New York City) engaging with crabs, conducting egg density surveys, coring the beach, censusing crab populations, evaluating shell quality, measuring carapace size, surveying shells for numbers and types of fouling organisms, counting juveniles, and measuring sediments. I have attended international meetings of crab-monitoring and endangered species designation workshops. The traditional methods of qualitative interviews and ethnographic fieldwork are combined with physical and emotional engagement with thousands of horseshoe crabs.

Layout of the Book

Each chapter of this book takes up a different theoretical framing and geographical location of horseshoe crabs.

As many scientists attest, we are in the midst of the sixth mass extinction.[34] In order for the rate of extinction to be deemed a significant ecological crisis, scientists use the fossil record to calculate the changes in biodiversity on the planet caused by meteorological and geological events such as asteroids hitting the Earth and volcanic eruptions. In chapter 2, "Endangered," I interpret the evaluation of the species health of the horseshoe crab while simultaneously interrogating the debates of framing our current time period as the Anthropocene, the epoch that attributes massive climate change and species decline to human activities, not just to nonhuman events.

Every 4 years the International Workshop on the Science and Conservation of the Horseshoe Crab is held for scientists and educators to exchange information about the species. In 2015, I participated in this conference in Sasebo, Japan, the largest to date, with over 130 presenters from Japan, the United States, Hong Kong, Taiwan, China, Malaysia, Singapore, India, the Philippines, Mexico, Denmark, and Poland. One of the main reasons for these meetings, in addition to the scientific exchange of data, is to establish protocols for classifying horseshoe crabs on the scales of extinction. The International Union for the Conservation of Nature (IUCN)—a team of concerned humans, including marine biologists, microbiologists, ecologists, ecotoxicologists, paleontologists, and conservationists—is the oldest global conservation organization. A primary objective of its work is to support biodiversity and create species specialist groups for vulnerable organisms.

The IUCN Horseshoe Crab Specialist Group formed to collect data to evaluate the conservation status of the four living species of horseshoe crabs for placement on the IUCN Red List. The Red List is IUCN's comprehensive evaluation of global plant, fungi, and animal species and their relative threat of extinction. The procedure for assessing the risk of species extinction involves monitoring and compiling empirical data. The Red List categories are Extinct, Extinct in the Wild, Critically Endangered, Endangered, Vulnerable, Near Threatened, Least Concern, Data Deficient, and Not Evaluated. Currently, the North American horseshoe crab *Limulus polyphemus* is listed as Vulnerable. The three Asian horseshoe crab species are listed as Data Deficient, which means that they have not been critically reviewed. Red Listing an organism doesn't guarantee protection, but the Red List status informs policy makers of the situation and may add greater power to conservation efforts.

"Endangered" takes up the meta-analysis of humans measuring species decline. How is it that particular species becomes a concern for humans? It has become somewhat of a given that humans care about charismatic megafauna, those large mammals of popular appeal—think of cuddly stuffed animals cementing our lifelong relationship with animals we'll never meet in the wild. But how do ugly, weird, spiny, or spiky animals come to matter? How do we make them count? The literary critic Ursula Heise cogently argues that when humans "discover" endangerment, it is first and foremost through a process of human storytelling. These stories frame our perception of what animals come to matter and why and guide scientific techniques and measurements.[35] My book is an attempt to understand the story of how horseshoe crabs have come to be understood and designated as Vulnerable.

The sexual reproduction of horseshoe crabs is the basis of chapter 3, "Amplexed." Horseshoe crabs do not successfully breed in captivity. Therefore researchers attempt to collect as much data on crabs in the wild and establish laboratory-based experiments in order to examine the their reproductive cycle. Horseshoe crab reproduction, also called *spawning*, is an event that excites humans—field biologists, other professionals, and laypeople. In fact, in the Northeast United States in May and June, conservation groups and individuals plan spawning field trips to visit nesting habitat and watch the crabs come to shore in amplexed pairs. When pairs of male and female horseshoe crabs reproduce, they do so by amplexing, or clasping in a "copulatory embrace." This chapter examines the ways humans study, present, and represent these reproductive events.

I use my own participation in, and analysis of, mate choice experiments, horseshoe crab spawning field biology data collection, and juvenile counts as data in this chapter. I analyze interviews with horseshoe crab reproduction scientists to understand how they construct normative reproductive practices despite outlier data.

Turning to blood, chapter 4, "Bled," explores the dangerous world of endotoxins, molecules that form on the external membrane of Gram-negative bacteria like *E. coli*, *Salmonella*, *Shigella*, and many others. Endotoxins are pyrogens, fever-causing agents that are heat stable (these toxins aren't destroyed when heated). In the right dose, endotoxins are lethal to humans and livestock and companion animals, and they are ubiquitous. Horseshoe crab blood keeps us safe from these endotoxins, but at a cost. This chapter examines the growing tensions between the field biologists and the conservationists and the pharmaceutical companies and medical professionals in how horseshoe crab blood is harvested and used. It explores the issues surrounding the amoebocyte lysate tests that are used to detect the presence of endotoxins on both local and global scales. North American horseshoe crab blood is used for the *Limulus* amoebocyte lysate (LAL) test, and the blood of Asian horseshoe crab species is used for the *Tachypleus* amoebocyte lysate (TAL) test. Testing the safety of biomedical devices that go inside the human body requires the LAL test. Even though there is a synthetic alternative, it is bureaucratically untenable. Despite the fact that bloodletting for the LAL test causes stress to individual crabs and the species as a whole, human discourse narrates it as harmless and safe.

Humans create a safer world and generate profit from horseshoe crab blood. Beginning with an analysis of the discursive and material scaffolding to affirm crab bleeding as a donation, I explain the stakes in how humans characterize the extraction of blood from another species even when our own intraspecies donation is not as simple as we might believe. Next I explain the biomedical significance of the product generated from horseshoe crab blood, *Limulus* amoebocyte lysate, and how humans have attempted to protect themselves from a world teeming with invisible bacteria through the biopharmaceutical manipulation of horseshoe crab blood. I consider the geopolitical terrain of biopharmaceutical marketing, human population dynamics, and global horseshoe crab endangerment and describe how the crabs (and their valuable blood) are potentially becoming a contested resource between nations and continents. I end with a discussion of how, despite the synthetic alternative to LAL being available, there is no pragmatic, political, or economic will to switch to this product, thus ensuring the continued bleeding of horseshoe crabs. Ultimately, this chapter traces how human and nonhuman matters bleed into one another, whereby nonhuman animals fortify our bodies in anxious times of disease transmission and our treatment of nonhuman animals inflame, fortify, nuance, or trouble the intrahuman matters of worthiness, global stratification, and commerce. The pharmaceutical industry represents an intensification of the human-crab relationship. It is in a sense a speedup of globalization and biomedicalization in which tensions between conservationists and biotech companies weave an interesting story.

Finally, chapter 5, "Enmeshed," considers habitat and space as meaningful, albeit in different ways, to horseshoe crabs and humans. Using Timothy Morton's notion of hyperobjects—global warming, in this instance—as a backdrop in this chapter,[36] I explain how site fidelity and reclamation projects increase the vulnerabilities of both species. As access to shoreline and coastal habitats are under threat, both crabs and humans must adapt to changing environmental stressors.

Site fidelity refers to horseshoe crabs remaining faithful to, and to returning to, their specific spawning ground year after year to breed. Their site fidelity both increases their vulnerability to harvesting and makes them an excellent species for field biologists to study—you know where to find them. Musing on the term and behavior of site fidelity, I describe the ecological land/seascapes of horseshoe and human habitats in decline and how horseshoe crabs become a sentinel species for human interpretation of ecological health.

This chapter also examines the practice of *reclamation,* which refers to human engineering to change lakes, rivers, oceanfront, or marshes into usable land. Habitat destruction through reclamation projects such as beach armament and embankment destroy geomorphical continuity. For example, in Japan more than half of Japanese beaches are covered by artificial structures to address sea-level rise, to fortify shorelines for tsunami protection, or to extend the coastline outward and backfill to create industrial, agricultural, or residential land. Globally by 2025, it is predicted that 75% of all human populations will live at the coastline. This massive concentration of population at the coast as sea levels rise creates conditions for hot, sour, and breathless bodies of water. Algal blooms will continue to suffocate seas, with hypoxia and acidification of the oceans, combined with runoff of heavy metals and pesticides into the sea, creating conditions that are toxic to horseshoe crabs. According to Mattei, it isn't egg predation that is killing urban horseshoe crab eggs—it is contamination: Eggs are poisoned by lead and other pollutants. Juvenile crabs also suffer from lack of food sources owing to contamination. Horseshoe crabs' long maturation process means that a single "missed" generation could have massive population effects. Creating a "living shoreline," or urban estuaries, is one possible solution that I discuss in this chapter.

In the conclusion, "From the Sea," I speculate on the future of the horseshoe crab. I also consider its remarkable ability to survive as a species for millions of years, and I make a case for its continued persistence. Furthermore, I also suggest that the sentinel data that we are generating from studies of horseshoe crabs and habitat destruction might actually indicate that it is humans who have more to fear from our engineering of the shorelines than horseshoe crabs. I end with a reminder of the themes that were explored throughout this book.

Over my lifetime, and more intensely and carefully over the last 4 years, I've probably handled thousands of horseshoe crabs. I've dug for their eggs, flipped them over, and followed them in the shallow surf, trying to keep pace with them as they glide out to sea. I love the feeling of holding active older crabs; as I slip my hands underneath their bodies, they grab onto me as if they are hugging my hands, and I feel that we are physically connecting. Their gripping is reassuring to me. And as I demonstrate in this book, I'm also implicated (as are you) in their capture, relocation, and bloodletting. I feel responsible to represent these nonhuman others, unlike other research subjects or informants, in ways that garner compassion, concern, and action from humans. At the same time, I must admit a certain quality of relief in that these subjects don't talk back. Both literally and figuratively, I hold the crabs and their stories in my hands. They can't talk back to me in a way that I can completely comprehend, but I must muster all my skills of observation and interpretation, as Carl Shuster suggests, to understand both the material and symbolic lives of horseshoe crabs as well as our becoming with them.

2

Endangered

Anyone vaguely knowledgeable about horseshoe crabs immediately and dramatically proclaims that they are hundreds of millions of years old.[1] Even the popular media fetishizes time with respect to horseshoe crabs. For example, people interviewed for the National Geographic Wild film *Alien Crab* claim that "dinosaurs saw the same species I am seeing" and "these ancient mariners crawled under the feet of *Brontosaurus*." Truthfully, I have been told that horseshoe crabs have phylogenetic roots in the Cambrian Period and that fossils have been dated from the Upper Ordovician so many times that I have often feigned understanding the significance of this lineage and mustered what I thought to be the requisite astonishment. I have been shown charts to see what Cambrian means and how the geologic divisions of time—eons, epochs, eras, and periods—differ. During the Cambrian, horseshoe crabs—or more specifically, their distant relatives—were living among sponges and algae, some other marine invertebrates, and other arthropods, but there were no hominids. But once I walk away from these charts and my enthusiastic lecturers, I often quickly forget the ordering of this time, as if all were erased.

For me, understanding horseshoe crabs has meant getting a grip on my idiosyncratic, socially functional, and personally rewarding relationship with time. If we're going to consider the horseshoe crab, as I have often been told, we'll need to take a few steps back (and a deep breath) to understand the big picture and context of the crab's existence; the implications of a species being labeled vulnerable, threatened, or endangered; and the process of being identified as a species. This chapter examines how, in addition to understanding horseshoe crabs in geologic time, we are forced to confront the destroyer-rescuer role that humans play. I am

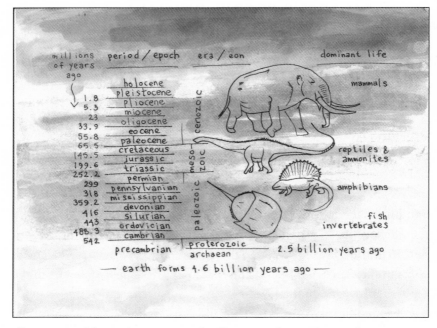

millions period / epoch era / eon dominant life
of years
ago

holocene
1.8 pleistocene
5.3 pliocene
23 miocene
33.9 oligocene
55.8 eocene
65.5 paleocene
145.5 cretaceous
199.6 jurassic
252.2 triassic
permian
299 pennsylvanian
318 mississippian
359.2 devonian
416 silurian
443 ordovician
488.3 cambrian
542

cenozoic

mesozoic

paleozoic

mammals

reptiles &
ammonites

amphibians

fish
invertebrates

precambrian proterozoic archaean 2.5 billion years ago

— earth forms 4.6 billion years ago —

Illustration of the geologic time scale. Illustration by C. Ray Borck, 2016.

grappling here with geologic time and the contrasting time scales of the species—humans and horseshoe crabs. I argue that, in apprehending the horseshoe crab, humans experience enchantment, the magical interruption of route mindless repetition. At the same time I relate the crab directly to some very hard truths about our present ecological moment, including our being complicit in mass extinctions and horseshoe crab endangerment.

* * *

Since starting this project, I think of my life as before and after horseshoe crabs. Before horseshoe crabs, time was either immediately personal and measured in task-based increments or generational and measured in interactions with my parents, kids, or students. My everyday simplistic relationship with time was in the human, immediate, and egotistical sense, based on what I could personally experience. And it's a good relationship from my perspective. My entire life I have been described as a fast person, a quick talker, an impressive multitasker, a speedy walker. I've always felt that time was similar to money: something to be thoughtfully spent, conserved for desired things, and managed to lead to optimal outcomes (e.g., doing laundry while making dinner as I entertained a toddler with pots and pans meant more time for reading a novel). Pride swells whenever someone says, "Whoa, you are such a good time manager," or "I can't believe how fast you are," or "You get so much done." And perhaps somewhat inhumanly, I've never truly empathized with the explanation "I didn't have enough time." In my more grandiose moments, I believe I can control time.

I admit that historical thinking, for me, has been of the generational nostalgic variety. I am susceptible to glamorizing a past as less complicated, kinder, slower. I drift into visions of an unspoiled, pastoral, bucolic landscape of harmony.[2] Yet this peaceable kingdom is always a past where humans existed and where I place my species-specific facsimile into a (not so) distant past. In the same vein, as part of my gender location and racial privilege, I can also lapse into idealizing decades or centuries ago as being so much safer and simpler.

There is also the familial time of experiencing and then watching childhood. Reflecting on the gendered norms of my own childhood, I often tell my daughters how I was able to be a lanky, boyish girl playing soccer with a bad perm, scraped knees, and tube socks well into my sixteenth year. Yet my daughters, at younger than 16 when I started this project, are negotiating Snapchat, thongs, bikini waxes, and midriff shirts. I don't think I could have handled the constant social media self-surveillance machine combined with hyperspecific tween/teenage body projects narrated in real time. Years ago, there seemed to be more places to hide and room for self-discovery without witnesses. Ironically, I don't want my girls to grow up too fast or for time to pass us by.

It is a personal paradox: In my everyday life I believe I have mastered time, but in geologic terms, I struggle. Geologic time is mind-blowing because of the limited capacities of human ontologies and epistemologies to apprehend it. Like many people, it's hard for me to grasp concepts that have no solid measurements. Being properly socialized as human beings means we have to come to terms with how to communicate through measurement. These human inventions of measuring time have made it bend to our needs. Therefore understanding geologic time requires a completely different conceptual/affective apparatus.

In the case of time, we assign measurements to seconds, minutes, and hours. I cling to these measurements as if they are real and as if we didn't make this all up. I must be reminded that measurement of time is what humans concocted to explain phenomena such as aging or the rising and setting of the sun. Solid measurement of mass is materially more tangible because common sense dictates that an entity's mass is never going to change and that, in its stability, it is secure. But time is always changing, and we can never talk about the present, since once we have, it is already the past. Even though human measurement of time is constructed, it becomes naturalized and then applied to all living things; we place all other things on our time scale. We assign time to biology-specific orientation to orders, routines, cycles, or life spans in all biological entities. I have found that humans are supremely interested in the life span of other species. When sharing the fact that worker honeybees live for about 6 weeks, I've often heard a sort of tragic astonishment from humans—"It's so sad that their lives are so very short. They work themselves to death." This anthropocentric empathy doesn't consider time's relevance to the bee or even how "6 weeks" is experienced by the species. *Our* time becomes *all* time.

Deep time, alternately called *geologic time*, is defined as the time frame of the earth's existence, the multimillion-year time frame. At first, I though that the failure to understand deep time was actually an idiosyncratic, personal failure. But I have come to understand that it's not simply that I don't get it, it's that humans can't access it in the same way that we can access the intensity of our regular lived time, the immediate time we can experience. But there are consequences of not understanding geologic time. For example, despite overwhelming evidence, in everyday life humans seem to be unable to fathom the enormity and catastrophe of global warming. The sociologist Kari Marie Norgaard expresses how we humans are unable to cognitively keep global warming at the front of our consciousness; we are collectively living in denial of climate change and manage our fear through emotional management strategies.[3] Maybe my (and others) lack of apprehending geologic time is part of this emotional management—it is very hard to confront how my species has completely, irrevocably harmed the planet for all living things. Part of the larger argument of this book is trying to come to terms with how humans come to care about things, ideas, objects, and animals. Time is one of those things. I am trying to understand how people care about time or become invested in deep time as a concept that enhances the value of horseshoe crabs.

As a species, we humans, it seems, are deeply wrapped up in our own embodied, affective relationship to time because we feel it. It's what we use to measure our own lives, our worth. We can't feel geologic time in the same way as we can immediate or experiential time. Being with the crabs helps me (and probably others) to approach and experience an affective resonance with deep time; perhaps this is why I (and others) have come to think they're magical. They blow our minds because they transcend our capacities for apprehending time. They push us to think of time differently. It's not that simply that I don't "understand" deep time—we all are challenged and make up myths, stories, sciences, and religions to address the idea of what's come before us and what remains after us. Deep time and immediate time are both measurements that I've learned, and as such both are constructions. For me the difference is not really cognitive but affective. I can connect my body to immediate time through my hunger levels, my sleepiness, my wrinkles, my kids' artwork. But I have a harder time connecting my affective self to the Cambrian.

Horseshoe crabs somehow make decisions as individuals and as a species in both immediate and geologic time. Individually, crabs practice going to the shoreline, burrowing in the sand, laying eggs and eating. But over vast millions of years horseshoe crabs as species have also done these things on the changing terrain of earth. Their orientations are perhaps toward changes in light, seasons, water temperatures, tides, and geography. Do they remember through temporality or location? Are our almost theological beliefs in the separation of space and time even relevant to them? Are they nostalgic for another eon long ago when their companion species were different, when they didn't have to share the planet with grabby humans? It is these very questions that function like an ethnographer's fumbling "imponderabilia" of a crab's everyday life.[4] The founder of social anthropology Bronislaw Malinowski urges ethnographers to plunge into "natives' games" as a means of getting at the "culture" of other humans—the task is even more tricky when plunging with the crabs.

I am unable to speculate about the crabs' relationship to experiential time. When time is measured in meta or deep terms, it is challenging for me to grasp, and I am re-assured by the evolutionary theorist Stephen Jay Gould, who says that "deep time is so difficult to comprehend, so outside our ordinary experience, that it remains a major stumbling block to our understanding." He continues, "Deep time is so alien that we can really only comprehend it as a metaphor."[5] In geologic time, the extent of human's history is like a blade of grass on the far end line of a soccer field, and horseshoe crabs would be at about the top of the goal box.

Deep time is based on geologic theories extrapolated from evidence found in strata, rocks, or fossils. On this geologic time scale, I rarely admit that I don't really know if humans lived in Pangea (we didn't), or, more embarrassing still, I am not precisely sure when the Neolithic Period was (also known as the New Stone Age, it occurred around 10,000 BCE). We have existed for but the slightest fraction of time of the Earth's 4.6 billion years. In the case of deep time, part of why we want to know about the deep past is because it helps us to infer about the future. We want to understand the dinosaurs and their extinction because we want to infer things about ourselves. We interpret the geologic matter of dinosaurs to be a big clue for our essential questions: How did we get here, and how might we endure? Horseshoe crabs precede dinosaurs by 200 million years, and as such they might harbor many clues. The paleontologist Richard Fortey wonders what has led them to be "ancient survivors." He asks, "Is being a survivor a question of having some very special features or nothing more than pure chance?"[6] Indeed, what, if anything, do horseshoe crabs tell us about the past and our future?

For the remainder of this chapter, I toggle back and forth between the descriptions of my fieldwork—the *being in it* with scientists—and my interpretation of how these scientific projects work to construct things. This toggling is between the actual work of making horseshoe crabs known through time, speciation, and counting and then the meta-analysis of what this knowing reifies about the singular and absolute concepts of Time, Species, and Census. In what follows, I am both engaged in the fieldwork and then telescoping out to interpret what the fieldwork, the science, constructs as foundational.

The Magic of "Geologic Time, Baby"

Walking though the halls of dioramas in New York City's Museum of Natural History, my youngest daughter pulls on my hand and whines, "When do we get to see the people?" She's bored with seeing taxidermied animals and wants to go to the exhibits of human scenes and especially the miniature renderings of human civilizations. Once we arrive she runs to her favorite "families" and makes up fantastic stories about what the people are doing, paying close attention to the babies and children.

Perhaps it is a sign of our ultimate anthropocentricism that there is something so difficult for us to conceive about time before humans. I suppose I am species-solipsistic when it comes to time—my species wasn't there, and so I somehow struggle with the time before humans existed. Yet I see how dangerously close this cleaves to creationism. Indeed, while studying horseshoe crabs, I came across photographs of a gigantic insulated foam and fiberglass model of a horseshoe crab temporarily owned by the Freedom Worship Baptist Church in Blanchester, Ohio. Erected

The World's Largest Horseshoe Crab in Blanchester, Ohio

in 2006, "Crabby", the 28-foot wide, 68-foot long model was originally
part of a nautical museum. The church subsequently sold the structure
when it declared bankruptcy, and it was re-assembled as a roadside at-
traction. When interviewed about the relevance of the horseshoe crab to
his church, Pastor Jim Rankin stated, "The fossils found of the horseshoe
crab are the same as they appear in the waters today. The crab never
evolved, so the creation account must be true."[7] The ancient existence
of horseshoe crabs and their stasis, or morphological stability over time,
are both used as evidence among creationists to testify to Genesis and to
intelligent design over evolution.

I am not a denier, though. Technologically sophisticated media shifts
my consciousness and invades our senses. Hollywood pushes this along
with the massively produced Jurassic-ish worlds that have further cor-
rupted my ability to truly believe anything. I find myself uttering, "That's
so fake," as if the scientifically grounded yet theoretical descriptions of

the past are some CGI-generated cinematic entertainment. Paradoxically these mediations, fantastic and scientific, produce increased skepticism about geologic time, making it imponderable for us. And why must we care about deep time and how long horseshoe crabs have lived?

My friend Pat gave me some insight. When she was teaching her daughter Ryan about geologic time, it both awed and reassured her. There is some odd existential comfort in the interpretation of deep time being profound and the revelation of our human existence as insignificant, repetitive, or mundane.[8] Our lives and the collection of ordinary worries are dwarfed by deep time; we might feel some liberation in understanding that our existence really is inconsequential. Pat recalled:

> I know this sounds simple, but we did one of those to-scale paper time lines. When you draw it all out, including both major extinction events, the scale of it is truly mind-blowing. And then how it has all been pieced together recently. The pure randomness and variety of what existed, and what persisted. Against all of it the unassuming horseshoe crab is a miracle that swam across a whole chunk of that time line. And yet, given the whole time line, they (and we) are a blink. And that means our blizzard is meaningless. This is what makes me happy. Not academic enough for any article or book, but the wonder of it exploded for me when I broke it down to teach a fifth grader. And I've been hooked on it ever since. "Geologic time, baby," is the shorthand phrase Liz and I use all of the time in our household. The emotional equivalent for me of that "Let It Go" dopey Disney song.

Pat's explanation triggers an *aha*. Yes, I was reminded that horseshoe crabs are an enchantment for so many humans. They are a magical reminder of something larger than the self and the endless worry about getting by in late capitalism. Life happened well before you, and it will go on without you. Unlike contemporary humans, horseshoe crabs have been able to exist and traffic outside of the systems of capital accumulation, though they are enrolled in capital enterprises all the time. For humans, our recent time is not only culturally constructed, it is also powerfully fetishized by market forces. As the anthropologist Michael Taussig argues, human cultures tend to represent time as "elemental and immutable," a process he called *phantom objectivity*. "A commodity-based society produces such phantom objectivity, and in so doing, it obscures its roots, the relations between people."[9] If we build on Taussig's observations, perhaps humans are drawn to horseshoe crabs and deep time because this relationship reminds us that other ways of being are possible. Humans are not naturally or immutably forced to experience time in this way, as having particular use or exchange value.

When I teach, I spend a great deal of time on a present-day interpretation of Weber's theory of the iron cage of rationality and our collective disenchantment. Max Weber, a German sociologist working in the early 1900s, developed the theory of the iron cage in an attempt to explain the massive social, economic, and political changes brought by modernity. He was concerned with how rational calculation has come to order all of social life and how humans have become estranged from their own humanity. He wrote that humans have become "specialists without spirit, and sensualists without heart."[10]

Over the last 20 years, most of my students have been first-generation college students, middle-class to lower-middle-class, at a publicly underfunded college. They have a keen awareness of the effects of rational bureaucracy in late capitalism. Ironically, when we discuss how every minute interaction is a means to an end in their busy lives, they come to life. Sitting in a circle, I often feel like I am leading a support group for beleaguered millennial students. Speaking in turn, they are able to admit their own realizations that their lives lack imagination, meaning, and purpose. Slowly they admit that any affective or intimate human exchange seems to have some ulterior motive or rational calculation. These lessons depress us all in the collective acknowledgment that there is no magic, no enchantment. In my critical animal studies class, students often point out that even our domesticated animals are manipulating us to get us to do their bidding. It's all a means to an end—transactional, not transcendent.

There can be quite a sense of disillusionment and drudgery among my college students in their ongoing calculus of how to get from point **a** to point **b**—how to navigate an anxious life in perpetual estrangement. How do I get my degree while working a job, commuting to campus, doing an internship, and researching graduate school programs? Where has the wonder and magic gone? Where is that sweet playful abandon, getting lost in the moment?

It is striking to me that when I bring in the horseshoe crab carapaces for students to handle, a certain palpable giddiness, inexplicable joy, and visceral fear takes over the room. As they handle the crabs' carapaces, *time as usual* is interrupted, and something about this traveler through deep time undermines the dread. The short lecture in which I narrate my own burgeoning knowledge of the species can shock them—"Professor Moore, you are blowing my mind. They do look prehistoric. Older than dinosaurs?" I experience this breach of routine time even more fully when I am on the beach, holding a live crab, turning over its body. A pragmatist at heart, I am often taken with my own being overcome by the crab—and witnessing my students' gleeful rupture of the mundane is a delight.

I do believe my students and my friend Pat, and in some respects myself, experience a sort of hopefulness when considering horseshoe crabs. Thinking about them can be a break from everyday rationalized routines and an opportunity to linger in the wonder. I speculate that we find relief in the fact that nothing we have experienced in time as a species even compares to the horseshoe crab. There is something impressive about their durability, longevity, and constancy. Richard Fortey suggests we might owe our lives to horseshoe crabs in some ways. He claims that "we are all children of the Cambrian, whether we know it or not."[11] The Cambrian was a time of great primordial soup and a flourishing of life forms. Not all survived. So am I related to a horseshoe crab? Can an invertebrate become a vertebrate? Or is that a different branch of the tree?

Yet the enchantment is fleeting. We can't simply stay in a state of astonishment at the endurance of the crab—not because we are human but because we are humans produced and reproduced under systems of global capitalism. There is a use value to be mined from the crab beyond their exchange value as blood, carapace fertilizer, and bait, and it has to do with time. Our desire to operationalize the crab's mastery of deep time for our own purposes co-opts the moments of magical transcendence. Theories abound about how crabs have accomplished this mastery—their 10 eyes that serve wide-ranging sensory-based functions, their ability to adapt to water with variable salinity and oxygenation, their compact bodies and hard-shelled exteriors, their copper-based blood that produces massive clotting, their scavenger-based diets.

The horseshoe crabs' experience of deep time leads them to become useful to humans in still another way. The crabs give us speculative power in explaining long-term survival, and as such they are dissected, measured, modeled, and sequenced to uncover the secrets of deep time. Over and over again we take from the crab, perhaps as we are primed by children's books like *The Giving Tree*. In this classic story, the apple tree is always giving to the boy—apples, branches, and trunk. It is clear she is happy in this sacrificial relationship. The human boy never gives anything to the tree, and the tree never asks for or takes anything.[12]

This act of placing the horseshoe crab on the rational geologic time line seems like an attempt by humans to steal some of its magical qualities. It's as if the awe and affective stimulation of this alien critter is something humans attempt to possess and "master," obscuring that very quality of wonder. Scientific scaffolding is constructed to determine if they are 450 or 510 million years old, or if they are cousins of trilobites, morphologically homologous or genomically related. The rational calculations squeeze out the mystical beauty, and my eyes glaze over.[13] In our efforts to know and categorize, we humans recast horseshoe crabs as valuable to natural history, evolutionary theory, and paleontology, and this intraaction thereby makes us both—crab and human—more rational, logical, and knowable and less irrational, unpredictable, and magical.

Becoming a Species

I look at the term species, as one arbitrarily given for the sake
of convenience to a set of individuals closely resembling each
other.—Charles Darwin[14]

Standing on the beach, horseshoe crab in hand, I've many times asked different scientists, "So is this the exact crab that existed over 400 million years ago?" They reply, "Not exactly. It's like a lineage." Or they launch into dense explanations that boggle my mind. There are "relatives in the fossil record," and they can be recognized as related to the modern species but not the same crab. Paleontology claims that horseshoe crabs are related to another ancient marine arthropod, the trilobite. There is evidence to suggest that trilobites emerged at about the same time as horseshoe crabs, but trilobites have been extinct for hundreds of millions of years. Over dinner one night, while we discussed geologic time and crabs, the marine biologist Mark Botton clarified that "relatives of *Limulus* were contemporaries of trilobites." They were similar in that they had larvae that were similar, they cast off their carapaces in the same way when they molted, and they had compound eyes that were part of the body—those eyes did not stick out above the bulk of the body.

Requiring more explanation about horseshoe crab and trilobite connections, I reached out to the paleogeologist Yumiko Iwasaki, who studies horseshoe crabs as a proxy for researching trilobites. During lunch and cheesecake at Junior's Restaurant in Brooklyn, Yumiko explained the relationship of trilobites to horseshoe crabs. Using our dining area as a map, Yumiko placed utensils as symbols across the table. "If you map out the phylogeny, you know the tree of life, the trilobites are on this end—a really, really far end here." She placed a fork. On the other far end of the table, she placed a spoon. "And this would be insects and crabs on this end. Next to them, the trilobites." She placed a knife down about 6 inches from the fork. "These would be scorpions and horseshoe crabs and ticks. They are more closely related if you compare trilobites to crustaceans. You can say they, horseshoe crabs and trilobites, are distant relatives, but they did not evolve from one another—they share a common ancestor." Trilobites are important because they are used to gauge the rate of speciation—how species become differentiated or, as paleontologists say, how species *radiate*.[15] Trilobites were so prolific and covered such vast terrain of the Earth that they were literally everywhere. Speciation happens over vast and gradual time and creates new branches of the evolutionary tree. So horseshoe crabs and trilobites are different groups, but they have certain features that are the same— their mouths, for instance, are the same.[16] In my experience talking with biologists and paleontologists, I have gotten the impression that there continues to be a sense of surprise that trilobites went extinct and horseshoe crabs lived—a great deal of the research attempts to explain why this might be so.

A foundational organizing principle in biology, the concept of *species*, tries to wrangle biological life into different categories. The definition of species is not stable. At first *phenotypic* difference (the characters that make up the appearance of individuals in a group) was used to categorize groups and was soon refined into a criterion for defining a species. Then the *biological species concept* defined species as a group of individuals that can produce offspring that are themselves fertile and that are reproductively isolated from other groups.[17] Most recently, with the advent of genetic testing, defining species has become more complicated. Genetic testing of what were thought to be distinct species has shown that genetic lines are often blurred—what was considered a distinct species may turn out to be two different types of species or more. There are species that interbreed and produce viable offspring (those offspring can reproduce), and lots of genetic information is shared between these groups. Significantly, our techniques for identifying species change over time—but this identification does not necessarily result in any greater knowledge about the species.[18]

As a graduate student in the 1990s, I was trained in feminist science studies at a time when cultural studies was alive in the critique of any discursive mechanism that naturalized differences. Everything that was purported to be of nature or natural was actually a discursive production that "naturalizes" what is really a cultural product. For example, alternative interpretations emerged against the standard linguistic and visual scientific representations of "sperm cells," a cultural view that reinforced that these cells were naturally programmed to fight one another to get to the passive egg.[19]

Species is another of these terms that is doing a type of hegemonic labor in the service of biological essentialism, built on the scaffolding of systems of stratification. However, the move toward feminist new materialism suggests that while discursive, the construction of *species* is still an important descriptive device because it allows social action to be organized. Rather than jettison the term, as suggested by Timothy Ingold,[20] the anthropologist Eben Kirksey argues for the need to understand discovering species as a project in becoming: "As entangled beings rediscover each other in intergenerational dances, species persist across time and space."[21] Rather than seeing the creation of a species as an exclusively anthropocentric dominating act of classification, creating and then recognizing a species, as the remainder of this chapter explores, can also be a potential exercise in its survival.[22]

Censusing, the procedure of counting and recording populations, is done for the formulation of policies and plans. Within contemporary life, census projects can involve humans, nonhuman animals, and plants, and they rely on the determination of species categories. In 2010, for example, the Census of Marine Life, an international effort to assess the diversity, distribution, and abundance of global marine life, released its results. The 10-year effort coordinated 540 expeditions and included over 2,700 scientists from over 80 nations and discovered over 6,000 new species. From its own description, "The Census investigated life in the global ocean from microbes to whales, from top to bottom, from pole to pole, bringing together the world's preeminent marine biologists, who shared ideas, data, and results. During their 10 years of discovery, Census scientists discovered new species, habitats, and connections and unlocked many of the ocean's long-held secrets. They found and formally described more than 1, 200 new marine species, with another 5,000 or more in the pipeline awaiting formal description."[23]

On this grandest scale, to me, there is an absurdity to the choreography undertaken by a group of international human experts establishing criteria to count and measure the entire contents of the global ocean. Modern apparatuses of finding, catching, tagging, and counting offer humans some illusion of control. Now that we know what species exist, somehow we can reverse the hyperobject of global warming or rescue species that are disappearing—even tricky ones like the horseshoe crab that have demonstrated perspicacious versatility to all previous threats. The notion that making something knowable through scientific discovery, just as it is on the precipice of being lost, is a worthy use of resources suggests that the creation of a knowledge base about all marine species can lead to action plans. Or has, as Timothy Morton points out, global warming already happened; is our mobilization of massive international efforts to find out what we are going to lose really about other social processes? It brings to mind the human tendency when in the midst of a tragedy—be it global warming or an individual disease diagnosis—to scurry around in a frenzy of busy-ness, creating tasks and meanings to ground and comfort.

As explained above, at every turn there is potential controversy in classifying a species. Even at the very level of keeping track of biotic life on our planet, the term *species* is simultaneously very useful and vexingly partial. The historian Simon Pooley calls on us to problematize the notion of species when mobilizing the discourse and practices of conservation. "Conservation is the science and art of the possible, but when we decide what is endangered, and prioritize conservation action, we should be reflexive about the limitations of our fixation on species, and the role of our values in shaping our choices. So many living beings remain unclassified and beyond both our scientific comprehension and our ethical consideration. Essentialist conceptions of species may elide our interrelatedness and conceal our culpability in endangering life on our planet."[24] As a counterpoint, Eben Kirksey suggests that "stabilizing the existence of species in techno-scientific worlds can help them endure hostile or indifferent political and economic forces. We are only dimly aware of how our own existence, as a species, is contingent on the lives and deaths of others. Abandoning the notion of species would mean losing a useful tool for grappling with other animate beings."[25] Horseshoe crabs come to matter as a species not just because of human use for capital accumulation but also for the sense that we are entangled with animals in liberation projects—if we save the whales, the bees, the horseshoe crabs, we can save ourselves.

The Making of the Anthropocene

My exercises in learning and relearning the meaning of human's categories of time and classifications of species are crucial to entering the sociopolitical ecological worlds of species conservation. Species and time are interrelated in conservation sciences: When did a species emerge? How long has a species existed? When did/will it be extinct? There is an irony about the relationship of deep time and horseshoe crabs as it is the story the improbable long-lived survival of such a non-threatening and clumsy species. They are one of the most vulnerable of creatures; during spawning season we can see them trying to turn themselves upright as each wave knocks them back and forth, seeing their carapaces, up and down the beach, insides ripped apart by birds, smelling their rot in the dry heat of a summer day. And yet, simultaneously, their hardiness extends across the supreme perils of deep time. How is it that this species is one that has survived when practically all other life has gone extinct? And how can we survive a lethal extinction event—even if we are creating the conditions that cause it? If we can save horseshoe crabs, can we save ourselves?

Herein lies another hook, capturing my attention and giving me more reason to care about time with respect to the species. The horseshoe crab has survived the previous five mass extinctions.[26] Mass extinctions are

Horseshoe crabs turned over in the shoreline waves at Plumb Beach during a spawning event. Photo by Lisa Jean Moore.

characterized by unusually high numbers of species dying out at the same time (greater than 50% of all species) and are caused by meteo-rologic or climate-related events. These five mass extinctions are the Ordovician-Silurian extinction, the Late Devonian extinction, the Permian extinction, the Triassic-Jurassic extinction, and the Cretaceous-Tertiary extinction. Yumiko suggests that "horseshoe crabs have lived so long because they are a generalized species; horseshoe crabs didn't specialize as much as trilobites which meant they were less vulnerable to threats from massive changes in the Late Devonian period. Horseshoe crabs are really so adaptable—and they have the blue blood, which is very efficient to survival."

As many scientists attest, we are in the midst of a sixth mass extinc-tion with massive loss of global biodiversity.[27] To conclude that such a significant biotic crisis as a mass extinction has occurred, scientists use the fossil record to calculate the changes in numbers of life forms on the planet caused by meteorological and geological events such as asteroids hitting the Earth and volcanic eruptions. Horseshoe crabs are one of a handful of species that have managed to survive despite these kinds of cataclysmic events. So to learn that we are in the midst of another mass extinction event and that horseshoe crabs might in fact be unable to make it through this time is distressing for humans, even more so because there is overwhelming evidence to suggest that we humans are the cause.[28]

What we are told is that the human use of the biosphere is unsustainable and that humans have induced habitat loss that deeply threatens terrestrial biodiversity. We humans have transformed the planet in ways unlike other those of other organisms. Until quite recently we have been living in the epoch called the Holocene, the last 11,700 years since

A recently dead horseshoe crab drying out on the shoreline. Photo by Lisa Jean Moore.

the "ice age," or the time "when evidence of significant human capacity for ecosystem engineering or niche construction behaviors first appear in the archeological record on a global scale."[29] Our domestication of plants and animals is the boundary of the Pleistocene–Holocene epochs.

Owing to "stratigraphic, atmospheric, and biotic variables,"[30] we are now considered to be in the Anthropocene, a heuristic device used to denote the epoch of geologic time that attributes climate change and species decline to human activities. It is forecasted that during the Anthropocene we will experience a mass extinction event that could wipe out 30%–50% of all living species.[31] Somewhat controversially dated at starting at AD 1800, typically the consensus date for the beginning of the Anthropocene is also called the Industrial Revolution (1760–1820). If we are "all the sons and daughters of catastrophe," as explained by Richard Fortey when discussing mass extinctions,[32] are we also the parents of catastrophe in the dawning of the Anthropocene? We claim that we are the first species to be aware of causing planet-wide environmental changes,[33] but our understanding of the Anthropocene is necessarily limited because it is still in process and might lead to our extinction. Or, as the historian Dipesh Chakrabarty suggests, there is a great irony in the Anthropocene in that humans can name and construct the dimensions this geologic shift and that "we can experience specific effects of crisis but not the whole phenomenon."[34]

The notion of the Anthropocene is promiscuous. Lists of contributors to species die-off and ecological degradation proliferate. These lists include the use of materials in modern agriculture, aluminum, concrete, plastic, nuclear fallout, landfill, urban structures, and dams. While theories abound about the precise timing of this epoch transition, Erle Ellis argues that anthroecological change is the best explanation of the Anthropocene, a time where humans first transformed global ecology in attempts to increase the environment's carrying capacity for human life.[35] Five different human activities are identified as potential sources of early anthropogenic methane, a gas that traps heat in our atmosphere: (1) generating human waste; (2) raising methane-emitting livestock (e.g., from belches and flatulence); (3) generating animal waste from raising livestock; (4) burning seasonal grass biomass; and (5) irrigating rice paddies.[36]

As is the case with certain academic terms, *Anthropocene* is a "hot" term at this moment. It is well traveled and deployed in the humanities, social sciences, and natural sciences. People like the ring to it, and it seems to satisfy some species-specific sadomasochism—we can feel powerful in our self-destruction, attempt recovery, and relapse into demolition. While the Anthropocene may become the popularly accepted term for this epoch of time, and its acceptance may possibly (but probably not) lead to a sense of deeper human responsibility for global ecological sustainability,[37] it is not without problems. The term itself is anthropocentric in that it elevates humans to being the ultimate cause— the force—the supreme destroyer of the Universe. And in our self-anointed position as extinction maker (in the impressive company of asteroids and volcanoes), we can also consider ourselves the generators of the solutions. It is as if the Universe is waiting for the great human knight to come to the rescue. Simultaneously there is a counternarrative that we will cause our own extinction and be just a blip on the geologic time line.

Stated more academically, Kathryn Yusoff calls this phenomena of naming geological, temporal and social time as the Anthropocene a form of anthropogenesis. We have produced a mythic Anthropos as the geologic world maker/destroyer, or in Yusoff's words, "Anthropogenesis is the institutionalization of this originary moment (or genesis story) for humanity as an organism capable of geologic force on a planetary scale and of an epochal duration."[38] I have witnessed some of this bravado in my fieldwork, as humans describe saving honeybees or horseshoe crabs as a form of saving the self and temporarily interrupting the ecological crisis.

Working on *Buzz*, Mary Kosut and I frequently witnessed the circulation of this Anthropocene guilt through constant references to planetary destruction among beekeepers, honey lovers, and urban homesteaders.

They also suggested that there is potential hopefulness through species intraaction. Urban beekeepers spoke of their attempts to ameliorate apiary decline through making space for colonies on their rooftops, fire escapes, and backyards. The potential emergent and becoming of these intraspecies relationships quickly turn into humans believing they are stewards of the species. The deployment of their human status is somehow the key to species overcoming environmental threats even though the human species is also the most likely suspect in ecological destruction.

Obviously the alternative to species stewardship is a nihilistic acceptance of the inexorable forces of capital leading to inevitable ecological destruction. The hopeless might say, "Let's take, use, and waste, all we can while we still can." This approach is also deeply problematic. The anthropologist Anna Tsing, the theorist Donna Haraway, and the sociologist Jason Moore use the alternative term of the *Capitalocene* to express how the political economy belongs in the heart of the Anthropocene.[39] The Anthropocene is an explanation that is too easy, neat, or sewn up, and it relegates all humans as equally situated agents of destruction. Moore argues that, "above all, the Anthropocene argument obscures, and relegates to context, the actually existing relations through which women and men make history with the rest of nature: the relations of power, (re)production, and wealth in the web of life."[40] Capitalism is a particular way of organizing nature and has resulted in superexploitation of natural resources for the temporary benefit of a very select group of humans. Not all humans are equally to blame, and often humans are forced into systems of ecological harm.

Becoming Endangered? Humans to the Rescue

I'd like to shift the focus from horseshoe crabs in deep time punctuated by the repeated extinctions of other species to this particular moment of human–horseshoe crab intraaction. During these 4 years of fieldwork with conservation biologists, ecologists, environmental scientists, and citizen scientists, I've wrestled with how we narrate humans' threat to the Earth and, in particular, the "rescue" of the horseshoe crab. When feeling exasperated during one particular conversation about time with Yumiko, I said, "Well, why should we care about these crabs, anyway?" She smiled and replied, "Oh, because we are the newcomers, and they are our seniors." These interactions are on the microsociological, but they exist on a meta level. From bureaucratic scientific quantification of massive swaths of data to manual labor on urban beaches, humans are imagining themselves to be working against their own historic legacies of destruction toward salvation for humans and the horseshoe crabs (and bees, and polar bears, and others).

Examining the work of biological conservation from the 1980s through the 2000s, the political scientist Rafi Youatt sums up a chief challenge of the task of how to identify and count all species as we are in the midst of "a major extinction event in which we do not even know what or how much is being lost."[41] He uses Foucauldian theories of biopower to explore these operations of classifying and categorizing to produce a sense of normative and healthy global biodiversity. Our project of categorizing and counting species is a part of national projects, as he concludes, "The rise of biodiversity as an object of global environmental governance has meant attachment to things well beyond conservation, biodiversity more clearly becomes a natural and economic resource, attached to national sovereignty."[42] Whose responsibility is it to count and assess the health of the species? Is it a national project? For the horseshoe crabs, if their survival (as examined in chapter 4) is of pharmaceutical and vital value, then their importance is calculated by both national and corporate actors. Furthermore, horseshoe crabs don't maintain geographic borders, which is depicted very clearly by the fact that the species *Tachypleus tridentatus* can be called the Chinese or Japanese horseshoe crab, depending on which human is speaking.

Getting on the List

On April 26, 2014, I entered a dingy, fluorescent-lit office space to join a team of concerned humans including marine biologists and microbiologists, ecologists and ecotoxicologists, as well as paleontologists, conservationists, and middle school science teachers. Dispensing with our introductions, we rolled up our sleeves and began the daylong workshop of the Horseshoe Crab Specialist Group of the International Union for the Conservation of Nature (IUCN) at the Center for Environmental Research and Coastal Oceans Monitoring (CERCOM) based at Molloy College. The IUCN is the oldest global conservation organization, and it "provides public, private and non-governmental organizations with the knowledge and tools that enable human progress, economic development and nature conservation to take place together. . . . [The Union is] organized into six commissions dedicated to species survival, environmental law, protected areas, social and economic policy, ecosystem management, and education and communication."[43] The IUCN Horseshoe Crab Specialist Group began in 2012. A primary objective of its work is to support efforts to study and conserve horseshoe crabs and their habitats.

To be more specific, at this meeting the agenda was to summarize the progress made in Red Listing the species of horseshoe crabs. The Red List is IUCN's comprehensive evaluation of global plant, animal, and fungi species and their relative threat of extinction. The procedure for assessing the risk of extinction of a species involves monitoring and compiling empirical data. These are measurements of species health that are also deeply dependent on longitudinal data. Scientists must demonstrate that over time a species has experienced a change in its population density in order to categorize its relative "health" in an ecosystem. Doing this work for the Red List is on a temporal scale that includes both immediate time as well as, in the case of the horseshoe crab, deep time.

The categories used by the Red List are Extinct, Extinct in the Wild, Critically Endangered, Endangered, Vulnerable, Near Threatened, Least

Concern, Data Deficient, and Not Evaluated. Recall that globally there are four living species of horseshoe crabs. In 2014, the one in North America was deemed Near Threatened, and the three in Southeast and East Asia were deemed Data Deficient (meaning there has been no critical review of the species owing to lack of data). The IUCN's Species Survival Commission reviews reports submitted by species specialist groups to approve recommendations and create species designations on the Red List. While I was speaking to one biologist, he suggested that "it is really more like environmental law than science when you get to the level of convincing the Commission."

Red Listing doesn't guarantee species protection, but it informs policy makers of the situation and may add greater power to conservation efforts. There is no legal force behind the IUCN. Bureaucratic hoops are jumped through in a complicated series of forms and spreadsheets, and a species is given a designation somewhere on the continuum of Extinct to Least Concern. As Mark Botton, co-chair of the Horseshoe Crab Specialist Group, explains, there is a "paradox [in] that we have had meetings, and all people are telling us that the horseshoe crab population is going down the tubes all over Asia. So clearly we have to update the status, but there hasn't been a group to advocate for putting it in a higher level of threat, and this poses an impediment to conservation efforts. We need to have people to speak for horseshoe crabs with the best data we can obtain."

Beyond these regional meetings, every 4 years the International Workshop on the Science and Conservation of the Horseshoe Crab is held for scientists and educators to exchange information about the species. In July 2015, I participated in this conference in Sasebo, Japan, the largest to date, with over 130 presenters from Japan, the United States, Hong Kong, Taiwan, China, Malaysia, Singapore, India, the Philippines, Mexico, Denmark, and Poland. One of the main reasons for these meetings is to establish protocols for classifying horseshoe crabs on the risk of extinction.

Like much of this chapter and the entire book, my overarching question is with why some species are a concern for humans while others are not. It has become somewhat of a given that humans care about charismatic megafauna, those large mammals of popular appeal like polar bears, pandas, and baby seals. Think of cuddly stuffed animals cementing our lifelong relationship with animals we'll never meet in the wild. We care about charismatic megafauna because we have done the cultural work to instill them in our consciousness as spiritually or emotionally valuable. But how do ugly, weird, spiny, or spiky animals comes to matter? How do we make them count? I often wonder how the crab could possibly compete with furry mammals and cute animal babies on kids' calendars, folders, and screensavers. While I am arguing that these campaigns to save animals (any animal) is based on a stratification system—vertebrate over invertebrate, furry over scaly—I also question the very idea that we can "save them." Polar bears and giraffes will become extinct. And it is not improbable to imagine that humans will die out before horseshoe crabs or honeybees. Nonetheless, there are people who have established ways to assess the horseshoe crab population's health and chart a rescue mission.

Importantly, and even ironically, this rescue mission of the crabs is happening during the persistent signs of the fragility of human life in myriad ways—the anthropologist Anna Tsing calls it "the global state of precarity—a state of acknowledgement of our vulnerability to others."[44] The use of precarity is a nod to the philosopher Judith Butler's observation that humans are predisposed to vulnerability; we have precarious subjectivity in that, since we are social beings, our lives are always in the hands of others—our companions, other drivers, and international politicians, for example.[45] I want to extend this idea beyond our human others.

Here are a few examples of our precarity with respect to nonhuman animals from just over the last couple decades. As I write this, the Zika virus, transmitted by mosquitoes, is threatening human reproduction in the Global South, and the range of infected mosquitoes is moving north. Every few years, there are health scares detailing how viruses jump species and are transmitted by through our raising, slaughtering, and eating animals. Farm animals serving as vectors transmit avian or swine flu to humans. Mad cow disease (bovine spongiform encephalopathy, BSE), linked to the fatal brain disease variant Creutzfeldt-Jakob disease (vCJD), is caused by eating contaminated beef, and it has killed over 200 humans in 12 countries. Periodically since 1986, yet unpredictably, BSE has been confirmed in cattle (France in early 2016), and vCJD kills someone (Texas in 2014). Colony collapse disorder, a mass die-off of honeybee colonies that began in 2006, threatens the production of over 75% of the fruits and vegetables that Americans consider dietary staples.

This human precarity indicates our deeply enmeshed and highly dependent relationship with nonhuman animals. We rely on these animals to work for us, and yet we have created unsustainable labor conditions for them and for ourselves. We innovate factory farming to optimize profit and construct conditions for disease propagation. We employ animals for industrial pollination of crops and weaken their immune systems to the point of massive die-off of a generation of "workers." As we will see with the horseshoe crabs in chapter 4, we use them for health protection and deplete their hearty populations. Even when we manage them as pests, we pollute the environment through pesticides, thus increasing global warming and polluting their breeding grounds.[46]

Despite the current time replete with examples of ongoing and pending destruction, humans continue to construct a narrative of themselves as masters of the planet's welfare. We encourage younger generations to "take responsibility" for particular species. An educator from the New York Aquarium explained her strategies for teaching New York City schoolchildren about horseshoe crab conservation: "We explain to them they are surrogate parents of the horseshoe crabs. We are working to make a program where horseshoe crabs are released by elementary school and middle school children." Here we are passing the responsibility on to children—perhaps encouraging them to be ecologically minded and/or making them increasingly anxious about things they cannot control (which was illustrated by my 7-year-old daughter waking me up one night to say she couldn't sleep, she was "worried about animals dying all the time").

In order for an existing species to be classified as endangered, human scientists must be able to document long-term persistent threats to it. Scientists must be able to articulate the species's taxonomy and geographic range, analyze its population, and determine what the major threats to it are. Yet managing an inventory census—that is, counting—horseshoe crabs is difficult because they are usually visible only when they are spawning. In the case of the upper regions of North America, this happens during about a 6-week period of time in late spring. Otherwise, their locations remain a bit of a mystery. Surveillance innovations are being beta tested where juvenile animals are tracked via passive integrated transponders, but there is limited longitudinal data (where the same population sample is tracked at different points in time over time).[47] Being able to track horseshoe crabs could provide information about where they go when they leave the shoreline—perhaps leading humans to identify their practices and create new means of counting them.

During the Japan meeting, Malaysian marine scientists unveiled their development of a smartphone application for geolocation tracking of horseshoe crabs.[48] That's right, horseshoe crabs have an app. After the initial explanation and astonishment from the audience for the app's ability to provide GPS location of crabs, people suggested that these apps might potentially aid those with poor intentions with respect to crabs. One scientist worried aloud, "There are those out there that would exploit this app and use it for harvesting horseshoe crabs. You know, telling people where to get the crabs."

Logistically speaking, horseshoe crab conservation is confronted with several challenges. The crabs themselves are difficult to find when they are not spawning. Their habitat spans far-flung regions of the continental shelf. There are vast differences in the presence of scientific experts in key locations and the lack of availability of resources for research in these regions. Among humans there are language barriers, disciplinary differences, and cultural heterogeneity. Furthermore, the threats to the Asian species of horseshoe crabs are slightly different from those threats to the North American species. Again Mark Botton sums it up: "First, there is human consumption in Asia, second, there is massive habitat loss, similar to the beach hardening like we see at Plumb Beach but more intense, and unlike in the United States, there is 100% mortality rate when bleeding crabs for biomedical use [in Asia]."

During the Monitoring and Data Collection Workshop at the Japan meeting, our charge was to discuss

- What is the distribution of horseshoe crabs (past/present)?
- What is the rate of reduction? and
- What are the habitat requirements?

But before we could even get to operationalizing the measures and gathering the quantitative and qualitative data, we were met with issues of variability in the data. For example, some people were measuring the carapace from head to tail, others the width from side to side. This discovery led to much discussion of how to establish global guidelines for consistency of methods and standard operation protocols. Furthermore, there was a call to proselytize new scientists to care about crabs and join the struggle. Pleas were made to create local campaigns to raise lay and scientific awareness of horseshoe crabs. This turned to conversations about branding, slogans, and marketing—"What if we developed a global message about horseshoe crabs that could travel, similar to 'Save the whales'?" one scientist asked.

Another specific objective of this workgroup was to put together an international directory for horseshoe crab researchers by country that includes contact information like email and direct links to websites. The members of the workshop believe that this process would identify regional gaps in horseshoe crab data and representation. I was struck by my own fatigue at paying close attention, an ethnographer's most valuable tool, during these discussions and how I yearned to get back into the field to actually be with the crabs. Global census-making is bureau-cratic and tedious work.

Most of my fieldwork sites are in the United States, specifically in New York and Florida. As to be expected, North America is where the preponderance of horseshoe crab conservation data are gathered and analyzed. The members of the IUCN realizing this imbalance of data continue to strategize about how to best train human members of the international community to be partners in data collection. It was very clear from the Japan meeting that other countries support programs that monitor and release crabs (e.g., Japan- and Hong Kong–based laboratory-bred juvenile horseshoe crabs are released to suitable habitats). There has been such great success with integrating citizen science into outreach programs that the Singapore programs actually have had to turn away volunteers because human volunteers far outnumbered the horseshoe crabs to be counted and measured. But what type of work is done to measure crabs and standardize a system for counting and assessing populations?

Citizen Science

For the last 3 years, I have worked with the biologist Christina Colon and several of her undergraduate students on Plumb Beach. As a professor at City University of New York's Kingsborough Community College, she requires students to engage in fieldwork with horseshoe crabs through the Jamaica Bay Institute for Science and Resilience. Christina is an expert on citizen science and has written widely on the topic about the challenges and benefits from training laypeople in the methods of data collection.

With biodiversity declining and the pace of climate change increasing rapidly, ecologists are quickly seeing more and more connections between local species and global trends. The size, scope, and far-reaching implications of these connections necessitate long-term and geographically extensive studies. Such megastudies on wide-ranging or migratory species

This photograph shows me holding a horseshoe crab at Plumb Beach. This crab has been tagged as part of an Atlantic coast-wide tagging program organized in part through the U.S. Fish and Wildlife Service. See the "Horseshoe Crab Resighting Form" (posted at www.fws.gov) for the kinds of information collected on each crab. Photo by Paisley Currah.

take decades to complete and require a virtual army of researchers collecting data in perfect synchrony over thousands of square miles. Citizen science has the potential to provide that army of researchers to address large-scale questions.[49] Christina is one of several interdisciplinary horseshoe crab researchers who use these deputized scientists to assist in longitudinal and labor-intensive data collection.

As a means of educating and mobilizing individuals to understand the ecology of the Long Island Sound horseshoe crab, Jennifer Mattei, an evolutionary ecologist and professor at Sacred Heart University, founded Project *Limulus* in 1997. Mattei is concerned by what is happening to the ecological health of Long Island Sound and is specifically examining the relative health of the horseshoe crab population. She articulated her reasons for caring about horseshoe crabs: "One day they were cockroaches of the sea, and what gets me going about it is that it would be a shame to lose a species like this due to overharvesting or habitat loss. They have survived these mass extinctions. We should care about these guys because they have survived all these things but [are] not surviving us very well. And if we have to wait for an animal to be listed on the endangered species list, then it is too late." There is a sense of futility in my conversation with Mattei, for she is correct that, once a problem is bureaucratically categorized as existing, it is probably too late. The frustration of trying to convince the public of the dire predictions for nonhuman animals is perhaps illustrated in the example of the polar bear. Many scientific experts suggest that, even if emissions of carbon dioxide decrease, certain endangered species like the polar bears are already likely to go extinct in the next few decades.[50] And yet humans are a stubborn species that innovates ways to ameliorate environmental threats (even the ones it creates itself).

Project *Limulus* is part conservation program, part scientific protocol for species census. Jennifer describes the early days of the project, when trying to tag horseshoe crabs. Initially she used a "T-bar tag like the kind you find in clothing, so we put up these little tags and punched a hole in the carapace." Unfortunately, this turned out to be the wrong tool for the job,[51] and as Jennifer shares, "The T-bar had a design flaw in that it got tangled. So we made cinch tag, and we ended up putting a hole in the shell and cinching it up." These cinch tags close up firmly on the body of the crab. Jennifer describes how, through trial and error and innovation, a process for tagging was created: "I contacted a company, and they gave me a discount—this was in 1997, and we put out like 50 tags. So we made this awl and we started conservation groups training. We would train people, laypeople, to become beach captains, you know, to be in charge of a beach, and we would have them take care of volunteers in their area because we couldn't do it all. We had hundreds of people working for us. It was fantastic."

As the program became increasingly successful, Mattei created partnerships with federal agencies such as U.S. Fish and Wildlife Service. But as she describes, owing to budgetary cuts, the program peaked in the early 2000s and is now in decline:

> Each cinch tag has a unique number, and we now have demonstrated a 10%–12% return. The U.S. Fish and Wildlife issued tags from about 2000 and asked if I wouldn't mind switching over to their protocol. It was to take a power drill out to the sea. Can you see me handing out power drills in saltwater and sand to children I have trained? All you have to do is design the opening of the hole so that they [the tags] can fit in, so we switched in 2006 to the federal tag system. But now they are losing money through budget cuts, so they are shutting down. They will only give us 3,000 tags a year. In the past, we have put out 14,000 per year with all our volunteers.

From these humble beginnings, about 15 years ago, thousands of volunteers and approximately 95,000 tags later, Project *Limulus* is an exemplar of a successful citizen science project. The project has a 22% recapture rate, providing data about the spatial and temporal patterns of horseshoe crabs in Long Island Sound in the United States.[52] These longitudinal data are crucial for establishing an assessment of the species population health.

My own experiences as a citizen scientist have taken place in New York, Connecticut, and Florida. In 2016, I joined a team in Cedar Key, Florida, led by the prominent horseshoe crab and marine biologist H. Jane Brockmann. She taught me how to tag a crab, and here are my descriptive field notes:

After I take the female from the bucket on the shoreline, I balance her on a makeshift table on the sand (an over turned cooler with a bath mat to keep the crabs from slipping). Facing the crab toward me, I pick up the awl and find the "meatiest" part of the crab to poke into—I am nervous because Jane is standing over me, and I don't want to disappoint her. But I am not sure how firmly I should push in the tool. I place my left hand over the carapace of the crab and with my right I begin to push the awl into the shell. There is a slight popping feeling as I pierce her shell with the awl, and I spin it gently to make the hole a little wider. When pulling out the awl, the crab bleeds a little and I wonder what it must feel like. This is the blood that helps us, and I am wasting it to put in a tag. Plus, does it hurt? Jane reassures me that any bacteria I am introducing is probably not a problem for the crab given the wonderful qualities of her blood, but I feel guilty. And then an egg also pops through the hole. I quickly pick up the plastic tag and push it through her shell. I then kiss her and say sorry as I put her back into the ocean. She might be tracked if another person sees her—some weird new human/crab message in a bottle for future beachcombers.

* * *

From these data, scientists create working groups to establish reports for the Horseshoe Crab Specialist Group of the IUCN. The lead investigator on the team assigned to *Limulus* is Dave Smith, a biological statistician who works for the U.S. Geological Survey. During an interview with Dave, he explained the blend of mathematical calculation and social assessment that goes into determining a species' risk tolerance. He summed it up: "All species on the planet are on the risk of extinction. If you look far enough into the future, many, many species have some probability of risk, so many that you can't expend enough resources to figure it out. So there are other social concerns in addition to just the pure probability of extinctions that have to be taken into account. Even [with] endangered species, we must consider the values to things like ecosystems and recreation when making our assessments. So some species might get an additional bump in terms of worth. Some contribute to more value than others." I nodded rigorously since, for me, it was quite validating to hear Dave explain the procedure as if it were not just some purely scientific or statistical endeavor. Rather, he affirmed that measuring the worthiness of a species is interrelated with a social assessment of its value.

He continued, "The question is, then, at what level of risk does it warrant protection as an endangered species to the IUCN? We have to figure out what threshold falls into the categories of Vulnerable, Endangered, and so on. That threshold is a normative in that it is the risk we are willing to tolerate in those categories." There is not some hard-and-fast objective number but a mixture of quantitative scientific assessment, statistically modeling, and psychosocial qualitative evaluation of worthiness and tolerance.

In July 2016, Dave Smith's team published with the approval of IUCN the new designation of *Limulus* as Vulnerable.[53] This significant development is an upgrading of the level of concern about the population of North American horseshoe crabs. According to the IUCN, the Vulnerable designation is appropriate when the animal meets particular criteria to be "considered to be facing a high risk of extinction in the wild." When I spoke with Dave about the report, he was very circumspect and explained to me that certain areas along the East Coast of North American had strong populations of crabs. It was at the geographical edges of their habitat where they are endangered. He added, "It would be a great tragedy if we lost them in the New England area or in the Gulf—any range contraction would be tragic." Even in the time that I have spent writing this book, the status of the horseshoe crab has been changed. This shifting status is meant to highlight the vulnerability of their time left as a species.

Hope in Unlikely Places

This chapter, and perhaps this book, is about the ambivalence of what it is that humans do when they come to realize and affirm that they have ecological interconnectedness with species and geographies. This ambivalence is combined with an unwillingness to give up hope—but it is a deeply skeptical hope. I believe humans yearn to see their position in geologic time—what came before us—as a way to increase their human perspective. For others, including me, learning and teaching about objects like crabs brings back wonder and a sense of something larger than mundane existence and calculated rationality. When we play with horseshoe crabs, consider them, hold them, imagine their deep past, we experience the enchantment of a world that's hard to come by in late capitalism.

Across the globe, there are people working together to address problems that our species have caused—this activity of conservation, or husbandry, is hopeful, but at the same time it is also an anthropocentric thing in itself. Just as there are virtues and problems related to species classification, classifications of endangerment often elevate humans to be ultimate villains or heroic saviors. With respect to the Anthropocene, there lies an aporia of sorts—humans at least partially created the problem, and fixing the problem is part of our same old ways of self-aggrandizement. But, anthropocentrism itself is bad. It can provide some tools that offer us a way out of further destruction and maybe a way to fix some of it—an act of taking responsibility.

* * *

What does hope become when we talk beyond generational or human time (my kids' and students')? What does it mean to talk about endangered species and saving some of them within the *longue durée* of geologic time? Working through these ideas, especially for this chapter, has been fraught with greater-than-expected anxiety. As the philosopher María Puig de la Bellacasa explains, "The everyday experience of time is one of permanent precariousness: an ongoing sense of urgency and crisis calls to act 'now', while the present action is diminished, mortgaged to an always unsure tomorrow."[54] We have to act now to help save the horseshoe crabs, but these actions seem cumbersome, futile, and even preposterous in the wake of the inexorable crushing ecological destruction.

I am trying to figure out how to hold these seemingly contradictory ideas in my head—one is that we humans are just a speck in deep time, and our immediate time has come and gone, so it is ridiculous for us to go through this work of putting plastic tags on crabs and having international meetings to negotiate self-imposed bureaucratic minutiae. Or we humans can pull it off by counting, measuring, and tagging—we can get out of this mess through the processes of re-enchanting the world and making it thrilling and wondrous.

Much like the Earth is geologically formed from strata, this chapter attempts to negotiate the stacked material temporalities (personal, familial, generational, historical, human, crab, geological, deep) as a way of revealing how we co-habit the Earth. We are attempting to learn and live in times of catastrophe. This moral horizon is so complicated and frustrating in trying to figure out how to be a better resident of the Earth and neighbor to its other inhabitants while we are also so deeply enmeshed with them.

3

Amplexed

Sitting in a room full of college students, scientists, and conservation-ists at an event for Earth Day 2016, I stifled a laugh—an uncomfortable but not uncommon situation for me, as I am sometimes overtaken by inappropriate giggling in professional settings. We were watching *Alien Crab*, a National Geographic program about horseshoe crabs, when the following narration came on as footage of horseshoe crab reproduc-tion was shown: "Males are ready to jump any females that come near. Our female hides in the sea grass, she won't give in to the first male that comes along. . . . The males get carried away. The females play hard to get, making sure only the fittest males will carry on the primordial legacy. . . . Jousting with his telson, the male asserts his dominance."[1]

Listening to this, I leaned over in my seat and whispered to the pale-ontologist I had recently befriended, "You play hard to get, girl." I rolled my eyes, but then I was chagrined when she, this very paleontologist, was next on the screen as an expert scientist to explain the relationship of horseshoe crabs to deep time. I quickly changed my demeanor to be a more serious audience member and sat thinking about the variety of narrators of the horseshoe crab's life in this short video and their varying degrees of legitimacy.

Nature programs, such as these, are just one type of narration that humans produce to explain biological reproduction.[2] Some narrations are more predominant than others, and sustaining an ability to observe and explain reproduction—be it human or nonhuman—can be a chal-lenge without invoking the master narrative punctuated by statements that support the heterosexual imperative or male prerogatives. Even when we feel our consciousness has been raised to "enlightened" and we can identify the ideological workings of biological explanations, those master narratives are so predominant that they may prevent us from "seeing" all the possibilities of what is going on. Rather, we fixate on one truth that supports the dominant cultural narratives, and we erase the social and cultural work of manufacturing that Truth, and affirm it as objective.

As the anthropologist Matei Candea has written, animals can become "symbolic ciphers"—we interpret their behaviors as the key to how our social worlds are really naturally put together; how we interact comes from nature. Candea urges us that in our fieldwork with animals we must be open to being with animals in the field rather than exclusively narrating their lives as if we can use animals as some confirmation of inherent pan-species behaviors. Through fluid movement across a continuum of attachment and engagement on one side and detachment and distance on the other,[3] social scientists, like myself, must see our role in the field as engaging with horseshoe crabs (or bees or other animals) as a form of co-producing knowledge with these animals, rather than taking data from the animals as some confirmation of a universal truth.

In this chapter, I attempt to self-consciously engage with the project of being with horseshoe crabs in their reproductive practices. Their reproduction occurs when the marine species comes to shore and is therefore the most studied component of horseshoe crab lived experience. I consider this being with, this becoming, as a form of enmeshment, which I explored in the previous chapter. There are multiple dimensions of enmeshment, including material, discursive, and psychological. Material enmeshment with horseshoe crabs is evident in this research on their acts of reproduction, the handling of the eggs, the digging of the sand, the management of their habitat. Discursive enmeshment is demonstrated through the inevitably anthropomorphic descriptions of their behavior—clearly something humans can't help, which we can then deconstruct and mine for meaning. The psychological enmeshment, which runs the risk of appearing to be essentialism, is the deep internal way humans identify with other species. These dimensions of enmeshment work in a network with one another to reinforce

Signage near a playground in Cedar Key, Florida, informing
people of the spawning habitat for horseshoe crabs. Photo by
Lisa Jean Moore.

and constitute what we come to know as ourselves and horseshoe crabs.
At a very superficial level, I reveal the discursive assumptions of universal gendered behaviors, as I have done previously with sperm cells
and honeybees. In this book, though, I want to delve more deeply and
be more attentive to the dimensions of enmeshments and unintended
consequences of how we make cuts, decisions about what to pay attention to and what to ignore, in what to include and what to exclude, as
significant in our observations.

Pity the Queen

In 2012, I completed the collaborative multispecies ethnography *Buzz* and installed five beehives on my Crown Heights rooftop. In the subsequent years, when socializing or in casual conversation, it comes up that I have expertise in urban beekeeping. Beyond requisite conversational norms, it's often surprising to me how many people seem truly interested in talking about honeybees. Most people I come across have never seen inside a beehive in real life; rather, they have a generalized sense of what goes on in the hive from movies, books, or grade school science classes. People are overwhelmingly interested in the *queen bee* and what they imagine to be her fantastic life. A collective sense of the queen bee's enviable existence is repeated by many of my friends and acquaintances; she is a social dynamo, the leader of the hive, and a powerful taskmaster.

During a summertime dinner party, while watching bees on my roof, a friend said with obvious admiration, "The queen bee is basically the alpha bitch, right?" These ideas are definitely generated through leaps of extrapolation steered by popular representations of notable *queen bees*, for example, Beyoncé (also known as Queen Bey and her fans as the Beyhive). As a sociologist doing critical animal studies, I am fascinated by this space between overt human anthropomorphism, which we believe we can identify, and actual animal behavior, which we believe exists as knowable. Humans use their observations and narration of animals to express all kinds of wishful thinking and social anxiety from heterosexual imperatives, to traditional gender norms, to patriarchy, and to matriarchy. Simultaneously, humans are forever hopeful that we can get outside of our own narration and understand the true ontology, the true essence, of animal behavior—typically we elevate scientific methods and quantification as the closest we get to singular reality.

But try as we might, we really can never get outside of our own narration. The feminist science studies scholar Karen Barad explains that "objectivity, instead of being about offering an undistorted mirror image of the world, is about accountability to marks on bodies, and responsibility to the entanglements of which we are a part."[4] Our entanglements in the world are at the same time material and discursive. Barad instructs us that, when we observe something in the natural world, it is essentially to acknowledge where we make the cuts. We are continually making decisions when we do science, observe natural phenomena, or study animals—a cut is the place where we decide what we will consider in our observation and interpretation and what we will exclude. Differences materialize because of how we make cuts—there is a difference between a queen bee and a worker bee because we make the cut around biological reproduction. We then create the terms *queens* and *workers*, producing discourse to represent and produce material reality. It is both material—in so much as something is physically happening (an egg is being laid)—and discursive in that we come up with words, definitions, and descriptions for how to represent the materiality. Discursively we believe the queen bee to be powerful because we consider that she lays all the eggs and we exclude observations and interpretations of the constant surveillance of her.

In this case, the vast majority of people interpret what they think to be the queen's experience through a cut that glorifies reproductive labor. This cut is ironic to me since it doesn't seem in line with our own misogynistic species. In human everyday life, I don't typically see or experience amazed reverence for women's work or reproductive labor. But our species' misguided admiration of the queen bee is tricky. On the one hand, I don't want to take away from what I perceive to be some nascent feminist celebration of grrl power—even if it has to happen in another species expressed through queen bee love—but, on the other hand, I feel an urge to gently share my own opinion of the queen's life. I feel as if I am performing a kind of corrective even though it might steer people away from some feminist empowerment.

I explain to friends and acquaintances that the queen bee is really living a life of nonstop reproductive labor. Normally a queen bee only leaves the hive on one mating flight for her entire life. Returning to the hive with all the sperm she needs to lay up to a million eggs over her lifespan, she is, to a great extent, imprisoned in the hive as her attendants, up to a dozen worker bees, follow her. These attendants, while feeding and cleaning her, are also assessing her reproductive capacities and making decisions about her worthiness to the colony. If she is not keeping up with the reproductive needs of the hive, the attendants and other worker bees will begin to rear her successor. This successor, called a *virgin queen*, is the queen's daughter, and she will emerge from the cell and kill any other virgin queens created by workers. Often in this process of installing the new queen bee, the workers will "ball the queen"— this means they will surround the reigning queen and either sting her to death or suffocate her. If she's lucky, in the northeast of the United States, a queen will live up to 4 years, although she generally makes it to only 2.

Empathizing from my own limited experience in reproductive labor (giving birth to three daughters), I don't envy the queen, I pity her. I feel her reproductive labor is endless and highly scrutinized. She is shackled to her offspring with limited autonomy with others making decisions about her well-being and fitness—much like the oversight of human women's and girl's reproductive lives. And in my effort to be completely reflexive in my analysis, my own "reading" of the queen's life is still another layer of human exceptionalism, that filtering we do when assessing the perception of a desirable life. In thinking about the queen bee, I attempt to offer from a perspective of critical anthropomorphism, or "humanizing animals with care."[5] As a human, a sociologist, a mother, an ethnographer, and a feminist, I am situated in my particular positionality, which both enhances and limits my ability to interpret the queen bee's life.[6] These are my cuts. Is my pity any different from others' admiration? Is this endless empathetic layering of anthrocentric explanations illuminating to anyone? Obviously there is no extra-human— what Donna Haraway calls the "god trick"—interpretation of animals' experience. But I live in the world with an awareness, a psychological vulnerability and resilience to certain triggers. The way we represent queen bees, and my experience of being with them, trigger certain capacities for me to come to understand the queen bee.

I share this example of competing human interpretations of bee reproductive labor because I have seen again and again how the explanations we create about biological reproduction in nonhuman animals
recapitulate our own fixations. Our fascination with other species, and
especially their reproduction, means we plan eco-wildlife vacations to
observe Costa Rican sea turtles, California sea lions, or Canadian polar
bears.[7] In particular, there is a great deal of narrative flair used when
we are learning and exploring reproduction, be it our own or even
nonhuman animals.[8] Humans are drawn to discussions of sexual and
reproductive behavior of humans and nonhumans, and we revel in descriptions of birth, babies, and "childrearing." Each articulation of what
animals or cells are doing, from vacation guides and YouTube videos, to
feature films, high school lectures, and children's books, is richly layered
with meanings ripe for sociological interpretation.

As I explored in *Sperm Counts*,[9] cultural expectations are transmitted
to humans through the androcentric explanations of the natural world.
In the case of human semen, over and over again, we describe semen in
ways that socially reproduce ideologies of male dominance, heterosexual
drives, and animalistic instincts that lodge our interpretations into cells
as if they are enacting some universal, biologically mandated program-
ming. As an assignment in my undergraduate classes, I have students do
a deconstructive exercise after reading children's books about reproduction. This class is typically the most engaged, lively, and hilarious of the
semester. Students share their astonishment at how the children's books
describe sperm as "fast swimmers," "hard workers," and "winners,"
whereas eggs are "attractive," "waiting," and "fragile." They count the frequency of verbs used to animate sperm versus egg action and the types
of adjectives used to express sperm or egg characteristics. These human
reproductive cells are on a gender-normative date. Once you are taught
to understand the reinforcement of the heterosexual paradigm, it is relatively easy to see it layered over the descriptions of chickens, dogs, and
sperm cells. But it is important to me as a teacher and a scholar that I
don't suggest that there is one way to peel away each layer and get to the

Truth. There is only layer upon layer of description when we narrate the natural world. Our entanglements in the world mean that we make the cuts of what to consider in places that reinforce existing stratifications.

Simply put, the scientists' job is to study the horseshoe crabs. They study horseshoe crabs for a variety of reasons including conservation (to make better conditions for the species' survival) and commercial interests (to effectively mine them as raw materials for industrial profit or professional advancement). My job, as an ethnographer, is to study the horseshoe crab scientists, the environments, and the crabs, themselves— the mesh (as I detail in chapter 5). There is a certain type of training that comes with doing my job where I concentrate on deconstructing socially situated assumptions such as science's gendered or speciesist taken-for-grantedness. But I can also get absorbed into their subject position as scientist and must learn the language and skill sets of studying horse-shoe crab reproduction—thus I simultaneously enact horseshoe crab reproductive researcher and horseshoe crab scientists' research.

While I do vigorously identify as a sociologist, I must engage with and adopt scientists' tools (such as calipers to measure crabs, or vocabulary to identify the anatomy or the behavior of the crab). At the same time that I use their tools, I also categorize their tools as constructs. Sometimes during fieldwork, this can feel traitorous, as if I am betraying the trust of the scientific informant. When scientists demonstrates their method and technique of interpreting crab reproduction, I nod in agreement. But internally I also feel "Oh, this is so good," because I will transcribe my notes as juicy evidence of gendered constructions of reproduction. I am just as implicated in a messy entanglement including my loyalties to human informants, dedication to the crabs, responsibility to sociological tenets, and pressure to be a clever analyst when I analyze scientific explanations of *how horseshoe crabs reproduce.*

By being aware of my own (and others') entanglements, I'd like to explore how any emergent description of horseshoe crab reproduction is illuminating and limiting. And my observations are always partial because of those entanglements. I want to also consider the way we make cuts with respect to horseshoe crab reproduction and imagine what we are excluding. How can we account for the essence of horseshoe crab reproduction, their ontological status while they mate, without slipping into androcentric narration? How do the current renderings of horseshoe crab reproduction limit our potential of learning what the horseshoe crabs have to teach us?

Spawning Ground

Horseshoe crabs are one of the few marine animals that live submerged in the ocean—in this case, on the continental shelf—only briefly coming to the sandy shoreline to reproduce. During mating season, they may arrive at the shore attached, or *amplexed* (from the Latin *amplexus*,

Three amplexed pairs of horseshoe crabs, with satellite males maintaining positions to disperse semen at the shoreline at high tide on Plumb Beach. Photo by Lisa Jean Moore.

or embrace). In amplexus the male horseshoe crab grabs ahold of the female's opisthosoma (abdomen) with his pedipalps, sometimes called boxing-glove claws. The male grasps tenaciously to the female. In my own human interpretation, my own cut, it seems to me like the male wants to make sure he is not going to lose his chance for his sperm to be deposited close to her eggs.

Most of us are probably more familiar with images of sea turtle reproduction, having listened to dramatically narrated perilous journeys of hatchlings waddling to the ocean. But crabs also reproduce under circumstances that leave their offspring vulnerable to shore predators. In fact, it feels miraculous to me that an egg develops, hatches, and grows into a living horseshoe crab. In the mid-Atlantic region of horseshoe crab habitat, roughly three larvae per 100,000 eggs make it to fourth instar.[10] *Instar* refers to a phase between two periods of molting in the development of an arthropod. Horseshoe crabs will molt between 16 and 17 times before they reach the status of reproductive adults, which is after their final molt.[11] The fourth-instar stage would typically be reached at the end of the summer/beginning of fall of their first year of life (scientists refer to this time as *year o*). That is, if the embryo hatches out in June as a "trilobite larva" (or first instar), it would likely become a fourth instar by the fall of the same year. To reiterate, out of 100,000 eggs laid in the spring, only three horseshoe crabs are expected to be alive in the fall.[12]

From here, it takes about 10 years for horseshoe crabs to reach sexual maturity, which occurs after their final molt. In molting, horseshoe crabs emerge from the old shell by basically crawling out of the front of their old carapace and emerging as a fully formed larger crab.

At first, once they have molted, the crabs are soft and wrinkly. When handled, they feel squishy and tender—you feel as if you must be gentle with them out of concern for their safety. Over time they will swell up with water and increase their size, and their shells will harden, forming the seemingly indestructible armor. During molting, horseshoe crabs are more vulnerable to predation, mostly from birds, so normally they

Spawning horseshoe crabs at Plumb Beach, New York. Many crabs don't make it back to the water and either die or wait, at varying stages of being buried, surrounded by litter, to return to the sea at the next high tide. Photo by Lisa Jean Moore.

dig themselves into the sand to hide from their predators. Because it takes a relatively long time for horseshoe crabs to become sexually mature, management and conservation of the population can be tricky. If crabs die en masse at a particular instar owing to massive shoreline nourishment (when sand is added to a beach to remediate erosion), as described in chapter 5, then a generation of crabs can fail to mature into reproductive adults, leading to extinction vortexes.

Throughout most of the year in the northeastern United States, it is uncommon for people to see horseshoe crabs out of the water, unless they are in pursuit of a mate or actively mating. My observations of the mating season, which in North America varies slightly depending on the latitude of the local population, are from particular field sites in Cedar

Amplexed horseshoe crabs coming to shore at Plumb Beach. Photo by Lisa Jean Moore.

Key, Florida; Sandy Point, Connecticut; and most consistently Plumb Beach, New York. As described in the previous chapter, horseshoe crabs have site fidelity and generally return to the general spawning vicinity year after year. At Plumb Beach, I often wonder if I am seeing, handling, or measuring the same crabs year after year as they come back to the debris-strewn urban seashore.

Although the mating behavior of all four living species of horseshoe crab is fairly similar, I am most familiar with *Limulus*. At the end of April through May and June, at high tide, adult horseshoe crabs roughly 9- to 12-years-old glide through the water and climb up the beaches singly or in mated pairs. Mated pairs are attached female and male horseshoe crabs. Male crabs appear to be going for a ride on a female's back. They are fiercely bound together despite the perils of constantly crashing waves, eager encroachment by unattached male crabs, and variegated littered terrain. Since the female is generally 20% bigger than the male, to a neophyte an amplexed pair might look like a parent and child. But it is not the aquatic version of maternal koala bear clutching, the crabs are amplexed.

For me, the female horseshoe crab's size is affirming. Size can be intimidating or impressive, and within human psychological and cultural/ historical context large women generate a plethora of thoughts and feelings. Personally, her being so much bigger than the male resonates with my own lifetime of being an above-average-sized woman. Watching an amplexed pair, I find her large body leading the way and determining the speed and direction of their movement thrilling. I am almost 6 feet tall, I am muscular, and I have been bigger, taller, and heavier than every single sexual partner. My own complicated relationship to femininity, my internal dialogues of what gets to count as a girl or woman, the challenges of taking up less room than my body demands, the struggle of finding flats that look good with a dress—these all come to mind when I watch female crabs, measure their bodies, weigh them, photograph them.

This tight gripping of amplexus typically creates "mating scars" on female crabs. When I first heard this term, *mating scars*, I was struck and started researching the terminology. With the help of my librarian Darcy Gervasio, I discovered that *mating scar* or *mating scars* does not appear at all in the *Oxford English Dictionary*. We also could not find anything in online biology encyclopedias or dictionaries. Google's Ngram Viewer, which tracks occurrences of words in published books from 1800 to 2008, shows the first occurrence of "mating scars" around 1950. Even today, it's not a very commonly occurring term at all. *Mating scars* isn't used idiomatically and doesn't seem to have as much cultural relevance as a term like *queen bee*, for example.[13] Outside of horseshoe crabs, the term *mating scars* is often used when discussing the courtship bites on the pectoral fins of female sharks during reproduction. The term *scars* brings to mind a sense of attack, as in battle scars, suggesting nonvoluntary or forced copulation. As we consider where to make the cut, I wonder, could these marks be thought of as more embellishments or ornamentations or adornments from contact?

I can relate to this idea of being marked by reproduction. Just as the mating scar indicates to others that a female crab has participated in reproduction, I have had this experience of realizing others could tell I had given birth. After I had my first daughter, I met with a new gynecologist. During a routine pelvic examination, she said to me, "I see your cervix is smiling." I was confused. She clarified, "When a woman has had a baby, her cervix changes from the circular os to a more of a slit with upturned edges." She grabbed a mirror to show me my cervix and explained the os to me, the passage between the vagina and the uterus. My smiling cervix revealed something about my reproductive status similar to the horseshoe crab mating scars.

Mark Botton points to mating scars on a female carapace. This female also has a wound below her mating scar area on the left side of her carapace. Photo by Lisa Jean Moore.

Horseshoe crabs engage in external fertilization—meaning that even though the male is attached to the female, his body does not enter hers to fertilize the eggs. The female will dig herself into the sand and lay batches of eggs at around 10–20 centimeters in total.[14] A batch, or *clutch*, as it is called, is roughly the size of a golf ball and contains a couple thousand to 8,000 eggs.[15] She returns to the sea after several days of nesting, and the males let go and search for other mates. Since the spawning season, in the Mid-Atlantic region, is about a month to 6 weeks long, in a given year, a female horseshoe crab can lay some 80,000 to 100,000 eggs. During spawning season, as part of my assistance in a research project, I have picked up adult female crabs for measurement. I was taught how to manually stimulate their gonopores, the two slits in front of (anterior to) the book gills (these gonopores are nublike protrusions in males). Book gills enable the horseshoe crab to breath in and out of water as long as they are moist. These gills absorb oxygen through leaflike membranes and the five sets that flatten out when the crab is on land and become more full when in water. Gently massaging and applying pressure to the gonopores can cause a bunch of eggs to pop out of her body. The eggs resemble small, green ball bearings.

As the female is laying her eggs, the male will release his sperm. We presume that the eggs are laid through a big cloud of sperm. As stated by one horseshoe crab scientist, "Sperm of the horseshoe crab does not swim until it is capacitated, and it is capacitated when it comes in contact with [the] chemical coming off the eggs. It only begins to swim very close to the eggs. Otherwise it is carried in currents. Once it gets very close, it swims very hard, and the eggs have a large jelly layer on them, and the sperm has an acrosome [a hat-like structure that that forms over the head of a sperm cell and releases chemicals during fertilization of an ovum], and it's kind of coiled up inside, and it has to penetrate the jelly." I was thrilled by this explanation of the horseshoe crab eggs, as they enabled capacitation of the sperm. In horseshoe crabs, as in humans,[16] eggs have more active participation in reproduction than they are typically given credit for in popular explanations of fertilization.

The attached male is in a prime position to have his sperm fertilize the eggs, but he is often not alone in fertilization. Attracted by visual and chemical cues, other male horseshoe crabs often follow the amplexed pair around at the shoreline; these unattached males are called *satellites*. Not all amplexed pairs have satellites, as there are *monandrous* females—those who mate with only one male. It is the *polyandrous* females who attract satellites. Walking down the shoreline during spawning season, I've become aware of my strange compassion for satellite males. I find myself strangely rooting for them in their attempts to get close to the amplexed pair even though I now know it is rare for a satellite to overtake the attached male's position.[17] There is something compelling about the ever-hopeful interloper waiting in the wings; it's reminiscent of the perennial underdog. When I shared this with Jane Brockmann, she reminded me, "But the point is that he fertilizes a lot of the eggs as a satellite. Our paternity analyses show that a male in the no. 1 position over the female's incurrent canal can expect to fertilize half of the eggs she is laying; when there are two males in that position, each can expect on average to fertilize 38% of the female's eggs. They don't need to take over the attached male's position! When we conducted the first paternity analyses in horseshoe crabs, we were very surprised by how successful the satellites were." My human interpretation of crab's "underdog" behavior is changing to "crazy like a fox"; instead of seeing satellite crabs as bumbling losers, perhaps these crabs' reproductive strategies of staying on sidelines is an effective way for their genetic materials to get into the mix.

Buried in the sand, the embryos develop limb buds, and roughly 3 weeks later they emerge from their outer membrane to become larvae. This post-hatch stage is called the *trilobite stage* because of the larva's superficial resemblance to a trilobite, the earliest known marine arthropod, now extinct. Horseshoe crabs forming in the egg are really exciting to look at under a microscope; all of the legs are fully formed, and they swim around in a clear membrane as if they are encased in a clear marble.

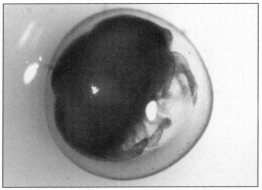

Horseshoe crab embryos inside clear eggs. Photos by Jennifer Mattei.

Female Mate Selection

In April 2016, I took a research trip to Cedar Key, which is in Florida, located on the Gulf of Mexico. The purpose of my trip was to meet with two experts on horseshoe crab mating behaviors, H. Jane Brockmann, an animal behaviorist and evolutionary biologist with a substantial record of horseshoe crab research, and Mary Klugh Hart, a behavioral ecologist. I had first met these two scientists when they presented a riveting paper entitled "Condition-Dependent Mate Choice in the American Horseshoe Crab (*Limulus polyphemus*)" in Japan during the 2015 workshop.

At this point, I had spent 2 years in the field and had never come across work such as theirs—lab-based experiments of mate choice. As Mary shared, "Female mate choice is a well studied concept in behavioral ecology, but hasn't been so much in horseshoe crabs." During the meeting in Japan, I was struck by how people (those much more knowledgeable about horseshoe crabs than myself) were also very taken with Mary's explanation of the female horseshoe crab's role in reproductive pairing. The basic finding of this experiment was that monandrous females and attached monandrous males choose high-quality mates, whereas mate choice is weak for polyandrous female and attached polyandrous males. I wanted to ask more questions, but Mary and Jane were in high demand at the meeting, and I felt it best to just observe.

I had hoped that this Cedar Key trip would be an excellent opportunity to have some time to interview Mary and Jane. But work came first. After recovering from being slightly lost in my rental car and overcoming spotty cell service, I met Jane at my hotel. I quickly changed into my water shoes, grabbed my fanny pack full of camera, sunscreen, and water, and jumped in her car, whisked off to the beach. The tagging and measuring of crabs must be done at high tide, and we were in a bit of a rush since I had made us late. But we were able to measure and tag 25 crabs that afternoon; Jane had three field sites working that day along the key, so I felt lucky to be paired with her. With skill and patience, Jane explained her process for tagging crabs and the tools needed to measure them.

As I handled these Florida Gulf Coast crabs I was astonished by how incredibly clean they were. Unlike the barnacled, scarred, and pitted exteriors of their New York peers, these crabs' carapaces were gorgeous, smooth, almost silky.[18] A mucusy slime covered younger crabs, secreted from pores in their shells, which, Jane explained, had properties to prevent fouling organisms (like barnacles and other organisms) from growing on the crabs. I had never felt this slime in New York, but I tagged many crabs in Florida that were slippery and filmy. Beyond the crabs, the habitat at Cedar Key was incredibly beautiful and slightly unreal

Back of a vehicle on Cedar Key, ready for measuring and tagging crabs: Styrofoam bucket for weighing crabs, scale, ruler,
awl, and two tags (smaller for males, larger for females).
Photo by Lisa Jean Moore.

to me, like a movie set. Warm sea breezes, no trash, mangroves on the
shoreline, pelicans perched atop empty docks.

During a late afternoon snack after tagging horseshoe crabs, Mary,
Jane and I sat down on a verandah overlooking the water. I asked them
why in Japan there was such an interest in Mary's presentation. "It
seemed that people were really interested in your work," I said, while
drinking a cold beer. Jane responded,

Yes, they were very interested in it. Everything [that] has always been done on horseshoe crab reproductive behavior has been very largely done on males because they are perceived to be the active ones. The females sort of come ashore and dig in, and the males are the ones that are crowding around the pairs, and so forth. In fact, most of the scholarly work has been done on males. When I give talks I used to say, "Well, I don't have much to say about females—there isn't any research." And it doesn't look like the females are doing anything, they just walk along and the male grabs ahold of her.

I believe Jane was being modest when she claimed not much research has been done on female horseshoe crabs. Jane's research on the subject spans decades, and she is a confirmed expert in the field, although her research on females did not start until 2010.[19]

I continued, "What struck me most during your presentation at the Japan meetings was the commentary that people gave at the talk. It was almost as if people found it titillating." Mary grinned. "Sure, yeah, people always do that. They love sex." Jane chimed in, "Yes, and they love these satellite males—I mean whenever I talk about the satellite males people go crazy. They all have fun." I sheepishly shared how I also felt sort of an affinity for satellite males. They laughed, and I asked, "Why do you think people identify with the male crabs?" Taking a sip of her drink, Mary thought for a moment. "The males definitely identify with it. When you give talks to the public, they joke about it—they go home talking about it. People do that about animal behavior all the time." We continued to discuss the challenges of describing animal reproduction without slipping into human-biased assumptions. I brought up the role of empathy and how it can create a way of connecting cross-species divides.

"I guess like me they feel sorry for these guys, like they are the hangers-on, the losers," I added. Shaking her head, Jane corrected my assumption: "Satellite males are actually very successful. When they are on shore they get themselves into particular positions where they are able to fertilize eggs. There is some jostling for the male-attached position, but there is relatively little takeover. I don't even think they are trying to take over most of the time. They settle in, in this area between the prosoma [the front part of the horseshoe crab's body] and the opisthosoma [the bottom half of the horseshoe crab's body, which is connected to the telson]—they have this very particular place they like to be and want to go to. The very particular place, we have shown, in that position they have very high paternity." Surprising. I felt embarrassed by my assumption of the satellites' buffoonery. I misunderstood their strategies, their wisdom. My empathy was misplaced? I wondered out loud, "The one that is attached has high paternity, too?" Jane continued, "Not as much as you would think, he does when he is alone since an attached male has 100% paternity. When there is one attached and one in this position it is 40% for the satellite and 60% for the attached male. But when there are two it is 40%, 40%, and 20% for the attached male. So they do very well in this satellite position, even some further out positions—they tend to do less well but do take some away from the satellites."

Since a great deal of horseshoe crabs' lives take place out in the ocean away from readily available viewing it is difficult to know what precisely is going on with respect to amplexus. We have to guess at some of these questions: At what depth to crabs attach? How long are they attached before they come to shore? As Jane states, "My impression is that most of the pairing is done further out in the water. It's not done real close to shore." So some of horseshoe crab reproductive research is done within a laboratory instead of being "in the wild." Observing animals in the laboratory, while certainly limited, does lead to discoveries. Jane continued, "We know something else which is quite interesting—one of my grad students and I noticed that when we were keeping these animals, they poop a lot. There is a lot of poop when we keep them in these tanks. But we noticed that the attached males didn't poop much. And we noticed that indeed they did not poop because they don't eat."

Now my concerns shifted to the attached males as being deserving of my concern. I blurted out, "How long do they not eat?" Jane smiled again. "Our animals only stay attached for a couple of weeks at the most. Occasionally you will see an animal that has been attached for longer than that. I picture them attached in advance of coming to shore—1 week to 2 weeks. However, in some of these northern populations, they can stay together the whole season. And he doesn't eat the whole time. Occasionally a little grass gets in there but the female's tail is covering his mouth. He really can't eat—whereas the satellite males and females are eating a lot and even when they are breeding." It doesn't appear to harm younger males to not eat. But perhaps it is worth it to be a satellite male, I thought. You get some paternity, you get to eat, and you have your freedom to move around to different females at will.

I learned that males become reproductive after their terminal molt and that, on average, attached males are younger than satellites. Jane and Mary believe this suggests that older males can't go without eating for that long. Turning our conversation toward females, I asked about female mate choice and the presentation in Japan again. I reminded Mary of the description of the female behaviors of swimming away or bucking off males. She recollected her observations during her experiments. "It was surprising to see the female resistance. It was a bucking where she looked like she was trying to avoid having the male attach. Most of the time he did eventually attach. But it appeared to be resistance—in the wild, maybe she could get away from him. But we had her enclosed." Jane chimed in, "It was also a hard bottom so we don't know if she would have scurried away." "Or," Mary added, "even buried."

Do female horseshoe crabs have reproductive agency? Can reproductive experiments reveal some behaviors of female horseshoe crabs that go beyond a description of her passively getting mounted? As Mary and Jane continued to explain their lab experiments to me, they pointed out that there was evidence that female horseshoe crabs appear to be resisting the male attaching. Jane shared, "Some females do not like satellites and won't tolerate them, and she will leave the beach if one joins her. She will not nest. Some females attract males and some do not. This is based on an experiment we did with cement models." This experiment that Mary describes involves a cement model decoy used to observe horseshoe crab mate behavior in the laboratory. The scientists have determined that male crabs use different cues to find a single female or amplexed pairs in their reproductive quest. Mary continues: "And they [the male crabs] use visual cues to find pairs and some chemical cues. So we know that when you place a cement model of a horseshoe crab pair over the site of a polyandrous female [that has been removed] and a model over a monandrous site, the satellites will be attached only to the site where a polyandrous female had been nesting. It was just the odors in the sand that attracted males—that is all it could have been. Something in the sand is different, and they know to come or not come." In other words, the female crabs leave cues that the males read, cues that indicate female mate preference—monandrous or polyandrous.

"So," I asked, "what is the significance of this research?" Jane continued, "Some females are attractive to satellite males, and some are unattractive to males. We have done an experiment in which we guide a male into a particular female. For a female that doesn't want to attract additional males, he will hang out for a few minutes and jostle with the attached male to get himself into the special position, and she will get up and leave. These are the intolerant monandrous females." I felt as if my head exploded. *What*? I thought, *Intolerant Monandrous Females sounds like the name of a punk rock band. Up there with my other favorites the Incompetent Cervixes and the Hostile Vaginas.* I stifled a desire to share my private chuckle while Mary spoke:

Oh man, people love that. I don't know why people love it. I gave a couple talks and I remember running into people who saw the talk and they were joking about these intolerant females who wouldn't have other males except for the one attached. It is really common in behavioral ecology—you have higher density, and more sperm competition—satellite males are a well-known concept. But these people [in the audience] want to make it match to their life. As scientists, we have to be very careful about being objective and not trying to make some decision or declarations about what the females are doing based on what we would do as a female—and yet when you give a talk—you use a lot of metaphors.

I sympathize with Jane and Mary in their challenges of trying to figure out the reproductive patterns of horseshoe crabs, especially given the dearth of prior research on female horseshoe crabs. They are simultaneously attempting to elucidate the mechanisms of reproduction and represent the range of variations in reproductive possibilities while figuring out the why of these differences. In creating classifications like *polyandrous* and/or terms like *intolerant females*, these horseshoe crab researchers' choices of words are not without politics.

Unable to control myself, I quickly burst out, "How did you come up with the word *intolerant*?" Sensing my judgment, Mary answered, "Jane tried to come up with the least leading terms possible. She really thinks about it." Jane thought for a moment. "I think it was Sheri, my post doc," she said, "who came up with it. Or maybe we talked about it. It just seemed like a good explanation of what was going on. They just don't tolerate it. A good description." And I couldn't really at the moment think of anything to say, so I nodded. It was true they didn't tolerate the options available, so the females leave the beach, presumably to try laying eggs at the beach again another time. What if they had come up with other terms instead of *intolerant females*? Possible terms that occur to me are *highly selective females* that were wisely rejecting *deficient males* or *mediocre males*—scientists really don't know why certain males are rejected. But given the context of our species adherence to heterosexual imperatives and misogyny, the term *intolerant females* emerges as a term that "makes sense" because it fits within our sense-making culture. Females who don't want to mate are intolerant of business as usual with satellite males.

What happens when I ask scientists to reflect on the ways they make these determinations (or cuts)? In the case of Mary and Jane, I tentatively ask for an accounting of the term *intolerant females* since clearly I am more struck by it than they are. I am tentative because I deeply respect and appreciate the very detailed, painstaking labor-intensive and under-recognized work that they do. They cannot get hung up on discourse every time they do research or make a field observation, or they would never get anything done. They must move past the term to attempt to understand the animal's behavior. However, in the process of doing science, there is disregard, erasure, or minimization of the term's particular history or politics. We often don't consider fully how the term we use actually frames what we see.

As part of my methodological and factual checking for this book, I shared my interpretations with Jane Brockmann, who offered,

> I completely agree. [In] some studies in animal behavior, the entire field has been turned around when someone thought to change the metaphor. For example, the term *pair bonding* was very popular when referring to birds in which male and female were nearly always found together during the breeding season, but Janis Dickinson watched the behavior closely in her bluebirds, and she realized that it was the male that was always following the female—so she changed the metaphor to *mate guarding*.[20] This completely changed the way people thought about the behavior, and entirely new hypotheses emerged as a result. However, what is missing in the description above, is our objective definition of *intolerant* [it is when a female leaves the beach within 2 minutes after an unattached male touches the attached male or the female].
>
> These are females that don't attract satellite males, so we determine this with an experiment in which we guide an unattached male over to the monandrous pair. By this definition, some monandrous females are *intolerant*, that is, they leave the beach, whereas others are *tolerant* of the satellite, that is, they remain on the beach and continue nesting when the satellite joins the pair. We explicitly use this specific definition in all our studies.

It is obvious that Jane and her team of researchers are extremely specific in their definition of descriptive concepts for animal behavior; however, as Max Weber would point out, it is the unintended consequences of how these terms travel and are used that sociologists must investigate.

The narratives we create to explain animal behaviors are inevitably infused with our human understanding of nature. Our individual lived experiences and learned outlooks inform the "cuts" we make in gathering and interpreting information about the "natural" world. These cuts are important to acknowledge for their trickle-down cultural, political, and social consequences. I have argued that it is not possible to avoid making cuts, but we can be aware of them and better account somehow for our own existence in the mesh when doing natural science.

Specifically, this chapter has demonstrated the different ways we make cuts when studying the reproductive practices of horseshoe crabs. Not all cuts are created equal since there are hierarchies of knowledge. For instance, my valorization of female horseshoe crabs because I identify with their girth and weight is not as relevant as a scientific explanation of their egg-density production. Cuts matter since they have politics and can reinforce and reify the social stratification that exists in our everyday lives (e.g., that heterosexuality is natural because we see it in almost all species). Our enmeshment with horseshoe crabs—material, discursive, psychological—and our becoming and being with them means that we will continue to anthropomorphize our interpretations of them. It is a flawed skill, but it is the one we have. However, when we read the same narratives that are familiar to us back onto the animals, we then limit what is possible for us to imagine and learn from them. We are merely affirming our culture, naturalizing our beliefs. I'd like to push us to look for what is not traditionally celebrated and reread narratives differently or even to naturalize other, subversive narratives. I work to queer our cuts, be out about our anthropomorphism, and generate transgressive epistemologies.

4

Bled

Voluntary Donations

During my college's spring break, while my daughters were in school, I had hoped to make a great deal of progress on this book manuscript. One afternoon, feeling antsy and distracted, I pondered a drive out to Plumb Beach to just hang out with crabs for inspiration. I quickly nixed that plan since March in Brooklyn is still too cold for crabs (and possibly me) to be on the beach. I felt frustrated. I wanted to think about crabs differently—not just by staring at photographs, handling my collection of dried out carapaces, rereading my field notes, or transcribing interviews.

I recalled my graduate school methodology classes. Anselm Strauss, the founder of my program and developer of grounded theory, a methodological technique and deductive process whereby analysts incorporate as much data as possible to generate theories, had told a group of us that if we were feeling stuck and too immersed in our own research, we should put ourselves in an unfamiliar but analogous situation. This method is a way of making our field site new to us. So, when studying the everyday work of window washers who scale skyscrapers, go to the circus and watch how performers navigate the high wire. Being in novel locations, he argued, could generate fresh ways to look at social phenomena as emergent rather than fixed. I'd been thinking about how horseshoe crab blood, when described for its unique benefit to pharmaceutical safety, is characterized. Mulling over scientific articles and my own interviews, I was struck by the ongoing human construction of horseshoe crab bleeding as a *donation*—"a biomedical gift," as noted in a pharmaceutical giveaway notebook,[1] In particular, a statement from the documentary *Alien Crab* stays with me, that horseshoe crabs "take an arrow to the heart" in their donation for every man, woman and child.[2] This evocation of the willingness, even glory, of the crab's intentions was startling to me. In pure grounded-theory technique to generate ideas, I could write a coding memo about blood—or better yet, I could think of other sites of blood extraction and donation.

I heeded Strauss's advice, and on March 25, 2016, I was on the subway to downtown Brooklyn, heading to my blood donation appointment. I was working on my book by donating blood like the crabs, while also doing something I perceived to be an unqualified good and noble thing. A skip in my step propelled me down the sidewalk brimming with a toothy smile. The front door of the New York Blood Bank advertised, "Donate blood now, people can't live without it." That's right, I thought, as I pushed open the door.

As I filled in the requisite forms, I inhaled handfuls of jellybeans from an automated machine. I thought back to my last donation. I

New York Blood Bank, downtown Brooklyn. Photo by Lisa Jean Moore.

proudly remembered I was a universal donor, having O negative blood type; however, my previous blood donation wasn't as easy to recall as I thought it would be. Could it really have been over 20 years since I donated? Shocked at how time had passed, I justified myself—I was pregnant or breastfeeding for many of those years. I'd lived in England, which temporary disqualified me owing to mad cow disease fears. I'd gotten a tattoo, a nose piercing. I'd had a few surgeries. Shaking my head back to reality, enough excuses, I was here now and ready to give.

The receptionist asked if I wanted to be a plasma donor, but I had to pick up my first grader at the bus stop, and I couldn't spare the 2 hours. If I had a high enough iron content in my blood, I'd do a red cell donation, but a finger prick test revealed that my levels were too low. A nurse led me into the donation room for whole blood donation. Three people occupied eight of the reclined chairs, each equipped with television monitors and adjustable leg and arm rests. A young African American man dressed in a Desiigner concert T-shirt and black jeans was dozing off, an older African American woman focused on knitting, and a white woman, about my age, spoke on her phone. Nodding to my new friends in the other chairs, I made myself comfortable. The nurse painlessly tapped my vein while I shot furtive glances at the other people, hoping to strike up a conversation about how amazing we all were to be doing this together. I had no takers.

For the next 5 minutes, I busied myself taking selfies until the nurse told me that moving around so much was dangerous for my needled arm. Smiling and shaking her head, she gently took my phone and took a photo of me—handing it back, she softly said, "You can stop taking pictures now." After 10 minutes, I was done and happily eating cookies and drinking cranberry juice. As I left the building, I walked down Fulton Street, a bustling shopping district in Brooklyn, and looked at each person, imagining that *my* blood was coursing through *their* veins. Truly feeling at one with the other people, as if we all *were* the same species, it was a magical short walk to the subway. I believe this feeling of euphoria—or perhaps in less dramatic people, connection—is a great part of the motivation for people giving blood. Yes, the mundane donation of giving blood on a weekday with no real pressing cause is not as visible as the donations made in response to national tragedies. The televised images of lines around the block for blood donation after the Orlando Pulse Nightclub massacre or 9/11 attest to the human ethic of care in the face of deaths. We flock to help our fellow humans by offering our personal supply of elixir. Ironically, even though these crisis-driven blood donation responses may make us feel like we are doing something, evidence suggests that donating blood in a sustained, routinized, and predictable way is of much greater value than crisis donation.[3]

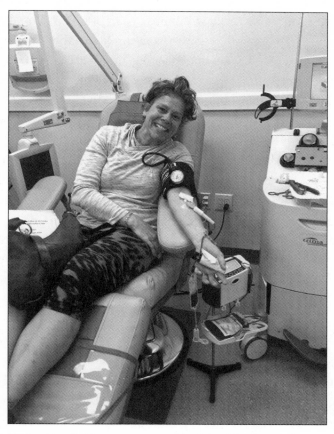

Giving blood. Photo courtesy of the blood bank nurse.

I am interested in this feeling that blood donation taps into, an example of what Marx meant by being in touch with your *species being*. Understanding the notion of the species being had always been elusive to me—like the Holy Ghost of my Catholic upbringing. I easily got how capitalism created conditions in which I was alienated from my labor power, my self, my fellow humans, but I never really understood this other category of species being. As Marx wrote, "To say that man is a species being, is, therefore, to say that man raises himself above his own subjective individuality, that he recognizes in himself the objective universal, and thereby transcends himself as a finite being. Put another way, he is individually the representative of mankind."[4] This type of grandiosity was never really within my realm of understanding—even when giving birth—but for some reason, thinking about my own blood or other human blood being shared among our species cracked the mystery. It was intoxicating to see oneself as outside of being a finite being, rather, being enmeshed with all other humans over the shared biological life force. Our blood, the blood of our species, was alive in me and in them and could be transferred between us. It was glorious to see this interconnectedness, and rather than walk down the street with typical irritation and impatience, I saw us, the people of the Fulton Mall in Brooklyn, as part of a bustling oneness. And understanding horseshoe crabs' blood enabled this entire experience to happen for me.

I've continued to reflect on my giving blood, something I have done several more times during the revision of this manuscript, while coming to understand human use of horseshoe crab blood. I contemplate the mesh of this specific biological transfer.

The Trouble with *Donation*

Humans have 10–11 pints of blood. Our blood is made up of transferable components including plasma (the clear liquid that holds the blood cells), red blood cells (oxygen-delivering cells), platelets (cell fragments involved in clotting), and other clotting factors (chemical and cellular parts that cause coagulation). Our blood is used strictly for intraspecies donation, and it is not used for any applications with nonhuman species.[5] Indeed, I haven't found any evidence of human bodily fluids or parts being used to enhance the life of nonhuman animals. The converse is not true—we've used female frogs for pregnancy testing;[6] honeybees for venom api-therapies, using bee stings to treat diseases like arthritis and multiple sclerosis;[7] and pigs' heart valves in human bodies via xenotransplantation, the process of transplanting body parts between different species;[8] to name but a handful. We've made horseshoe crabs indispensable to our human and veterinary biomedicine; we need their blood, and as health-care demand grows, we will need more and more.

Because many scientists and pharmaceutical representatives refer to collecting blood from horseshoe crabs as a *donation*, I want to dive a little deeper into the notion of a donation, defined as giving help to another. This deployment of the term *donation* performs specific cultural work and frames medical practices in a way that implies a certain consensual willingness to participate in a charitable act. A donation does not require compensation, it creates an air of noble generosity on the part of the giver, and it suggests that the giver has abundance of the resource and therefore is able to give some away.

A donation implies giving to another less fortunate than us—the receiver of the donation would typically have less power, resources, and status than the donor. During my donation of human blood, I thought of myself as a healthy, able-bodied human giving my blood to an imagined other who was sick, injured, and fighting for his or her life.

Despite powerful and dominant humans using *donation* as the model of understanding horseshoe crab bleeding in films, at conferences, and in popular media, not everyone understands the bleeding of horseshoe crabs as quite so altruistic. Perhaps in a broader sense, our relationship with horseshoe crabs could be described as parasitic. A heated exchange I'll recount here illustrates the contest to establish the acceptable definition of horseshoe crab bloodletting. In Japan while attending the 2015 International Workshop on the Science and Conservation of Horseshoe

Crabs, a pharmaceutical representative from Charles Rivers Laboratories presented a lecture on horseshoe crab blood. He described the industry's stance on the bleeding of horseshoe crabs: "We look at it like the Red Cross. They are making a donation. We care deeply about the animals and work with regulated harvesters. We do not buy injured animals." Pushing the representative beyond this seemingly prepared sound bite, a marine researcher and fellow conference participant whom I was sitting next to voiced concern: "But when you drain the crabs, what about the long-term effects of draining them? What measures do you take to insure their longevity beyond just placing them back in their habitat?" he thoughtfully asked.

The pharmaceutical representative cleared his throat, but before he could respond, Jack Levin, one of the key scientists responsible for discovering and innovating *Limulus* amoebocyte lysate (LAL) test immediately turned to face him. He looked exasperated. "Why do you use the word 'drain'? That is so dramatic and inaccurate. We are not draining the crabs," he said. Surprised by this direct question, the marine researcher shrugged. He asked, "Ok, then, what would you call it?" In a precise voice and stern tone, Dr. Levin stated, "I would say the crabs are being bled, but when you say draining you are misrepresenting it. The crabs rarely die, and it is astoundingly easy to get blood from them and not kill the animal as long as they are carefully handled." The session ended, and I turned to the marine researcher, who said with a smile, "I think I need a cup of coffee."

This interaction, which I've witnessed in some form or another several times, demonstrates the cultural work of establishing the legitimate and authoritative definition of how crabs are used by the pharmaceutical industry. The discursive skirmishes express the opposing viewpoints of crabs as either having their blood *donated* or *drained*. Indeed, the film *Horseshoe Crabs: Prehistoric Paramedics* features an interview with the same Charles River representative I met in Japan.[9] When describing the bleeding of crabs in the film, he explains, "When we received the crabs we have to do a couple things. We scrape off all the barnacles; we hose them down, so they get a bath as well. So we kind of like to say it's like a spa day for the horseshoe crabs. They get a manicure. They get a nice bath. Then they are wheeled into an environmentally controlled area where we actually bleed the animals." There is a concerted effort on the part of many humans to reinforce the description of bleeding of horseshoe crabs as easy, harmless, and quick. Creating this groundwork of the bleeding as safe and regulated makes the leap to a more lay explanation of horseshoe crab bloodletting as a *donation* is not a stretch. These different definitions are based on the question of horseshoe crab/human intentions: Can the bleeding of crabs be characterized as their altruism for us or our exploitation of them? And what are the stakes in these characterizations? If horseshoe crabs are capable of donation and altruism, then they are capable of decision making or some form of compassionate thinking. In the case of horseshoe crabs, this persistence of *donation* is more peculiar because the crabs do not consent to being donors in any perceivable way. They are actually harvested by fishermen through trawls or hand-harvesting methods, who then sell the crabs to a middleman or to the pharmaceutical industry. The role of donation falls on the crab, but the commerce stays with a variety of humans.

I want to pause here for a moment to be careful that my analysis is not too binary. Yes, I do believe, as will become more obvious through this chapter, that the biomedicalized pharmaceutical industry has some culpability in historic and contemporary poor treatment of horseshoe crabs. But the industry has made great strides, in responding to pressure from conservation biologists and others, in establishing standard operating procedures that minimize immediate physical harm to the crabs. In the words of one biochemist and technical director of an LAL facility, "I strongly believe all companies are well monitored and well disciplined to care for horseshoe crabs."[10] Truly, since there is great profit to be generated from horseshoe crabs, many actors in the pharmaceutical industry understand the necessity of horseshoe crab conservation. It is not insignificant that pharmaceutical innovators and horseshoe crabs have collaboratively given us the gift of protection and increased health through the LAL test. And it is not simply that pharmaceutical actors are bad and the rest of us are good; we are all implicated.

Importantly, I want to also resist the potential of blaming the fishermen for harvesting crabs. Most do not, as far as I have observed in my limited analysis, show disregard for the life of horseshoe crabs—they understand crabs are part of their livelihood. As fisheries have been depleted through the decades, maintaining a standard of living within the fishing economy has become increasingly challenging. Making a living in this contemporary world often means deciding how to do less harm while eeking out a living. In other words, in late capitalism, informal and illicit economies emerge not only out of pure avarice but also out of dire need and all the variants in between.

During a meeting in Japan, I asked the representative of Charles River, the largest manufacturer of LAL, what fishermen were paid per crab. He replied with a sly smile, "That's an industry secret that we keep close to our chests, but let's just say we make it worth their while." I absolutely felt like I needed to take a shower after that brief interaction. Later in the afternoon, different ecological scientists and conservationists sought me out and gave me ranges of figures paid for U.S. horseshoe crabs. The numbers were between $3 and $25 per crab. I have no verification of any financial figures, as it is also very difficult to speak with fishermen about fees because they enter into confidentiality agreements with pharmaceutical companies.[11]

Returning to human blood, the current voluntary, donation-based model is one that has emerged over time. Human blood donation was not always a charitable act. The British sociologist Richard Titmuss predicted that paying blood donors would run the risk of reducing the quality of blood donated (as financial motivation would lead individuals to conceal conditions of drug addiction or infectious diseases), which in the long run would make blood more expensive.[12] Titmuss believed that there was superior moral and economic value to altruistic donations over ego-driven (paid) ones, and a meta-analysis conducted in 2013 confirmed the hypothesis, finding that it is economically inefficient to pay donors for blood donation.[13]

In the present day, it is illegal to pay for blood in the United States. The legal historian and biochemist Kara Swanson dates the acceptance of blood donation and transfusion as a medical practice to the 1910s, afterward becoming more commonplace during World War II as a national blood supply was created. By 1975, payment for whole blood donations had been eliminated.[14] Blood donation is presently part of the gift economy.[15] However, it is still possible to value human blood through the ways it is priced within the U.S. Biomedical Industrial Complex—health insurers bill patients about $70 per unit of plasma. A unit of red cells is $180, and platelets are $600.[16] Our blood is used for a wide variety of intraspecies applications, such as transfusions during trauma emergencies, scheduled surgeries, platelet replenishment for people with clotting disorders, and plasma for autoimmune disorders. The Food and Drug Administration (FDA) limits refrigerated red blood cell use to 42 days, although some research is emerging that this limit should be made even shorter as fresher blood leads to better outcomes.[17] Furthermore, there are several blood products created from human blood, such as Rhogam (Rh_0[D] immune globulin [human]), an intramuscular injection medicine made from human blood that is used to prevent an immune response when humans are exposed to incompatible Rh blood proteins. Rhogam is most commonly used when maternal and fetal Rh proteins are different and has enabled healthier births.

Rarely do humans think they will ever need another person's blood. Yet our lives are unpredictable. Accidents, injuries, and disease always happen. Although there are surges in donations around times of national tragedies, trouble comes at all times, requiring mundane, consistent, routine donation. So as a species, we have difficulty meeting the need for human blood in our donation system. The American Association of Blood Banks estimates that at any given time 38% of the U.S. population is eligible to donate blood, but annually less than 10% of the population does so.[18] It is true that many people are eliminated from the population of eligibles owing to perceived risks. I use the term *perceived* because bans are not without controversy.[19] In particular, it has only been since 2015 that the FDA lifted its 30-year policy banning men from donating blood if they had had sex with men even once, providing that the men hadn't had sex with another man for 1 year. And as anecdotal reports from the aftermath Orlando mass shooting suggest, gay and bisexual men have been turned away even if they meet the 1-year restriction. But even among those deemed eligible to give blood by the homophobic policies and practices of the American Red Cross, donating blood is an altruistic act that most people opt not to do.

Our species has developed techniques to make human blood and blood products transferable. These technological innovations and our social practice of donating blood both represent social solidarity and enhance our personal sense of communion and kinship. But what of using horseshoe crab blood? It isn't an intraspecies experience for them, and there is no social solidarity argument to be made. Their blood is taken from their bodies by force and used exclusively for the benefit of other species. There is also no way of apprehending the crabs' own motivations or affective reactions to bloodletting. Whereas I have experienced the temporary euphoria of donating blood and knowing it will help another person, I don't imagine crabs experience this same feeling.

Thicker than Water

Horseshoe crab blood "donation" is indeed a different experience from human blood donation, but importantly, horseshoe crab blood itself is very different from human blood. Not everyone will get a human blood transfusion or a human blood product in their lifetime, but probably every human since the 1970s has directly or indirectly benefited from horseshoe crab blood through its ability to detect toxins. Unlike our blood, which is iron-based—containing hemoglobin and appearing red when we bleed—horseshoe crab blood is copper-based—containing hemocyanin and appearing blue when they bleed (as do spiders, crustaceans, and octopus). As the hematologist Jack Levin and the marine biologist Frederick Bang discovered in the 1960s, horseshoe crab blood could be used to make an actual clinical diagnostic test for such diseases as spinal meningitis and bacterial sepsis.[20] This blood-clotting defense in the crabs is one of the reasons scientists speculate that the species has lived through eons in seas teeming with harmful and pathogenic bacteria. The crabs have innate immunity, a defense mechanism that crabs are born with that creates an immediate reaction to antigens or infection. As Mark Botton explains, horseshoe crab immune systems "are rather basic and contain amoebocytes. When they get an infection, crabs don't have antibodies, but instead they release materials from the bloodstream that can create an immediate clotting to ward off infections before they become systemic." Amoebocytes are mobile cells that perform a role similar to our white blood cells in defense against pathogens. This clotting difference is what makes it so valuable for humans.

Horseshoe crabs are a commodity species "noteworthy because of their role in generating profit."[21] Ian Frazier, in a 2014 *New Yorker* article, wrote that horseshoe crab blood sold for as much as $15,000 per quart. He went on to share his frustration at getting any pharmaceutical scientists or representatives to speak for any duration or with any substance during his research.[22] This figure of $15,000, while oft-quoted, is not entirely accurate. As explained by Tom Novitsky, a microbiologist and biochemist who, until 2003, ran Associates of Cape Cod, a leading manufacturer of LAL, coming to a figure of the monetary value of LAL is a complex math calculation (akin to something one might see on a standardized math test).

Today a single horseshoe crab costs $2.50 on average. One crab can yield about 100–200 mL (milliliters) of hemolymph (invertebrate blood). From this you get about 10 mL of blood cells (amoebocytes). Adding 1 mL of amoebocytes to 6–7 mL of water yields about 7 mL of raw LAL. When multiplied by the amount of amoebocytes per crab you get about 70 mL as the final product. In other words, 1 mL of raw LAL will yield enough product for 10 LAL tests if the most common assay, the gel clot test, is used. The average cost of one gel clot test that uses 0.1 mL of LAL is about $1. Working backward, you can get 700 tests from a single crab with a maximum of 200 mL per crab. Since a quart is about a liter (no self-respecting scientist would measure anything in quarts), a liter of LAL would be about $3,500, nowhere close to $15,000, but the myth persists! Keep in mind, however, that the LAL business is extremely profitable. Some of the newer assays use less raw LAL, but the per-assay cost is not that much less since there are other chemicals added to the formulation to produce a color that can be read in a spectrophotometer. Subtract the cost of horseshoe crab, labor, marketing, sales, and FDA compliance (which is, by far, the largest cost, but it keeps new competitors out of the market so the manufacturers don't complain), and you still have a profit margin over 80%.

Horseshoe crabs are a commodity species, and the exchange of their blood in the market is a highly protected secret; finding out more about the who, where, and why of this valuable blood is not always easy to come by. It is clear that the *primary* use of LAL is for a pyrogen test (a test for fever-causing substances) used to check pharmaceuticals and medical devices. In our everyday lives, horseshoe crab blood is used to protect humans and other domesticated animals from our dirty world, making it incredibly precious. Endotoxins are pyrogens that are heat-stable toxins that form an essential component of the cell walls of a certain large class of bacteria—the Gram-negative bacteria. They are ubiquitous, and, in the right doses—*albeit extremely large doses never encountered in pharmaceuticals intended for therapeutic use*—they are lethal to humans, livestock, and companion animals. Gram-negative bacteria, the kinds of bacteria that contain endotoxins, are named for a particular laboratory-staining test that can distinguish them from other kinds of bacteria. Most Gram-negative bacteria occur in aqueous environments—even in the purified water that is an essential component of, or part of the process of producing, intravenous drugs and devices used to deliver these drugs. These bacteria include *E. coli*, *Salmonella*,

Vibrio cholerae, Shigella, and many others, some of which are human and animal pathogens—that is, they cause disease—but many more—for example, *Psuedomonas,* an extremely common bacterium in the aquatic environment—that normally do not cause disease. Even *E. coli*—which, depending on the strain, can cause severe disease—is normally simply part of the bacterial flora of our intestinal tract.

With the advent of intravenous therapy, physicians needed a method to identify when solutions were contaminated with pyrogens during medical procedures so they could avoid transmitting them to patients, hence causing unnecessary solution-related fever. Owing to the ubiquitous nature of Gram-negative bacteria, it is easy to see how water produced for pharmaceutical use, as well as various drugs (often initially made from natural raw materials or during a process using water) could be easily contaminated. Although these preparations were always *sterilized*—that is, any living bacteria were killed or removed before a preparation would be used as an injectable drug—the heat-stable endotoxins always remained.

Here's where the real value of LAL comes in. Just about every pharmaceutical is produced or processed using water. To remove contaminants, including endotoxins, pharmaceutical water is either distilled or filtered. Unfortunately, these systems, especially filtration, can become contaminated with Gram-negative, endotoxin-containing bacteria. In high enough concentrations, these bacteria (which grow in the water or on the plumbing and filter surfaces) produce and shed endotoxins in a sufficient quantity to cause a fever if injected into a human or animal. Keep in mind, the sterilization processes used to kill any living bacteria in a pharmaceutical do not destroy endotoxins, which are extremely resistant to heat and chemicals. Thus the Food and Drug Administration requires injectables to be tested for both sterility and pyrogenicity. But there is never enough endotoxin, even in the most poorly maintained systems, to cause severe injury, let alone death, if injected. At best, the regulations for pyrogen and LAL testing are another layer of safety for modern pharmaceuticals. As Tom Novitsky explains,

So when I see the inference that endotoxins cause "toxic shock" or "diarrhea," the statements have nothing to do with LAL use. In fact, the LAL test has been used in research to follow Gram-negative infections. Endotoxin is probably the direct cause of the symptoms of toxic shock but not the primary cause of the disease. One cannot get toxic shock or diarrhea from a pharmaceutical contaminated with endotoxin (a lot of drugs themselves cause diarrhea if you can believe all the TV ads). I should point out that our intestines have gobs of endotoxin and we are no worse for it. We also consume gobs of endotoxin in our food and drink every day. It is only when endotoxin is injected into our bloodstream or spinal fluid that it becomes a problem. Even then, however, there is no record of any deaths from injected endotoxin from a pharmaceutical except [for] several cases of death caused from blood transfusions, where a small amount of contaminated blood was stored until the Gram-negative bacteria grew to such great numbers that the endotoxin they contained killed the recipients in a matter of minutes. It is kind of sad that the FDA never saw a need to do LAL on stored blood prior to transfusions, albeit the incidence of endotoxin toxicity from bacterial blood contamination is extremely rare.[23]

So this leads me to ask, is the development of the horseshoe crab–bloodletting industry really out of proportion to the risks from endotoxin? Are humans constantly looking to generate more profit from LAL and therefore find uses for the test? There is ongoing research about potential applications of horseshoe crab blood. In the early 2000s, NASA scientists conducted research with LAL to prove that the immune response can work in zero gravity.[24] Additionally LAL tests are used in food-processing plants to assess contamination.[25]

The *Limulus* Amoebocyte Lysate Test

It was in 1964 that the *Limulus* amoebocyte lysate assay was formulated as an effective test. *Limulus* blood reacts to endotoxins by forming a gel that resembles turbid or cloudy uncolored Jell-O. The LAL test, constructed from horseshoe crab amoebocytes, has become the standard test in the United States, Europe, and Asia to test pharmaceutical injectable and insertables for biomedical and veterinary uses. The LAL tests do not "prevent" endotoxin contamination; they just reveals its presence. As described by the hematologist who innovated LAL, Jack Levin, endotoxin "is all over the environment, we produce enough of it daily to kill ourselves, and it's everywhere—just rub your finger on anything." The conventional and consistent presentation of the LAL test since the 1960s is that horseshoe crab blood may save our lives and the lives of animal others.

During the 1970s, the LAL assay was approved for testing drugs, blood products, and medical devices. In 1987, after a series of tests, it was mandated by the Food and Drug Administration to be used on all "human and animal parenteral drugs, biological products, and medical devices."[26] It became an internationally required test in 2010, when the European Medicines Agency, a part of the European Union and similar to the U.S. FDA, established guidelines and regulations for LAL-type bacterial endotoxin tests. Prior to the LAL test, from 1944 until the 1970s, scientists tested for pyrogens using rabbits. This testing method took up to 48 hours and required that three animals per test be injected with a sample batch of a drug intended for intravenous use. If an injected rabbit got a fever, it was taken as indication that endotoxin was present. This test was expensive, requiring resources to keep rabbit colonies alive, clean, and managed in the laboratory.

In contrast, LAL testing takes about 45 minutes, uses a small amount of extract made from the crab's blood cells, and the horseshoe crab, previously released to the sea, most likely survives. These tests can take different forms—for example, gel clot tests or chromogenic (color-producing) tests. Basically, a sample of test items such as vaccines or gene therapy treatments is taken and mixed with LAL to see if there is a reaction. The LAL test is a destructive test in this case, and therefore a sample from the vaccine batch is taken and tested three times as it is produced—once at the beginning, once in middle, and once at the end of the process. If the samples do not react with the LAL, the batch is deemed safe and released to the market. In the case of insertable devices, a wash of the device (e.g., a hip-replacement device) is mixed with LAL. As far as saving lives, one can accurately say that the LAL test has saved thousands of rabbits' lives as they were usually put down after they were used for pyrogen tests a few times. Colonies of rabbits were actually bred specifically for pyrogen test use, and now there is far less demand. So it is possible that the horseshoe crab is saving far more rabbit lives than human lives—although those rabbits might not have been bred if they weren't needed for testing.

Harvesting Crabs

Harvesting horseshoe crabs in the wild is the only way to get enough blood to make LAL in a cost-effective way. Juvenile populations can be bred in captivity, but these smaller crabs do not have enough blood to be profitable to the pharmaceutical industry. Horseshoe crabs are captured by fishermen using nets that trawl offshore of their known habitats, scooping them out of the sea to be bled and then released. As described to me by Ron Berzofsky, senior technical advisor at the LAL Division of Wako Chemicals,

> Fishermen go out in the Atlantic about a mile offshore and drag a net against the bottom of the ocean for about 30, 40, 50 feet. These are huge nets, and [they are] literally collecting anything alive at ocean floor—but it isn't digging in the mud or muck, just skimming the bottom, and it is getting things swimming close to the ocean floor. At the end of 30 min-utes, [they] will bring net to boat, and [they get] a lot of things, blue crab, skate, shrimp, just a ton of biomass, and they quickly sort through all the living things and return everything back to ocean. Everything except for horseshoe crabs, and then they take them back to laboratory. The horseshoe

A technician extracts blood from the Atlantic horseshoe crabs, *Limulus poly-phemus*. The medical profession uses an extract from the horseshoe crab's blue, copper-based blood, called *Limulus* amoebocyte lysate (LAL), to test the purity of medicines. Used with permission from the personal library of Ron Berzofsky.

crab[s] can live outside the water if they are kept moist and can get oxygen from the air, so we don't put them in water but keep them comfortable, and we return them no longer than 24 hours after capture.

I want to compare my experience giving blood to a horseshoe crab's. This comparison is difficult given the lack of information from the pharmaceutical industry. While I have been to the exterior of buildings that bleed horseshoe crabs, I have not gained entry. The closest I can come is to share the experience as recounted by fishery and wildlife scientists who study the bleeding of horseshoe crabs:

Throughout the typical biomedical bleeding process, horseshoe crabs are subjected to a variety of potential stressors (i.e., air exposure, increased temperature, handling, blood loss, trauma) . . . Animals may be held on the deck of a boat or in containers for several hours during collection, transported to the bleeding facility in trucks (that may or may not be air-conditioned), held in the coldroom of a laboratory for several hours at an air temperature of 16–18 degrees C, bled for a period of time, and then held in the coldroom or in a truck until transport back to the dock. Horseshoe crabs that are returned back the ocean are transferred onto a boat and returned to their approximate point of capture within 72 hours of their collection.[27]

Even in this clinical description, there is something reminiscent of the science fiction, anti-vivisection, H. G. Wells classic, *The Island of Doctor Moreau.* In order to bleed the crab, it is folded up over a bar, and the sinus is exposed. The sinus that runs down the back of the carapace is needled. Once inserted, the needle enters the heart of the crab (also known as the *hemocoel*); this procedure is called a *cardiac dorsal puncture.* The blood flows from the needle into a sterile glass container, filling it with light blue blood. Horseshoe crabs are then marked on their carapace to indicate they have been bled that year so as not to be recaptured and rebled.

The blood is then centrifuged, and technicians pour the hemocyanin out and retain the amoebocyte pellet that forms at the bottom of the container. Roughly 3% of the blood is the amoebocyte. Within the laboratory, technicians, in the words of Ron Berzofsky, "bust open the cells to get the lysate. So LAL is actually busted up horseshoe crab blood cells." The pharmaceutical companies then use their own recipes to magnify the chemical sensitivity of the blood's own reaction, making LAL more sensitive than what comes out of the crab.

While much is obscured about the collection of horseshoe crab blood, what we do know is that the biomedical bleeding of crabs uses cardiac puncture to collect between 25% and 40% of a crab's blood, and then it is released. This is roughly the "amount of a cup of coffee." By comparison, humans give about 10% of their blood during a voluntary donation. If we were to lose 30%–40% of our blood, we would be having what is called a class 3 hemorrhage (on a 4-point scale), requiring a blood transfusion. There is a species-management rate of a self-reported 15% mortality, or about 20,000–37,500 crabs per year, deemed acceptable by the Atlantic States Marine Fisheries Commission. These mortality data are collected based on an honor system, in which fishermen report the mortality data when they submit the paperwork required to receive permits to collect horseshoe crabs. Based on several interviews with marine biologists, ecologists, and environmental conservationists, it is widely believed that this percentage is arbitrary and not based on "good science." Furthermore, there are recent scientific studies to suggest that bleeding female horseshoe crabs after the spawning season significantly raises their mortality rate. Female horseshoe crabs, because they are larger than males and yield more blood, are more desirable to harvest. However, it is more risky for population dynamics if females are harvested, since their deaths leaves a void in egg production.

One study in Massachusetts demonstrated that unbled female horseshoe crabs had about a 3% mortality rate when harvested after spawning season, compared to a 22.5% mortality rate of bled females harvested after spawning.[28] The authors of the study argue that perhaps the assumed 15% mortality rate is not only inaccurate but that the harm to the crabs is not completely captured by our standard scientific methods and that the harvest and treatment methods should be reviewed.

Conservation scientists and environmental ecologists are concerned about what the LAL industry practices mean for the species, as I discovered during many interviews. The biologist Christopher Chabot described his collaborative research to me as an attempt to examine the long-term effects of bleeding on the crabs.

> Hundreds of thousands are bled to produce LAL, the most sensitive assay available for Gram-negative bacteria. We are interested in the mortality and morbidity of the crabs. It is hard on the crabs; they are captured, brought in, and are out of the water for up to 3 days. The law requires

they get put back where they were captured, but I want to look at the long-term effects. The bleeding throws them for a loop, especially if they are captured during the breeding season; that means they are knocked out for that year and can have a significant decrease in the population for that year. It takes a month for them to replenish their blood.

His fellow collaborator Rebecca Anderson continued, "You can tell when a horseshoe crab has been bled—a lot don't move at all for at least 20 hours, and there is significantly less movement through the fourteenth day of study." Both Chris and Rebecca concur that, while the 15% mortality rate is followed by the bleeding industry, the long-term effects of bleeding are just now becoming clearer, despite these scientific studies' not seeming to be an immediate priority of the industry.

Enforcing Regulations

The Atlantic States Marine Fisheries Commission (ASMFC) manages horseshoe crab harvest permits for bait (since 1998) and for biomedicine (since 2004).[29] Currently the 2011 best management practices developed by the ASMFC include rules for the handling of horseshoe crabs, including guidelines for capture, transportation, holding, inspection, bleeding and return to the sea.[30] There are differences in quotas and harvesting rules on a state-by-state basis from Maine to Florida. Beyond quotas, some regulations prohibit harvesting during peak egg-laying season in order to protect the reproduction of local populations. Additionally in 2013 through 2016, New Jersey, Delaware, Maryland, and Virginia instituted a regulation for male-only crab harvest in order to protect horseshoe crab egg production for both species regeneration and shorebird migration nourishment. In 2014, an estimated 452,014 crabs were harvested for biomedical use.[31]

Regulation and surveillance of horseshoe crab harvesting however is spotty, and the poaching of horseshoe crabs for bait and for bleeding is not uncommon. The federal, state, and local agencies charged with enforcement of oversight are underfunded and inefficiently coordinated. A dramatic *New York Times* story from 2013 reported that horseshoe crab poachers were observed near the New York City Belt Parkway. When enforcement arrived, a boat race ensued with the suspects getting away in speedier boat. Eventually recovering the captain-less boat at a dock, officers found 900 crabs.[32] Another incident reported in the *New York Post* describes an New York Police Department night-vision helicopter exercise observing four men illegally collecting 200 horseshoe crabs. "It's illegally taking wildlife from a National Park," said Lt. David Buckley of the U.S. Parks Police. "It's pretty common here and it's a lucrative business."[33] Two of the men were caught and charged a $500 fine.

Personally, over the 3 years and approximately 50 times I have surveyed horseshoe crabs, I have only once seen any form of active environmental enforcement. On an overcast June day in 2013, our small research team was measuring crabs when two armed officers from the New York State Environmental Conservation Police drove down the sandy grass line dune. It felt somewhat thrilling as these two military-garbed officers climbed out of their jeep with masculine swagger, holding their utility belts, and sauntered down to join us. Typically, I am wary of the police and have an irrational fear that I am always going to get either a ticket or arrested, but in this case, I was transfixed as a swoony admirer. There is something about being a defender of the environment that seemed, on face value, so indisputably noble and impenetrable to corruption. It is perhaps the first and only time in my life that I was happy to be "stopped by the police." Mark had his permit ready and was rather pleased to see some form of oversight, a rarity in his experience, too. Once they reviewed the permit, the officers were very curious about our research and stayed for a brief impromptu lesson about crabs. I asked them if they had found any horseshoe crab poachers, but their response was, "Mostly people fishing where they shouldn't."

There are reasons to believe that regulation of horseshoe crab harvest is not a significant concern for regulators. Furthermore, the

Two officers from the New York State Environmental Conservation Police observing Mark Botton describe the anatomy of a horseshoe crab. Photo by Lisa Jean Moore.

mandate of the fisheries commissions in many states is about the promotion of fishing for local economies and recreation. A scientist extremely knowledgeable about the practice of regulation shared his observations with me:

> Individual state members of the ASMFC are supposed to do their own regulating, but this also varies tremendously. In Massachusetts, the guy who is head of the lobster program is also supposed to do horseshoe crabs. Not sure how many patrol boats they have. Secondhand information says if they get a tip from a concerned citizen and they are in the area, they will check out illegal taking; otherwise, they spend their time watching lobster and shell fishermen and rely on self-reporting for horseshoe crabs. At least in Massachusetts, the Department of Marine Fisheries

is woefully underfunded and undermanned. Also because their charter is to promote the fishing economy in the state, new regulations are to sustain the fishery, not necessarily to protect anything.

There exists an inherent conflict of interest between sustaining human economic markets and recreation versus protecting a species that has not been deemed endangered. So even when regulations exist, there is spotty enforcement with real or tacit obstacles to surveillance. As I explore in the next section, the growth of the LAL market might present a greater need for oversight.

Global Pyrogen Testing and Economic Stakeholders

The interests of the pharmaceutical industry intensify the human-crab relationship, which is sped up by globalization and biomedicalization, ultimately creating tensions between conservationists and pharmaceutical companies that must be negotiated. But it's typically the supremacy of the biotechnical transnational corporation that overrides the underfunded ecological conservationists. There are four companies licensed by the FDA in the United States to make and sell LAL. The largest is Charles River Endosafe, owned by Charles River Laboratories operating in Charleston, South Carolina (although it gets a majority of its lysate from crabs in New Jersey). Lonza is the second-largest LAL manufacturer, operating out of Frederick, Maryland, and owned by Lonza Switzerland. Wako Pure Chemical is owned by Wako Pure Chemical, Osaka, Japan, and operates in Virginia. The fourth is Associates of Cape Cod, operating in Falmouth, Massachusetts, and owned by Seikagaku Corporation, Tokyo Japan.

During an Earth Day lecture in 2016, Mark told the Long Island audience, "Every person in this room, at one point or another, your life depends on this test. Everyone taking a medication—injection—vaccination—you have to be sure that those things are not going to introduce bacteria. . . . if you've had a heart valve or a stent put in."

Throughout my ethnographic research, this claim of horseshoe crab's blood saving human lives is made again and again to great effect. It certainly garners sympathy for the animal, as there is a greater sense that there's something in it for us. But the claims of the life-saving capacities of horseshoe crab blood is a bit of a leap, as described by an expert in the industry.

As Tom Novitsky shared with me, the LAL test might actually be most helpful for assessing the quality and sterility of pharmaceutical production, rather than a life-saving test:

All injectables are sterilized to kill living bacteria. Any endotoxin left would hardly be enough to cause septic shock symptoms let alone disease. THERE IS NO PUBLISHED REPORT THAT ENDOTOXIN ALONE IN A MANUFACTURED PHARMACEUTICAL PRODUCT HAS KILLED ANYONE. As I stated before, there is documented evidence of contaminated blood killing people after it was transfused due to the massive amount of endotoxin that was produced by living and growing bacteria while the blood was stored prior to transfusion. In the case of blood it is assumed that collections are sterile and then stored blood remains so until transfused. In the case in point, one donor had a subclinical Gram-negative bacteremia, and the bacteria in the collected blood happened to like the cold and dark during storage and grew to over 10^9 bacteria per mL. The amount of endotoxin associated with this number of bacteria was sufficient to actually kill the recipient. I actually tested a sample of the infected blood with LAL after the fact, and it contained a massive amount of endotoxin. To put this in perspective, the amount of endotoxin required to cause of fever in man is 100,000 to 1 million times lower than that required to kill. In fact, endotoxin in low amounts may actually be beneficial in stimulating our immune system, for example, keeping it tuned up. Thus the LAL test applied to pharmaceuticals is an indication of the quality of the product, more so than a 'life-saving' measure.

Even if LAL is not as much a life-saving measure, but rather a quality-control test, it represents a large market within the United States, where 70 million units of LAL are used annually.[34] For roughly the last 30 years, horseshoe crab blood has been the standard in the United States to meet FDA validation.[35] Whenever a biomedical company is applying for FDA approval, they must prove that all their products are free from endotoxins. Therefore, there are applications of the LAL test in all sorts of pharmaceutical preparations, including vaccines, bioproducts, intravenous muscular drugs, surgical tubing, and plasma protein. Beyond human medical use, there are applications of the test in maintaining safety in veterinary medicine, food quality, water supplies, medical devices, air quality, and aerospace (in the form of a portable gadget to see if endotoxins are present). While there is this open sharing of the value of LAL testing, there is some market-driven secrecy about crab blood as a commodity among LAL companies (how much they pay for crabs, where they locate crabs for harvest, who their customers are, how their bleeding facilities are designed). Through my fieldwork and document research I have pieced together an interpretation of the global market place.

A for-profit marketing firm claims that "globally the pyrogen testing market is valued at $462.38 million in 2014 and is expected to grow at a CAGR [compound annual growth rate] of 12.23% to reach $823.14 million by 2019."[36] This type of economic research analysis on the pyrogen-testing market is prepared for potential financial backers. Publications such as "Pyrogen Testing Market by Product Global Forecast to 2019" supply individuals with the data they need to figure out investment strategies for hedge funds, individual investors, and retirement products. As such, the data points of pharmaceutical forecasting is narrated for possible shareholders as pyrogen testing is positioned as a growth industry: "Pyrogen testing is used to determine the presence of bacterial toxins in pharmaceutical, biotechnology, and medical device products, which are intended for medical or veterinary use. Spot checks of all batches of pharmaceutical, biotechnology, and medical device products are mandatory for regulatory approval and market release. Pyrogen testing is carried out at all levels of pharmaceutical and biopharmaceutical manufacturing process to minimize the risk of product contamination. Growth in pharmaceutical and biotechnology industries will drive the growth of the pyrogen testing market."[37]

The growth is a potential bonanza for eager investors. The need for LAL consistently expands as new medical devices are innovated and human bodies are continually biomedicalized. Additionally, as the economies strengthen in countries like India and China, life expectancies increase, the demand for health-care treatments and pharmaceuticals escalate. Concerns from horseshoe crab scientists are beginning to emerge about the global supply of pyrogen tests—as one scientists shared with me, "Horseshoe crabs aren't going to be able to do all this heavy lifting for the globe."

In Asia, there is a similar pyrogen test for endotoxins that is synthesized through use of horseshoe crab amoebocytes; this is the *Tachypleus* amoebocyte lysate (TAL) test, referring to the species *Tachypleus gigas* (sometimes called the Malaysian or the Indonesian horseshoe crab) and *Tachypleus tridentatus* (alternatively called the Asian horseshoe crab, Chinese horseshoe crab, or Japanese horseshoe crab, depending on the human's geopolitical alliances). Zhanjiang A & C Biological Ltd., located in China, uses the Asian horseshoe crab (*T. tridentatus*) to produce TAL, and there are reports of TAL being produced from *T. gigas* as well.[38] Regulations protecting the harvest of crabs for biomedicine are not as successful in Asia as in the United States, in part because horseshoe crab habitat spans many countries. Additionally there is anecdotal evidence of crabs being drained to death. So while TAL is available, it is clear that it is far less abundant than LAL. There exists an oft-stated fear among North Americans that as the middle class grows in global economies of China and India and the access for biomedical procedures are more affordable, the demand for a pyrogen test will increase the demand for LAL as the availability of TAL cannot accommodate this demand.

As I continued my fieldwork, I began to notice a persistent yet muted anxiety repeated by informants. This apprehension circulated around the transnational supply of horseshoe crab blood and was expressed in discussions about the lack of regulation in the extraction of TAL in Asian countries, the shipping of LAL components to Asia, and the lack of conservation efforts in Asia. During a 2014 meeting of the Horseshoe Crab Specialist Group of the International Union for the Conservation of Nature (IUCN) in Long Island, Tom Novitsky, a retired scientist from Cape Cod Associates and now member of the IUCN, shared his photographs and fieldwork with the group. During his trips investigating the Chinese TAL industry, he found that "crabs are being bled to death, and then they are piled up, scooped away and sold for a secondary sale when their chitin is used or they are eaten. In fact, in some cases, crabs' blood is extracted, then they are re-injected with liquid because they are sold by weight to be eaten in restaurants." Tom continued, "These are mostly Vietnamese crabs, as they are purchased to be brought into China for bleeding."

While conducting fieldwork in Florida with Jane Brockmann, she shared with me a story and photocopies of a license issued in Florida to a man who applied for a license to bleed and ship crab amoebocytes to Asia. As Jane recounts,

There has been one license issued here in Florida for bleeding, and the man on his application says that he is working to sell that blood to Asian companies. The state gave him a license. This is because the Gulf side has it's own commission called the Gulf States Marine Fisheries Commission, and unlike the ASMFC, the Gulf States has zero interest in horseshoe crabs. What the license says is that [that] man should use best practices. He was going to work out of the back of his truck. So he has the license, there is no evidence yet that he is doing it. But he has to have the truck inspected if he is actually doing it.

Jane is expressing two concerns. One is the method by which this man is bleeding the crabs without the proper medical lab facilities and the sense that the license endorses his practice without sufficient oversight. But she is also expressing the undercurrent of fear among other horseshoe crab scientists and conservationists that LAL will be collected and synthesized in the United States and shipped to foreign countries.

Humans are able to work around any regulations by taking crabs from another state, in the case of *Limulus*, or another country, in the case of *Tachypleus*. The border/transnational anxiety, though, comes with a claim to property of wildlife off the coast of your state or country. This fall back to the position of state loyalty, in some cases, or nationalism, in others, is complicated. The fear is that once *Tachypleus* is extinct owing to the nonconservation practice of bleeding crabs to death, others (most often stated as "the Chinese") will come for the crabs off the coast of North America, "our crabs." And these anxieties are not without merit, since it is a material reality that Asian species of horseshoe crabs are threatened and that the demand for LAL is likely to grow as the human population increases and medical demands are more accessible. But these anxieties about "our crabs" also rely on existing discursive contests. In my previous research with Mary Kosut, multispecies ethnographies can reveal the stereotyping and racializing and xenophobic senses that infuse transnational traffic in nonhuman animals. For example, the ways Africanized honeybees are controlled as undesirable immigrants is layered over historic discourses and practices in migration among humans.[39] "The Chinese coming for our crabs" fear is part of this ethnocentric logic.

We live in a world where we are always and everywhere potentially contaminated. In the multinational quest for global fortification against one danger (endotoxins), there are leaking national resource borders wherein "bad practices" can emerge. We are vulnerable through the food we eat and water we drink, through daily interactions with fellow humans and companion animals, and ironically, through our reliance on medical interventions. To combat this contagion, humans have innovatively used other species, in this case, horseshoe crabs, as prophylaxis. Horseshoe crab blood protects against the growing fear of contamination, the notion of xenotoxification by bacteria of our immune system. Certain human bodies, enhanced by technoscience, are more capable of avoiding potentially lethal exposures because they gain access to biomedical resources. Many, if not all humans are a boosted, cyborgified species that deploys by-products of animal others to fortify us in this world teeming with toxins. But who specifically benefits from these boosts? Flexible corporate structures that can adjust to where raw materials can be extracted.

Ersatz Pyrogen Tests

In the case of LAL, there is a synthetic recombinant technology available and proven. As described by the biochemist Ron Berzofsky,

> If you wanted to make LAL in the laboratory, you must use the horseshoe crab as a basis and examine their DNA. The DNA codes contain the information of every protein the horseshoe crab makes. We looked at DNA in the horseshoe crab, and since we know amino acid sequence—we know how to translate that. So we found the segment that codes the clotting function and put it into another cell that expresses the LAL, and we can do it in a bioreactor. We can make the recombinant, and it works the same as natural, and we don't need to bleed [horseshoe crabs].

Ron pointed me to Lonza's product, advertised on their website, called Pyrogene™, described as a "reliable animal-free alternative to LAL," which is in line with a mission to reduce animal use in testing.[40] However, this technology is not widely accepted. The reasons are surprisingly bureaucratic—it is not that the synthetic test is more expensive or less effective than the LAL test. While it is true that the cost of switching from the natural blood of the horseshoe crab to the synthetic would involve some material equipment costs and retraining, the reason the

synthetic is not used has to do with the historical establishment of testing from the FDA. It sounds like an ultimate definitional Catch-22. Here
again is Ron describing the situation:

> LAL is regulated and licensed by FDA because in 1971 FDA published the
> law of the land that LAL is a blood product, even though it's not human
> blood. So it falls under the jurisdiction of the FDA Bureau of Biologics.
> So when we made the recombinant technology, we applied for a license,
> but we came to find out [it] didn't require a license because it is not
> blood, it is synthetic. As a result, they won't license it, so pharmaceuti-
> cal companies won't touch it. So there is a huge bottleneck here. Also,
> the FDA requires that, if the pharmaceutical industry wants to switch,
> they have to show FDA equivalent data comparing LAL testing with the
> synthetic for each item that is tested. The pharmaceutical industry simply
> does not have time to do this level of testing.

Thinking about the ways this perplexing situation exists, I asked Ron
if the FDA is just being difficult. He thought for a moment and then said,
"I don't think FDA is being the bad guy here. They have to show things
are performing the correct way to cover their ass and make sure that
the public is safe. The pharmaceutical companies say, There is nothing
broken with the system we have, so why would we do all this comparative data gathering to switch? We aren't going to save money. We aren't
sacrificing any horseshoe crabs. So there really is no driver to do this." In
all the human hand-wringing and anxiety politics about the crabs, many
are still being bled, and some are dying. Humans perform a great deal of
cultural work to frame horseshoe crab bleeding in terms of a *donation*,
but this donation is anything but. One of the big ironies of my blood
donation, and of all human blood donation, is that it is made safe by
LAL. Human blood donation is scaffolded on draining horseshoe crab
blood. The tools of injection are mandated safe through some intraaction with horseshoe crabs, and so I am implicated. The use of crabs has
become integral and routinized to global biopharmaceutical practices

and everyday human life (our clean water, flu shots, hip replacements). However, many scientists as well as other human actors do believe it is possible that in the long term we could run out of LAL. Yet they argue that the only way the industry of pyrogen testing will change is "if the horseshoe crab population gets depleted"—then we will need to have a back-up plan. Or, in the words of one Malaysian researcher, the synthetic will not be used "until all the crabs are dead."

5

Enmeshed

Although I drive this highway almost every day—sitting in traffic, going back and forth to work, cursing and anticipating those familiar bumps and nicks on the road's surface, August 2014 stands out. I was zooming down the Belt Parkway, already sweaty with the prospect of the day's work. The brilliant sunshine was burning off the metropolitan haze, the salty sea breezes mixed with exhaust fumes, and thumping music came in from passing windows. I crept off the painfully slow exit ramp and pulled my Volkswagen "clean diesel" Tubo Diesel Injected Jetta Sport-Wagen into the parking lot, arriving at the Plumb Beach, Brooklyn, comfort station. I grabbed my camera, slathered SPF 60 all over my face, and headed to the meeting spot, where a biologist, a paleontologist, an ecologist, and several undergraduate students were listening to instructions for our day's work. We were there to measure the size and assess the quality of the horseshoe crab's carapace. I was excited by the prospect of handling the horseshoe crabs again—wading through the bay and picking them out of the water as they bend, wriggle, and contort themselves in an almost comical motion, their twelve limbs wildly grasping in air. Smiling at the other humans, my fantasy was quickly interrupted as I looked down and saw a bloated rat, floating belly up, its body attempting to rest on the shore, ending the relentless tidal ebb and flow.

No doubt this is an "urban" beach, as marine debris is abundant—shiny tampon applicators, old car tires, colorful plastic bags, partial beach toys, twisted condoms, ripped candy wrappers, broken beer bottles, and the occasional dead rat. To many humans, the ever-present flow of trash and urban detritus must interrupt the "commonplace appreciation of nature" and prevent the loosening of social entanglements

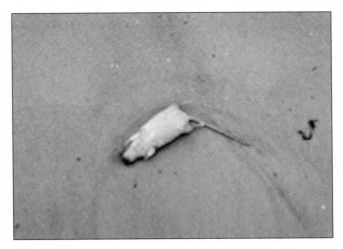

Dead rat on Plumb Beach. Photo by Lisa Jean Moore.

implicitly promised by our romantic notions of "a day at the beach." Indeed, the "natural-ness" of Plumb Beach is ironic, as it has been the site of concerted efforts at sediment management—the combination of strategies to "renourish" shorelines. The Belt Parkway is threatened by heavy beach erosion and sea-level change; sand has been pumped, rubble added, grasses planted, dunes constructed, and jetties erected.[1] We make and remake our homes alongside the horseshoe crabs on the coastlines, and this remaking has become integrated as a continuous loop of shoreline management.[2] For materially, we all, humans, horseshoe crabs, and others, are dependent upon outmoded infrastructure that makes us increasingly vulnerable to danger and destruction (see the discussion of precarity in chapter 2). New York City's weak infrastructure is exposed through media reports practically everyday. Subways shut down during storms, sewage backs up, parkways flood, sinkholes close down streets, and gas lines explode.[3] Daily, we are dwelling in the ruins of anthropogenic climate change on our planet, in New York City, and at Plumb Beach.

And yet these Brooklyn horseshoe crabs are intrepid. They crawl out of the water, over half-submerged car tires and broken glass, to get to the sandy beach. Even with their dexterity at navigating human-produced debris, the crabs must face shorebirds who wait nearby. I imagine the birds are hoping that a crab gets flipped over and is unable to right herself. Then the bird will rip out her insides. Horseshoe crabs are tussled by the waves onto their backs all the time, their tender bits open to the air. On one visit, as far as I could see, there were at least 12 crabs in a variety of vulnerable poses on the shoreline. Sometimes the beach looks like a graveyard, dead crabs up and down the beach. The inside of their carapace empty—stripped clean of anything edible as humans are engaged in their various seemingly less dangerous leisure activities of dog walking, sunbathing, kitesurfing and cruising.

This chapter investigates the contingencies of sea-level rise for the horseshoe crabs, the Belt Parkway, the scientists (including myself), and the beach in intraaction with each other and the hyperobject that is global warming through my participation in a research project about horseshoe crab eggs. At Plumb Beach there is an ongoing gestalt of entanglement making and unmaking ecologies. It is this enmeshment, this becoming with horseshoe crabs, and this entanglement, the ways our fates are linked to one another, that I play with throughout the chapter to indicate the working assemblage of Plumb Beach, horseshoe crabs, humans, sand, science, and parkway.

As a sociologist, a human, and an ethnographer, using this concept of *enmeshment* is invigorating to me since my framework is fundamentally different from those of scientists who are primarily moved by the doctrine of specific etiology—in other words, the Enlightenment principle of proving cause and effect is what drives scientific inquiry.[4] The sea-level rise causes the shoreline to change, causing animals to be in peril. Scientific narration of horseshoe crabs is hegemonic as a master narrative, so I must work both to take these scientific explanations into my ethnographic interpretation, but also to understand this narration as a situated knowledge.[5] Using intraaction is an attempt to show that there isn't a cause-and-effect logic—I'm trying to get at a different cut of human–horseshoe crab enmeshments.

In this chapter, after a consideration of the physical location of Plumb Beach, I describe an ongoing intervention to the landscape to abate sea-level rise and shoreline erosion. Since this sea-level rise is not unique to Plumb Beach but is a global occurrence, I suggest that there is a potential parable in the Plumb Beach example. Next, I turn to describing my ways of methodologically and theoretically apprehending horseshoe crabs through the lens of critical animal studies and intraspecies mindfulness. I then describe my own participation as a citizen scientist and ethnographer in an ongoing research project that examines the ecological consequences of the re-engineering of Plumb Beach on the horseshoe crab spawning beach. I telescope out from this labor-intensive and longitudinal observation of horseshoe crabs' adjustment to shoreline transformations to consider the larger impact of rebuilding environments. I close with my own frustration at trying to put into action conscientious personal and social change when foiled by larger neoliberal forces.

Dirty Filthy Beach

The place I refer to as *Plumb Beach* was acquired as a New York City park property in 1924. But it also became part of the Gateway National Recreation Area when Congress created it in 1972 as a part of the National Park Service. Both a city beach and federal park, Plumb Beach offers the dense metropolis of New York City a sort of natural refuge through access to the beach and Jamaica Bay, a tidal estuary. Jamaica Bay has also been the site of a restoration plan to create and restore habitats that benefit native biota. The Rockaway Inlet that borders the 3-mile Plumb Beach on the south and east is a dredged navigational channel.

This is a place I have returned to for 4 years as part of my research journey. What I originally considered a disgusting beach that I would never visit, the perfect representation of urban/ecological catastrophe has, over time, become more to me. I've taken my three daughters to Plumb Beach multiple times just to be with horseshoe crabs, swim, explore, and play in the mud flats and on the breakwaters and jetties. The

Daughter research assistants exploring mud flats at Plumb Beach, holding horseshoe crab molts, August 2015. Photo by Lisa Jean Moore.

beauty that the place brings is illuminating to me. My original assessments have shifted, and my loyalty to the place is affirmed, not as an instrumental barrier beach in the service of something else, but a place of value in and of itself. This chapter is about the places, the shrinking physical landscape, where humans and horseshoe crabs meet, and it is specifically about this spit of land in a teeming metropolis. It is also about how these places are sinking, constantly re-engineered for the human lifestyle of transportation and recreation. Human intervention poses specific challenges to horseshoe crab ecology, potentially exacerbating the erosion of living shorelines.

In addition to my returning to this particular place, it is also a place of return for horseshoe crabs, for they possess the characteristic of *site fidelity*—sometimes called *site tenacity*—a term used among horseshoe crab researchers (and ecologists and conservation biologists researching other species) to describe the repeated seasonal return of individuals, pairs, or colonies to the same location to breed year after year. Implying a sense of affective longing for connection to environment, the anthropologist Deborah Bird Rose calls it "the tendency or desire to return."[6] When the water temperature, tides, and other capacities are in alignment, intergenerational groups of horseshoe crabs come to this shoreline from the depths of the sea to breed (as described in chapter 3).

The horseshoe crabs and I now have this temporarily in common: a geographical memory, a seasonal return to this beach. My geographical memory is influenced by the crabs, but not vice versa. Thom van Dooren and Deborah Bird Rose have explored nonhuman animals engagement with places, also called *place-attachments*. These anthropologists convincingly demonstrate through penguins and flying foxes how "the capacity to experience places as meaningful and significant is one that is shared well beyond the human species."[7] While these horseshoe crabs have some affinity for Plumb Beach, their ability to be loyal to this location is changing because of the competing interest of humans' own site fidelity to New York City. Our re-engineering to stave off our displacement from New York City at times of sea-level rise has displaced horseshoe crabs and disrupted their attachment to Plumb Beach.

The beach has been geomorphologically transformed through years by tides, winds, dredging, sediment management, and perhaps most significantly through the creation and ongoing maintenance of the Belt Parkway in the 1930s. In the words of a research assistant, "The whole idea of beach nourishment was not for this habitat but for the Belt Parkway." At Plumb Beach, this section of the parkway cleaves the closest to the water—by my estimation at high tide, the parkway is about 20 yards from the edge of the water. Envisioned by the infamous urban planner Robert Moses, this parkway is a major access route between three of the boroughs of New York City, the connection between a metropolitan area and two major international airports, and the storm evacuation route for all of Long Island's 7.5 million human inhabitants. It's a road not unlike many others. It is not particularly scenic or residential; it is for going places, and it is policed, and it contributes to metropolitan haze. Over 150,000 cars travel on the Belt Parkway each day, making it the busiest principal artery between Queens and Brooklyn.[8]

Impressively, Plumb Beach has been restored eight times since 1972. This level of fiscal and cultural investment suggests that there will always be future plans to fortify the Belt Parkway—until such fortification can no longer be successful. Sociologically, it is both a mundane site of human-nonhuman everyday life and an extraordinary site of massive civil engineering intervention.

Hurricane Sandy, a devastating category 3 storm in October 2012, was followed by years of nourishment projects at Plumb Beach that have effectively dissected the beach. There are two distinct geographic zones now, referred to as *before the groin* and *after the groin*. A groin is a breakwater constructed of large rocks or cement positioned perpendicular to the shoreline to protect a coast by interrupting the waves. To protect the highway, 127,000 cubic yards of fill were added, in addition to the breakwater structures, to *before the groin* (also referred to as the New York City beach or the nourishment site). *After the groin* is also known as the reference site, and it is maintained by the National Park Service.

Taken as a whole, the constellation of Plumb Beach is continually becoming different things to different beings. It is a barrier protecting the teeming metropolis' crucial transportation route, a playground for neoprene outfitted kite surfers, a cruising locale for men who have sex with men, a site of variegated trash piles that double as domiciles for insects, and an aquatic habitat for flora and fauna, which includes varieties of seaweed, horseshoe crabs, sea gulls, fiddler crabs, hermit crabs, jellyfish, fluke and mud snails. And it is a spawning beach for horseshoe crabs who return here year after year to mate.

Before embarking on this research project, I drove this road, like most others, an ordinary driver making my everyday way here and there. Like most, my day was and is inflected with a great many things that go unnoticed. In this process of learning about another species as a sociologist—becoming a human in a world with other species—I entered into a new set of social-scientific relations. I acquired an appreciation and knowledge of a messy network of horseshoe crabs, the Belt Parkway, and the effects of global warming. This experience has in turn affected how I experience ordinary life as a resident and commuter in New York City. As the feminist physicist Karen Barad offers, "Humans are neither pure cause or pure effect but part of the world in its open-ended becoming."[9] This chapter is about my reflections on thought frameworks (my sociological ones, in particular, but also others) that humans invent and improvise in order to understand and control our places (environments), nonhuman beings, and other objects. I am sharing a revelatory moment of understanding my place as a researcher interconnected with a site of research, as I intraact with the objects of research, as well as global variables that are beyond human control (and possibly understanding).

The Rising Tide

Plumb Beach is the site of ongoing multiple biological, ecological, and (my own) sociological research projects to create or understand management strategies for the coming ecological crisis of global warming. Specifically, how do the everyday life experiences of humans and parkways coincide and intraact with the everyday lives of horseshoe crabs on an urban beach? While it is true that horseshoe crabs have no use on a daily basis for parkways, I show that the everyday wear and tear on the parkway, the encroaching seawaters, and human reliance on the parkway is deeply consequential to the crab's habitat. Humans go to great efforts to maintain the parkway for their daily activities, which in turn leads to changes in daily life for crabs. While this story is indeed a specific one tied to a particular location, there is explanatory power in this case study. Overwhelmingly, the habitats of all species of horseshoe crabs are a combination of estuaries, shorelines, and the continental shelves, with their precise locations depending on their migratory schedule. Human populations also congregate at shorelines, where the largest cities in the world are typically located. During our field trips at

Measuring the carapace of horseshoe crabs on Plumb Beach. This is a mated pair and satellite males covered in barnacles. Photo by Lisa Jean Moore.

the Japan conference, we learned that in Japan geomorphic continuity is nonexistent, as over half of all Japanese beaches are covered by artificial structures to interrupt the rising seas.

Is it all in vain? Can you stop the sea? Because of global warming, over the previous century the sea rose 6.7 inches.[10] Because of sea-level rise and other global warming consequences, it is predicted that we will experience storm surges and high tides that will escalate coastal flooding, threatening infrastructure, agriculture, fisheries, and ecosystems. As reported by the Intergovernmental Panel on Climate Change, a collaboration between the World Meteorological Organization and United Nations, globally "by the end of the 21st century, it is very likely that sea levels will rise in more than about 95% of the ocean area. About 70% of the coastlines worldwide are projected to experience a sea level change within ±20% of the global mean." Popular news reports claim that the sea levels will rise at rates faster than those since the founding of Ancient Rome, with estimates suggesting that by 2100 the sea will rise between 3 and 4 feet, estimating from 2016 rates.[11]

Based on these projections of rising sea levels, it is safe to assume that beach nourishment projects will be ongoing and amplified in an effort to maintain shoreline property and infrastructure along eroding coastlines. Humans and their shoreline re-engineering have continued, and continue, to seriously degrade ecosystems, resulting in oceans and urban estuaries that are "hot, sour, and breathless."[12] The phrase "hot, sour, and breathless," oft repeated at the Japan meeting, refers to the UN Rio +20 Climate Conference that took place in Rio de Janeiro in 2012 and the sponsored aggregate report on climate change: Climate change experts have demonstrated that sea levels are increasing and that we are seeing the trifecta of ocean warming, ocean acidification, and ocean deoxygenation. Terrestrial water is contaminated through runoff containing human and animal waste, fertilizers, heavy metals, and pesticides. Ocean waters become hypoxic, or deprived of oxygen. The overproduction of carbon dioxide and the increase of nitrogen and phosphorous in the water raises the algae and bacteria levels in bodies of water. Furthermore, the typical practice of managing sea-level rise through dredging, bulkheading, groin building, and seawall building often creates a hardening of the shoreline. Sand accretes near jetties, and new sand mixtures change the density and composition of the grains.

Importantly, horseshoe crabs have adjusted to previous changes in sea level throughout geologic (deep) time. As noted in chapter 2, horseshoe crabs' long survival through eons is a tribute to their talent for adaptation to dynamic ecological, meteorological, and geographical transformations. Specifically, horseshoe crab experts Bob Loveland and Mark Botton make it clear that sea-level rise has not been an insurmountable problem for horseshoe crabs in the past: "We hypothesize that shifting habitat for horseshoe crab spawning has always been a hallmark of the advancing coastline. Under most conditions, *Limulus polyphemus* (the American Horseshoe Crab) is able to find the new habitat and exploit it for the purpose of reproduction."[13] In other words, crabs have been adaptable to change in the past. So if it is not the rising sea that can threaten the species' survival and commitment to a spawning beach—what is the threat?

Handling Horseshoe Crabs

While some humans want to protect the highway at any cost, others see themselves as stewards of other species. Mark Botton, one of my key informants, sides with the crabs. Mark, a 60-something marine biologist from Fordham University, is one of the world's foremost horseshoe crab researchers, having dedicated over 25 years to understanding the species, its habits, behaviors, and reproduction. During 4 years of near-weekly summer visits to Plumb Beach, he introduced me to the species and showed me how to handle adults, locate juveniles, dig for eggs, evaluate the quality of the outer shells (the carapaces), and identify anatomical differences to sex the crabs. And he also taught me how to appreciate the size of females ("She's a big one"), marvel at the skillful swimming ("Look at how he navigates with his telson, gliding in the water"), worry about their daily challenges ("Now she's trying to flip herself back over, and she'll either dry out or get eaten by gulls if she doesn't right herself"), and fawn over the young ones ("Come here, Cutie, we just want to measure you"). Mark has mediated my understanding of the everyday life of the horseshoe crab, including its movements, routines, and struggles. In time, I have developed a burgeoning "feeling for the organism" and have earned Mark's highest praise: "You would have been a good field biologist."[14]

Having trained with Mark, I am now able to go out and observe crabs on my own. I have refined my own method of intraspecies mindfulness, the practice of speculation about nonhuman species that strives to resist anthropomorphic reflections.[15] In other words, in being with crabs I watch the ways they swim, crawl, eat, and reproduce, and I attempt to describe and understand them in situ. While I am limited by my own human position in understanding the crabs, I also try to allow the crabs to be emergent. I work to resist my own and others' narration that describes the crabs as possessing human motivations. It is an attempt at getting at, and with, another species in order to move outside our selves. Mary Kosut and I created the term and practice of *intraspecies mindfulness*, which is predominantly drawn from the work of Karen Barad.[16] Her articulation of intraaction is where worlds come into being through the mutual constitution of entangled entities rather than through cause-and-effect relationships. Relations between objects ontologically precede those objects. This mutual constitution of entangled agency is the mingling of people and things that creates action from within that mingling. So horseshoe crabs, the sand of Plumb Beach, the fuel of car exhaust, me, the other people, and other objects create the action that is around us. Sea-level rise and our response to it is the intraaction of all these forms of matter—nature, culture, and technology.

Walking up and down the shore, I've spent hours watching the crabs glide through the water, settling on the bottom to burrow into the sand. The slippery brownish carapace becomes its own ecology with barnacles, bryozoans, slipper shells, and flatworms living on the exterior surface. Male crabs attach themselves with a pair of clasper claws to the backs of females and travel sometimes for weeks piggyback style, moving up and down the shoreline with the tides. Spawning time at Plumb Beach thrills the research team as they monitor reproductive pairs and satellite males hoping to release their sperm over waiting eggs. This intensive focus on the trials and tribulations of the crabs over their life cycles has unmoored, slightly, my perspective. I've become more attuned to the *crabness* of these animals (what they are in and for themselves), and I have displaced, somewhat, my instrumental view of crabs (what crabs are to humans).

As discussed in earlier, I situate my work as part of the growing field of multispecies ethnography, located at the intersections of environmental studies, science and technology studies, and animal studies. In particular, I am intrigued by work that brings to light understudied organisms. Multispecies ethnography is a new genre and mode of anthropological research that seeks to bring "organisms whose lives and deaths are linked to human social worlds" closer into focus as living coconstitutive subjects, rather than simply relegating them to "part of the landscape, as food for humans, [or] as symbols."[17] I combine multispecies ethnography with other methods in my "toolbox"—grounded theory,[18] Baradian intraaction, and Actor Network Theory.

Originating in the work of the French science studies scholars Bruno Latour and Michel Callon, Actor Network Theory (ANT) treats objects as integral parts of social networks. I find value in considering the horseshoe crab in an entanglement in the classical Latourian or Callonian way, in which crabs and humans and highways and sand (as well as other objects and phenomena) are in a milieu and connected to, for example, urban transformation, general eco-urgency, shifts in more-than-human rights discourses, and commerce between scientific practices and local biologies. This framing would require that the horseshoe crab is re-animated as an actor, drawing from the lens of ANT and critical animal studies work. Moving beyond human interpretations of crabs, and anthropomorphic descriptions, I consider the possibility of the agency of the horseshoe crab: "A good ANT account is a narrative or a description or a proposition where all the actors do something and don't just sit there."[19] Emphasis is placed on accounting for the nonhuman others embedded within a research site and within larger sociopolitical networks. Using network analysis to understand the everyday workings of heterogeneous networks, I work to "find a way to treat all components in a system on equal terms."[20] My hope is to acquire a knowledge that is "for" humans but that can be used to inform human attempts to accommodate, in this case, horseshoe crabs and, by extension, other objects and phenomena. Another goal is to contribute to the burgeoning field of multispecies ethnography and to address the space between human/nonhuman by using the theories of ANT and intraspecies mindfulness to position the crab, the highway, and the sand through networks of ethnographic data and translation.

My blending of these methodological and theoretical approaches (ANT and Baradian intraaction) can contribute connective tissue, which, together, can help bring into relief the life of the horseshoe crab. I wish to move away from the implicit neatness that a network might imply because its linearity and implicit sense of logic seem inaccurate. I am inspired by Karen Barad's notion of the lives of everyday objects, humans, horseshoe crabs, highways, and sand grains as objects being as contingent on other objects. I'd like my work to be able to consider how things happen without humans being present and how that intraaction is extra-human. Without our often acknowledging it, these extra-human intraactions are often deeply consequential for human life.

Habitat Generalists

Horseshoe crabs are described as *habitat generalists* in that they are able to adapt to many ecological challenges, such as pollution. For example, in North America, they survive over a 4,000-mile shoreline with variable water temperatures, terrain, and water quality. They also are able to move to new locations over time. Thus, while the crabs have site fidelity to their spawning beach, they will change their behaviors over time if the beach starts to not meet their needs. It is this quality of site fidelity during spawning that can also create vulnerability for the species to humans. In the case of harvesting horseshoe crabs for bait, when humans know where to find crabs, they are easy to pluck from the shoreline.

From the 1990s, horseshoe crabs have been caught by fishermen to use as bait for eels (*Anguilla rostrata*) and whelks (*Busycon carica* and *Busycotypus canaliculatum*), worth an impressive $5 each.[21] The eels and whelk are shipped to "huge markets in Asia" and "fuel fishermen's livelihood here."[22] The harvesting of crabs is theoretically controlled, limited, and managed through a patchwork of intra- and interstate regulations, including the Atlantic States Marine Fisheries Commission.[23] Despite these regulatory apparatuses, many of my informants believe there is

Signage on a derelict building at Plumb Beach, Brooklyn, that explains the prohibition on harvesting horseshoe crabs. Photo by Lisa Jean Moore.

great variability in enforcement, and as a result there are several reports of a black market in horseshoe crabs.[24]

Jennifer Mattei, an ecologist from Sacred Heart University, admires horseshoe crabs as "habitat generalists," creatures able to live and survive across a lengthy and varied terrain, from Maine to the Yucatan Peninsula. Despite this expansive habitat and ability to adapt to a variety of environmental stressors, Mattei and many other scientists worry that crabs might face an "extinction vortex." Crabs need a critical mass to breed,[25] and with harvesting and changing shorelines, there is the potential for a lost generation of horseshoe crabs. Mattei explains, "They can tolerate low numbers but there could be a tipping point where they have local extinction because they can't find each other. Crabs, while not deemed threatened in North America, do experience the potential for local extinction."[26] Clearly certain humans are concerned about the reproductive habitat of horseshoe crabs as local populations are faced with shrinking shoreline for spawning. If several female crabs can't find mates, this lack of mates could exacerbate low density of horseshoe crab populations.[27]

The ecologist Christina Colon agreed with this prognosis as we walked along the beach: "I worry that we see no new young ones coming up. There appears to be a break in the chain, and if we miss a generation of juveniles, how will they find each other 10–15 years from now for mating?" Colon added, "Humans, like beavers and elephants, are really good landscape engineers and have changed the landscape to kill the shorelines and beaches through bulkheading and dredging." It is this threat that the research at Plumb Beach attempts to measure and interpret. The intensifying frequency of massive shoreline erosion episodes brought on by super storms, super moons or super high tides (also known as king tides) creates a human frenzy of activity—and we seem to be in for endless catastrophes. How has human engineering of the shoreline in direct response to sea-level rise affected the everyday habitat and reproduction of crabs? How have crabs' changes in reproductive practices affected the human enterprises of biological and ecological knowledge production?

Beach Nourishment and Horseshoe Crab Spawning

The nourishment of Plumb Beach provides a laboratory for sociological and biological analysis of the *before* and *after* beaches. Sea-level rise is one of the effects of global warming. Global warming in Tim Morton's lexicon is a hyperobject, an object that is "massively distributed in time and space relative to humans." He continues, "Global warming plays a very mean trick. It comes very, very close, crashing into our beaches . . . and yet withdrawing from our grasp in the very same gesture, so that we can only represent it by using computers with tremendous processing speed."[28] For Morton, there is no doubt that global warming has happened and is continuing to happen—and yet because of humans' limited abilities to perceive global warming in the immediate sense, it is difficult

Volunteers coring into a beach area by hammering PVC pipes into sand and then emptying the full pipes into plastic baggies to capture the horseshoe crabs' eggs inside. A census of these eggs is performed after the sand is filtered in the lab. After they're counted in the laboratory, the eggs are returned to the bay. Photo by Lisa Jean Moore.

to materially apprehend it. As a result, global warming is present in the everyday while at the same time withdrawn from our apprehension. We rarely think of sea-level rise while sitting in traffic on the Belt Parkway going to work, getting home, making a flight to Kennedy Airport, or going to the beach. But it is there in the everyday as we occasionally register the "Evacuation Route" signage on the side of the road. The ever-present and yet invisible anxiety about the changing landscape has become ordinary or, in the anthropologist Kathleen Stewart's words, "a drifting immersion that watches and waits for something to pop up."[29]

One existing ecological research project at Plumb Beach seeks to determine what the best sand habitat is for the horseshoe crab to reproduce and thrive. When Plumb Beach was "nourished," dredged sand was pumped to create a new beach—in the process, burying accumulated rubble, cinderblocks, and sand bags that had been added to stabilize the shoreline. The team of field biologists is measuring both the quantity and quality of crab eggs as well as the density and quality of sand at both the before-the-groin and after-the-groin beaches. Based on initial observations, the team thinks the sand at the new beach is too fine and therefore too tightly packed for the crab's reproduction. Mark Botton explained to me, as we were walking down the beach to do a juvenile count, "Once nourishment was completed, the horseshoe crabs weren't too impressed with the newly restored beaches—and preferred the reference site after the jetty. In fact, in the summer of 2012, this area of nourishment had absolutely no ecological value for horseshoe crabs. After Hurricane Sandy, and once they put the breakwater [jetty] in and added more sand, these sediments here were harder, and that harder sand is worse for them, and we know this from previous studies, that crabs can discriminate between different sediment type, and they prefer the softer, the better aerated sands." Thinking about this, I asked Mark, "So is a meta-goal of your work to figure out what is the best way to do beach nourishment and make the crabs have a healthy habitat?" Mark was cautious about making claims until all the data were collected and analyzed: "We don't really know if it is definitely the sand that drives them down the beach to reproduce, and we have to see the data from 2014 to see if they are coming back and what the sand quality is." He paused to assess the tides and winds for our work, and then said, "But a policy recommendation could be that beach replenishment needs to do a better matching of the sand to the type that works for horseshoe crab's reproduction. But then there are the financial constraints of where and how to get the sand, and that comes into play. The horseshoe crabs are never the priority." Here he is acknowledging that, while horseshoe crabs might be his priority, when the fiscal concerns of saving the beach for the highway for transportation come into play, crabs do not rank in most humans' considerations.

Marshaling the tools of a PVC pipe, a mallet, a penetrometer, plastic baggies, and sifters, humans both enhance and create their ability to measure differences between the two sites. We pound the pipes into the beach with the mallet as a means of collecting eggs. We arrange ourselves in one of the comparison areas and randomly toss the PVC pipes to land on the sand, then, taking the mallet we hammer the pipes in, pull them out, and shake their contents into baggies to collect the sand. A penetrometer is a gadget that measures the compression strength of sediments. As Mark explains, "It works like a spring scale in reverse. There's a spring with a calibrated scale; if you have a very compacted soil, you have to push the spring a greater distance before the soil gives way." Using this device, we are able to measure how compact the sand is. The more dense the sand, the less available oxygen is, and the less likely horseshoe crab eggs can develop and hatch.

These nonhuman objects—as well as the humans, the crabs, and global warming—"make the world" of research at Plumb Beach, operating in a constellation of the hyperobject of global warming. Nonhuman actors engage their capacities and properties in the process making sense of the everyday experiences of global warming, sea-level rise, traffic, beach nourishment, geomorphology, and crab reproductive and mortality rates. True to the Latourian ANT, all objects must be considered in this productive landscape to guard against anthropocentric ways of knowing. "Knowledge, morality, craft, force, sociability are not properties of humans but of humans accompanied by their retinue of delegated characters. Since each of those delegates ties together part of our social world, it means that studying social relations without the nonhumans is impossible."[30]

The nourished/before-the-jetty beach is composed of harder sand of more uniform texture, and over a 3-year period, fewer eggs were found at the before-the-jetty beach. During the same period, horseshoe crabs were reproducing on the after-the-jetty beach consistently. Using a penetrometer, researchers determined that there were "[no] immediate ecological benefits to the horseshoe crab" from the nourishment project possibly because "oxygen doesn't diffuse into the sediment." Importantly, based on egg counts for 2014, there was reason to be cautiously optimistic. Over time, as the wind pushed the sand down the beach and the ocean currents turned over the beach before the jetty, the beach was becoming more suitable for the crabs, and they were beginning to return to the before-the-jetty beaches as the sand changed. The beach is changing and becoming more suitable for the horseshoe crabs over time. However, in the arms race against rising tides, beach nourishment will happen at a quicker pace, potentially hampering the crabs' ability to adapt at such a speed. Horseshoe crabs may not be able to speed up their adjustments to spawn, and species decline when deaths are greater than births. If crabs are unable to lay eggs in places where they will develop, then clearly deaths will exceed births. Local extinctions occur more rapidly when generations of horseshoe crabs are not able to reproduce. The use they serve in the local ecology is lost.

Chris Ferullo, research assistant, explains,

> On the nourished beaches, we used the penetrometer to test how difficult it is to penetrate the sand. It is much more difficult, requires more force, to penetrate the sand on the side with the nourishment versus the side without the nourishment because the sand that was dredged out of the trench was very fine. It created a very compact surface. If we dig down 8–10 centimeters, the sand is black because no oxygen can get down there. So you can understand that when horseshoe crabs lay their eggs 15–20 centimeters deep, the eggs can't get enough oxygen to develop. We are trying to figure out how this beach nourishment is affecting the current and if the current and wind churn up the sand. This could, over time, make the sand less uniform, bringing more oxygen, and that's more favorable to horseshoe crab spawning.[31]

While beach nourishment extends the "life" of the Belt Parkway— the urban transportation, the human and vehicular traffic—research has shown that the horseshoe crabs do not use the newly nourished beach—at least, not for the first year or two after nourishment. They must make reproductive choices that steer them from this new sediment. Over time, as the sediment mixes up, they will, one hopes, re-adjust to breeding grounds that suit their needs. But if beach nourishment were to be practiced on the entirety of Plumb Beach, we can only speculate that the crabs would vacate the beach for the time it takes for the sediment to become less uniform. We could speculate about where the crabs would go. As horseshoe crabs have been unusually adaptable species, managing previous climate changes and radical habitat alterations, they clearly have had ways of adjusting their reproductive practices.

Objects Intraacting

If horseshoe crabs and humans are considered ontologically as occupying the same plane (without hierarchical stratification), our interest in crabs should not be limited to their value for humans. However, this is challenging because it is virtually impossible to interpret anything outside of the perspective of humanness despite actively engaging in intraspecies mindfulness. But even though it is not achievable to transcend our humanness, the practice of understanding our humanness as emergent with other species and objects is productive. Keeping in our consciousness how our very selves are only possible through massive intricate collaborations with constellations of other objects can shift our perspectives and motivate more holistic actions.

Furthermore, the Belt Parkway is deeply consequential to where crabs and humans live and reproduce. Landscape plays a role in their habitat, just as their existence plays a role in our ability to drive on the parkway. If, for example, the horseshoe crab were deemed Endangered by the International Union for the Conservation of Nature (as outlined in chapter 2 and defined as a team of concerned humans, including marine biologists, microbiologists, ecologists, ecotoxicologists, paleontologists, and conservationists), it could change the way the habitat bordering the Belt Parkway was managed. Since the crab is not classified as Endangered but merely Vulnerable, beach nourishment is not hampered by considerations of species maintenance.[32]

What might be some of the effects of global warming as a hyperobject on the everyday life of horseshoe crabs, humans, and the parkway? Sea-level rise has caused beach nourishment interventions to save the parkway. The saving of the parkway has caused horseshoe crabs to move down the beach to preserve their reproductive practices, and it may also mean that more people will drive by Plumb Beach than will stop there, or more waves will crash and erode the shoreline because the ecological barriers of oysters, crustaceans, and beach grasses are no longer viable. The field biologists manage apparatuses to create the perceptions or conditions, or both, for the life of horseshoe crabs in relation to humans and to their institutions, such as the Environmental Protection Agency, the National Park Service, and many others.

At a bare minimum, horseshoe crabs are appropriated in part for research as markers of shoreline health, for biopharmaceutical bleeding, and for transnational bait use. The species is connected to global flows of information and intellectual capital and academic research funding and pharmaceutical or biotechnological research and related to lobbyists and policy makers/legislators. There is a deep interconnected cascading of events that occurs at Plumb Beach. If the crab does something in one season, such as lay fewer eggs, that may send ripples throughout the whole configuration of participants. Fewer eggs mean fewer horseshoe crabs for the next generation. Fewer horseshoe crabs mean humans have less ability to harvest them for pharmaceutical companies and fewer crabs to count for census reports of species inventory. Humans might see this as evidence that the fill used for shore nourishment is the wrong type of shoreline engineering. Regulations about harvesting crabs might be amended. Economic projections from pharmaceutical marketplaces may change given the forecast of less horseshoe crab blood availability.

The horseshoe crab's shifting habits affect "our" everyday lives, subtly, in diffuse ways, over seasons and years. Changes can take on many forms because they are broadly constellated and widely diffused across space and time and order of phenomena, for example. Every single day people take the Belt Parkway and try to distract themselves from the monotony of the drive, the traffic, the drone, the exhaust, the boredom. And every day horseshoe crabs make their lives in the bay that borders the parkway. The crabs, humans, cars, sand, eggs, water, and wind live in a choreography of intraaction with ecologists, politicians, policies, regulations, pharmaceutical companies, and geomorphology.

As my project explores, crabs are being harvested for a variety of reasons. Is the point then to both make people aware of these exploits and to get them to start acknowledging and appreciating the relationship between human and nonhuman objects? What is my sociological intervention? Is it to raise awareness of appreciating roads, and cars, and sand grains, and crabs? Raising awareness seems vastly inadequate for the magnitude of the crisis of species decline and shoreline erosion. I believe this is why I have found in the summertime fieldwork a very real envy for the working conditions of the field biologist. Ecologically, Mark Botton, Jennifer Mattei, and Christina Colon have contributed substantially to what we "know" about the horseshoe crab, and their work offers concrete "so whats" for the results sections of research papers. Their work can change the way we re-engineer the shoreline. For example, Mark has suggested that the suitability of shoreline versus the water quality is limiting the breeding and thriving opportunities for horseshoe crabs, and therefore he argues for the very material increase in the amount of sandy beach for horseshoe crab spawning and egg maturation.[33] If my ethnographic work is about changing the minds and hearts of individual humans by trying to get inside of them with the horseshoe crab, the beach, and the parkway, what is the "so what" of my research? My deliverables feel both vague and enormous—we need to transform our conceptualization of ourselves as the ultimate beings and reconsider our ways of life.

The Impossibility of Doing Good

There is a tendency for certain academics and layfolk alike to approach animal studies projects either with a sense of awe and wonder or as part of a narrative of prophetic guidance: If the horseshoe crabs, honeybees, sharks, and cockroaches are supremely well adapted, we might do well to try and learn something from them. They've weathered the storm, the story goes, so let's understand their adaptations, while we also come to realize that we are their biggest threat and develop "clubs" to "help save the——." I am attempting to resist these sensational anthropocentric tendencies, however seductive it is to revel in details of other species' habits or to elevate oneself to savior—in this case by flipping over crabs.

I want to interrupt the tendency to think of crabs as the object of study. Rather, I call for a repositioning of the scientific narrator as actor, along with the objects of narration, so that we can understand the everyday (and ourselves) less as constructing a static narrative and more as enmeshed in a dynamic dialogue. The object is perhaps more the inter- and intrarelationships and our place and other objects' place in it—as well as its existence with or without humans. I have to resist thinking of myself and the beach as static, bounded, and permanently fixed entities. Instead, we need to see all—ourselves, crabs, the beach, the sand, the highway, and other objects—as bodies that are in the world and whose boundaries are created through entanglements and conflicts.

While waiting in traffic on the Belt Parkway, I think about how the enormity of the making and remaking of Plumb Beach transforms my everyday ordinary. According to Stewart, "The ordinary is a shifting assemblage of practices and practical knowledges, a scene of both liveness and exhaustion, a dream of escape or of the simple life."[34] The monotony of the drive is now my diesel car, pumping out fumes, adding to the already inexorable engine-generated sea-level rise. The ongoing shoreline management—through the coordinated efforts of humans, machines, and natural resources to protect the parkway—makes this drive possible.

But what is it for the horseshoe crab? My time with the crab is not sufficient to be able to speak to their everyday lives. But beyond that, my species' limitations means that I can never know their everyday lives. Maybe, though, I can know sea-level rise in a more affectively rich way, where there is something expansive here about being "in nature," about Barad's materiality, about being part of the worlds we study. The profound aspect of doing this research for me has been to experience how we share our worlds, even when we don't realize we're sharing them. Human everyday life is often deeply anthropocentric and also deeply technocentric—but not always organism-centric. In very material ways, humans are becoming with horseshoe crabs.

My project of everyday becoming with horseshoe crabs could be interventionist in a number of ways, beyond how it intervenes in the way earthly beings think about their co-inhabitants of this ecosystem. Sociological research participates in ecological interventions on both personal and public levels. On a personal level, in 2012 my entire family was deeply affected by my working on a book about bees, *Buzz*.[35] Part of our ecological, multispecies changes involved establishing six beehives on our Brooklyn rooftop and starting a composting project on our kitchen counter. And in 2014, after much research, we bought a used 2012 Volkswagen (VW) TDI (Turbo Diesel Injected) Jetta SportWagen. We reasoned that the increased expense of a diesel car and gas would be better for the environment during my commute to work, 70 miles round-trip. Some could suggest we were the perfect market—a "socially conscious" married academic couple with three kids—and in keeping with that script, we "drank the Kool-Aid" on the claims of "clean diesel": "Ultra-low sulfur diesel fuel, advanced engines and effective emissions control combine to achieve near zero emissions that is smoke free. Clean diesel has proven energy efficiency, and ability to use a wide range of renewable fuels that position diesel as a key technology for growing economies to achieve cleaner air, lower greenhouse gas emissions and a sustainable environment around the world."[36] Admittedly, I felt a certain white-lady smugness as I drove down the Hutch to campus. (The Hutch is an abbreviation of the Hutchinson River Parkway and part of my commute to Purchase College.) I had interpreted my enmeshment with the world around me as an intraspecies consciousness that motivated me to make better—or at least less bad—choices. Geez, I had bees, I was studying horseshoe crabs, I recycle, I was SAVING the environment.

Then, in September 2015, in the midst of my Plumb Beach juvenile horseshoe crab research visits, news reports started to come in that there was something rotten in Denmark (in this case, Germany) and that perhaps all the claims of VW clean diesel were not only untrue but that extreme and deliberate steps had been taken to hide ecological devastation. Volkswagen, one of the largest automakers in the world, had installed devices to cheat emissions tests, called *defeat devices*. As stated in the *New York Times*, "Investigators discovered that defeat devices, which activated emissions controls only when the cars were tested, were concealing the fact that its vehicles emitted up to 40 times the permitted levels of pollutants during regular use."[37] Defeat devices are as old as vehicle emissions standards—as one news report quips, "Almost as soon as governments began testing vehicle emissions, carmakers found ways to cheat."[38] In fact, this incident isn't even the first time Volkswagen was caught; the Environmental Protection Agency also fined VW for violating the Clean Air Act in 1973.

The current scandal, coined "Dieselgate," affected an estimated 11 million cars sold between 2009 and 2015 (including those of Audi and Porsche, which are part of the Volkswagen Group). For humans, Dieselgate has created excess mortality, and the lingering emissions are estimated to cost over $39 billion.[39] Calculations by a team of public health and emissions specialists suggest that in the United States 59 premature deaths due to air pollution have occurred because of Dieselgate, with the possibility of 130 more deaths if affected cars were not recalled by the end of 2016.[40]

My smugness has quickly turned to humiliation and anger at my stupid faith in the marketplace to actually create a purchasable solution to sea-level rise. Greenwashing, an advertising strategy, uses signs and symbols of ecological protection to make it appear that a company's ethos is in line with environmental conservation. Think of a truck commercial that depicts hipster hikers driving up a mountain with ambient music as a voice-over reminds us that celebrating Earth Day means "getting into nature." Foolishly, I think because of my ethnographic work, feminist consciousness, education, and political activism I am somehow immune from these media techniques. But greenwashing, which my previous book had completely critically examined, had worked on me, and I was duped. I am predictable; the machine of advertising algorithms and data mining created a purchasing script for me to pour in the contents of my identity. I am complicit in the guilty Global-North-white-woman-I'll-buy-my-way-out-of-this-mess-sense of activism, and as such I participated in making things worse for all living things. I collaborate in creating the conditions of what Lauren Berlant calls *slow death*, the prolonged destroying of the population from the institutional conditions that stratification (based on classism, racism, sexism) requires.[41] Driving my VW because that was a "responsible choice" for my social, political, and personal persuasion, I unwittingly added massive emissions to the air that kill vulnerable others through a long and gradual process of poisoning respiratory systems—these deaths won't be quick, and they will cause extended suffering. I've driven out to Plumb Beach and saved horseshoe crabs, but I've contributed to human slow death.

So enmeshment is not as simple as the choices we make when shopping because enmeshment isn't just conscious decision making—it's the interconnected, diffuse coming together in intraaction, where there are no distinct borders among people, animals, and objects. Clear motivations are not easily executed. My autonomous decision making as a green consumer who studies horseshoe crabs and wants to "help the animals and save the children" is enmeshed in a capitalist machine of algorithms that intraact to co-constitute all my identity, relationships, and actions. It's maddening. We are also ensnared when we are enmeshed—caught in a net of consumption. Enmeshment means I am tangled in complexities sometimes beyond my comprehension and often hegemonic in reinforcing hierarchies of worth. And in the case of Die-selgate, it might even work out to my economic advantage. Because I am human, because I live in the United States,[42] and because I can fill out multiple bureaucratically mandated forms, I will get my money back. Throughout 2016, for my inconvenience I was offered a $500 gift card from Volkswagen and $500 in dealer services, my car was bought back at its prescandal value, and I was given an additional $5,000 for my loy-alty. This money was then turned around, and we purchased a new gas-guzzling used car.

I must also question in a real way the city's dependence on the park-way. Perhaps if humans practiced intraspecies mindfulness, we could work to build environments with other species. New forms of en-gineering could be a win/win for (some) humans and the crabs if we found other ways to get through daily life besides driving to and fro on a sinking strip of asphalt. If horseshoe crabs were to be designated as an Endangered species (they are on their way with the Vulnerable categorization outlined earlier), the city might be forced to change how the parkway is used and managed. But even without the decline of the horseshoe crab, sea-level rise threatens the integrity of the road. Con-tinuing to pump sand and rubble into the shoreline is not ideal for the horseshoe crabs, who return every year but find the site they are return-ing to changed in undesirable ways. But it is also not likely to help us as we drive more cars, create more emissions, and change the climate. This dirty urban beach, strewn with debris, is easy to ignore during the commute.

Conclusion

From the Sea

On a warm April evening in 2016, my 15-year-old daughter and I arrived at the Mercury Lounge on the Lower East Side of Manhattan. Surveying the lineup, I frowned. There were three opening bands before we got to see what we had come for. Georgia and I exchanged knowing glances—it would be a long night. Neither of us are night owls, but we had agreed to work the "merch table" for my former Purchase College student Mal Blum, whom we were there to see. Since I had been so busy with fieldwork and writing, I felt I had neglected my girls. Georgia had kindly come with me on several field site visits, so I had arranged this treat for us. It was a way for us to spend some time alone together and see dear Mal play music. They had a sweet history, too—Mal had performed at Georgia's tenth birthday party, and Georgia made an appearance in one of Mal's music videos. We busied ourselves at the merchandise table, but by the third act, we decided to go inside and see the last act before Mal came on.

The lead singer of Slothrust (we later found out it's pronounced "slow thrust," not "sloth rust," as we'd been saying), Leah Wellbaum, took the stage and sang her first song. I smiled at Georgia, happy we were both impressed by Leah's voice and stage presence. Then she introduced her next song: "This one is called 'Horseshoe Crab.'" Convinced I had misheard, I turned to Georgia. "Wait, WHAT?" I mouthed, dramatically raising my eyebrows. She nodded, pursing her lips. I'd heard correctly. Transported, I felt what had been described to me in seventh-grade science class as serendipity—the unexpected discovery of dimensions of your project/problem in unusual locations, leading to inspiration and highly productive results. I've always practiced the advice of that middle-school biology teacher, Mr. Lewenthal; he repeatedly told us that in order to be good scientists we'd have to "have your brain primed at any time for the unexpected." Swaying back and forth with a sweaty crowd, waiting for the utterance of "horseshoe crab" at 11 P.M. on the Lower East Side of Manhattan with my 15-year-old teenager—was pretty unexpected.

Accompanying herself on the guitar, Leah sang,

> I learned that hunger is a symptom
> of adopting bad behavior
> I bit my tongue last night
> Woke up with blood on my pillow
> I woke up thirsty
>
> Words makes less sense to me these days
> Faces looks flat and unfamiliar
> Do you wanna rest forever?
> Underwater it gets better
>
> When I get better
> I'll treat you like I used to
> I'll do the things you want me to
>
> Sometimes I feel like I'm a seahorse.
> Sometimes I think that I'm a horseshoe crab.
> I don't have anything in common with myself,
> except that I came from the sea
> like everyone else did.
> But it is so unfamiliar now.
> Everything is so unfamiliar now.

I pondered these lines and the emotional depth Leah mined to express them. She got swept up in her passionate musical expression. I felt chills. Yes, I thought this is how it feels to think with animals, as

Lévi-Strauss opined. You change your vantage point, you see things you didn't see before, your ordinary becomes extraordinary, unfamiliar, and that has the potential to be thrilling, deeply strange. Thrilling if, I reminded myself, trying to write about theoretical interpretations of crabs weren't so abstruse. How do I translate my being with horseshoe crabs into my thinking with them—how do I put my affective and physical enmeshment into words? Doesn't my textual expression reduce the ontological experience to something epistemological?

It is a challenge to adequately express what happens when you become with crabs, as Karen Barad and Donna Haraway urge us to do. At the same time, it is astonishingly presumptuous and productively disorienting to think of oneself as a horseshoe crab. Writers like Franz Kafka use this fantastic exercise while writing to investigate existential questions. Why are we here? What is the purpose of existence? In *The Metamorphosis*, Gregor Samsa wakes up changed into an insect described as "lying on his back as hard as armor plate, and when he lifted his head a little, he saw his vaulted brown belly, sectioned by arch-shaped ribs, to whose dome the cover, about to slide off completely, could barely cling. His many legs, pitifully thin compared with the size of the rest of him, were waving helplessly before his eyes."[1] It is generative to imagine a human as an insect for expressing notions of what makes a self or an individual worthy of existing.

I, like others, can't shake the feeling that anthropomorphism is clumsy yet productive.[2] There is no way out of anthropomorphism, and as such we will always be anthropocentric. And although it is inevitable that anthropocentrism dominates our consciousness and actions, it is worth struggling with getting outside of our humanness. "Sometimes I think that I'm a horseshoe crab"—is this desire the ultimate expression of empathetic oneness, or is it an egotistical colonization of the other? I'd like to think the former—we are seeing ourselves as becoming with horseshoe crabs as a way to enhance our mutual entanglement in ecologies and be more mindful of who we are, what we are, what we use, and how we make.

I've been working to understand that, in the short time (relative to deep time) of researching and writing this book, humans have changed the *Limulus* species of horseshoe crab status from Least Concern to Vulnerable. This change in status is a cultural construct but it is also based on an empirical and material truth—there are fewer horseshoe crabs than there were, and their habitats are shrinking. We, as a species, have created conditions that are not healthy for crabs to maintain their epic longevity. Take, for example, the bleeding of horseshoe crabs and certain justifications in which humans claim that we know that the crab enjoys a "spa day" when bled and is capable of "making a donation." This construction of the crab represents the self-serving becoming with. We humans manipulate language in order to further exploit crabs' capacities exclusively for our benefit. When do we know we are becoming with the crabs in a just way? When is becoming with simply a strategy for our own selfish projects? When is it a deeply reflective becoming with that acknowledges how we are implicated? It might be impossible for us to sustain a consciousness about how our everyday lives—including our use of vehicles, land, and biopharmaceuticals—implicates horseshoe crabs.[3] But it is imperative that we try.

I am still concerned about the thorny ways epistemology, *what we know*, interferes with some apprehension of ontology, *what exists*. What is the relationship of what we know to what exists with respect to horseshoe crabs? Perhaps it is unavoidable that humans have to *think* themselves into becoming with horseshoe crabs. I don't know if we can just become horseshoe crabs in some nonconscious somatic way—maybe it happens as children? Growing up on the beaches of the East Coast, I don't remember a time when I didn't know what a horseshoe crab was. I've grown up catching and releasing horseshoe crabs, but I don't recall ever being formally introduced to them; they just always seemed to be there on the beach. I came to know them through touching them and tossing them. But something happened at some point where they became to me kind of like seagulls—"the scavengers of the beach"—ubiquitous and slightly distasteful. I am sure it was a form of socialization in which someone said they were gross, or ugly, or scary, and I started to think them a nuisance. I imagine I relegated them to the category of *trash animals*.[4] In assigning the label of *trash* to an animal, humans place negative value on the aesthetics of the creature, justify violence often through extermination, engage in eugenic practices of forced sterilization or management of female bodies, and elevate their own human status as preeminent. Smelly, rotting crabs or creepy moving live ones were messing up the day at the beach, and these crabs should be avoided or thrown farther down the beach.

Over time, my consciousness has shifted about horseshoe crabs, and I am not sure how I can access their ontological essence back to my naïve, playful, wonder with them—before the negative trash assessments were adopted. I understand that I am falling into the trap here of some romantic notion of an edenic past with nature, before the fall and before language. So I ponder my original enchantment—am I just chasing a retrospective, imaginary high? Trying to get back to the wonder of childhood—showing carapaces to students as a way to crack the monotony of market forces—spending hours on Plumb Beach with the crabs where there is no cell service—finding babies as some sense of "helping them" as I connect with my own children and "teach" them some environmental lessons?

Through this multispecies ethnography, I've come to know them in a different way. I now know horseshoe crabs as a species that provides humans some insight into the hyperobject of global warming, as an ancient animal that collapses deep time, as a pharmaceutical commodity of grandiose biomedical claims-making, as an animal model to make sense of endangerment and tensions over global ecological projects, and as a screen to project cultural understandings of sex and gender. The crab fans out beyond its apparent organismic boundaries into different temporalities, epistemologies, and ontologies. I am engaged with the complexity, embroilment, and enrollment of crabs in other projects and how the crab draws other projects into its spheres. It is enchanting to me to be with the crabs as an adult working sociologist in a different but similar way to a child playing on the beach. I've thought about what it means to be a scientist studying crabs and a scientist studying scientists. I've related horseshoe crabs to our shared experiences and vulnerabilities to environmental catastrophe. In mining the narratives about donation and voluntarism, I've explored the ways humans deploy language to exploit crabs even when it is no longer technologically necessary. Horseshoe crabs are not willing donors of their blood. They are forced to shoulder our pain and enhance our survival, often at the expense of their own. Human descriptions of crabs' reproductive habits reinforce certain long-held socially produced stereotypes about sex and gender and reassert essentialist stratification about human women either being open or *intolerant* of male sexual attention.

This *thinking* might be a prerequisite into becoming. In other words, I question whether or not we need to rationally think before we can get in touch with the ontological being of horseshoe crabs. Is epistemology, the knowing part, a necessary precursor to apprehending the ontology, the being part? My friend, the anthropologist Jason Pine, urges me to think that there is a way to have affective and sensory interactions with the materiality and being of objects where objects (including animals) are "strikingly expressive."[5] But, for me, I can't turn off the thinking so easily. And when apprehending an animal, the thinking is always socially produced, predominantly through scientific discourses, which are partial and biased. What can we actually know when our thinking is partial and biased?

Neither Leah nor I are horseshoe crabs, but as the song suggests, sometimes, we think we are these nonhuman animals. Or imagining we are them offers some creative power that humanness limits.[6] We are in a world of becoming with them—their blood has washed over our biomedical paraphernalia, their ground up-bodies have fertilized generations of soil, all this mixing up of horseshoe crab–human flesh and form. The crabs also become with us as part of the co-produced mesh. Our re-engineering of the shorelines, transforming the composition of the sea and changing the temperature of the planet alters their habitats, their reproduction, their movements, and their bodies.

Materially I can visibly see the borders between my body and theirs. We are separate entities, but we make each other up. When they latch onto my hands, when I wade into the waters and they scurry over my feet, when I breathe in their decaying stench at the shoreline—I am reminded of the work from the emergent interdisciplinary field environmental humanities claiming, "All living beings emerge from and make their lives within multispecies communities"[7]—and these communities are overwhelmingly dominated by humans in the Anthropocene.

Throughout this book I have collected, analyzed, and shared data about horseshoe crabs, and I have couched the data within theoretical frameworks. My goal has not been to make any kind of absolute or singular statements about the ontology of horseshoe crabs. But I do contend that it is only through rigorous radical empirical investigation, experiencing crabs in their habitat, collecting and analyzing data, and building a sensorial intraaction that one can begin to examine more theoretical questions of the epistemic significance of nonhuman entities. Empirical research is a good place to start, as ethnography and hard sciences do, but building a sensorial intraaction means more. It involves honing perception beyond the rational, logical method of inquiry that empiricism favors. Sensorial intraaction is embodied and empathic. This work, beyond the empirical methods of social science, is part of the womansplaining that I pondered in the preface to this book.

When I reached down and took horseshoe crabs out of the warm Florida waters, their bodies bent back and forth. I had to be careful not to get my fingers caught in the tilting carapace as I brought them to a firm terrestrial surface to tag them. To insert a tag, I used the awl to puncture the carapace. This puncture requires a certain amount of force. Through this repeated pushing and twisting the awl into the body of the crabs, I now know about a horseshoe crab's fortitude in an immediate way. Their carapaces are strong, their ability to heal almost immediate. And in the handling and tagging of the crab, I became a citizen scientist and a conservationist, but I was also someone who inflicted injury to an animal. I ran back to the waterline to put a crab back into the warm waters. My legs wobbled on the shifting sands. I wanted to offer some relief, to get them back to what I perceived to be more familiar. I licked my salty fingers, reminding myself of their aquatic environment. And while doing this, I had to consider how the process of tagging a particular crab does not help that crab, but in the future, it might help the species. I also had to know there was some type of futility in all of this physical and emotional labor. My use of theoretical frameworks assists in unpacking the social and cultural intersections between crabs and humans, but it is my sensorial intraacting with crabs that has allowed me to consider multispecies sociality.

I began this book with a discussion of my personal struggles and the clash between what is perceived to be the accurate mechanism to produce knowledge, classical, scientific, assured, and stable versus my own more situated, partial, embodied, and anxious method. This struggle is the integral driver in my investigation for this book—how the beingness of other nonhuman entities shapes and guides all of our collective existence and the modes through which humans are ever able to know it. For me, I have considered myself a post-Enlightenment feminist scholar who, with the knowledge of an extra-anthropic epistemic interrelationship, must return back to my original struggle over hegemonic ways of presenting knowledge. Ironically I must actually use the tools of science in order to clear a path for a more profound realization; this is perhaps a different science. It began with countless hours of fieldwork, interviews, and observations and getting my hands dirty. In this process of acquiring a massive collection of empirical data, I see myself caught in an epistemological/ontological struggle with nonhuman entities.

This is a methodology in which my own reflections count as evidence, a type of building block toward establishing epistemology. A central practice that undergirds the chapters of this book has been mining the personal reflections with crabs and scientists and other objects to make sense of these times. My anxious ways of knowing and being in the world are fueled by these times of normative gender scripts, massive biomedicalization, global warming, sea-level rise, and extinction, and horseshoe crabs offer me a way of understanding and finding relief from these systems of domination. Wellbaum's song, and its associative bodily reasoning, the all-encompassing feeling of being overwhelmed and taken up in a sweaty mass of people, feeling my species being, enchanted by rhythms and invocations of horseshoe crabs, liberates me from the traps of circular thinking. I am open to new ways of being.

Catch and Release investigates and grapples with these questions: How do humans exploit the horseshoe crabs, come to depend on them, and fret about their welfare? Humans exploit crabs within a biomedicalized world of late capitalism, and I believe that humans, if they themselves survive, will continue to use crabs until crabs are extinct. How is it that humans are simultaneously saviors and villains in stories about the crabs? A concerned group of humans have attempted to organize to protect horseshoe crabs. But their efforts are likely too late in the massive, inexorable sea-level rise that the planet is experiencing. Have the crabs met their match in humans after 480 million years? Or are humans, in their speciesist ignorance, insignificant to the crabs' geologic legacy? I do believe crabs will outlive humans.

NOTES

PREFACE

1 Solnit, *Men Explain Things to Me.*

2 Hartsock, "Foucault on Power," 164.

3 Alger and Alger, *Cat Culture*; Arluke and Sanders, *Regarding Animals*; Bennett, *Vibrant Matter*; Chen, *Animacies*; Haraway, *The Companion Species Manifesto*; Helmreich, *Alien Ocean*; Kirksey and Helmreich, "The Emergence of Multispecies Ethnography"; Lisa Jean Moore and Mary Kosut, *Buzz*; and Tsing, *The Mushroom at the End of the World.*

4 Haraway, "Situated Knowledges: The Science Question in Feminism and the Privilege of Partial Perspective"; Harding, *Whose Science/Whose Knowledge?*; and Hill Collins, *Black Feminist Thought.* Standpoint theory, emerging in the mid-1980s, posits that individuals come from particular situated places or positions in the world. Individuals' places in the world are deeply related to their social status, including their race, class, gender, sexuality, religion, and ability. Such a place is a standpoint, and it is deeply influential to how an individual interprets the world. Standpoints then, are, viewpoints or perspectives for how individuals see the world and are always partial.

5 Barad, *Meeting the Universe Halfway.*

6 Ingold, "Anthropology beyond Humanity"; and Morton, *Hyperobjects.*

7 Lisa Jean Moore and Mary Kosut, *Buzz.*

8 Haraway, *The Companion Species Manifesto.* The science studies scholar Donna Haraway uses the term *natureculture* as a way to resist and destabilize the entrenched binary thinking of nature versus culture. In everyday life, we often categorize things as nature/natural (an animal) or culture/cultural (communication). In contrast to this either/or categorization, Haraway innovated the term *natureculture* to encourage thinking of nature and culture as always entangled together and mutually reinforcing one another. My dog is neither nature nor culture; she is part of the natureculture of the life we have co-created. In our family, the dog is part of the family we have formed in collaboration with one another.

CHAPTER 1. FIELDWORK IN THE MUDFLATS

1 Qualitative research is emergent and in a sense, messy, as it focuses on meanings, interpretation, rituals, interactions, and so forth. In this context, I did not start with a hypothesis per se but with a set of ideas and questions that guided my

study in the initial phases of the project. As is common in qualitative research projects, I expected to modify and amend these questions over time to reflect what I had learned throughout the ongoing fieldwork process. I conceptualized questions revolving around horseshoe crabs as a species through the perspectives of scientists, conservationists, biopharmaceutical representatives, and layfolk. All data were analyzed based on a modified-grounded theory methodology. *Grounded theory* is a deductive process in which analysts incorporate as much data as possible so formative theories can be used as deductive tools. Through the writing and rewriting of analytic memos, this tool—the grounded theory— ultimately aims to incorporate the range of human experiences in its articulation and execution. According to Anselm Strauss, a key developer of grounded theory, it is through one's immersion in the data that these comparisons become the "stepping stones" for formal theories of patterns of action and interaction between and among various types of data. By triangulating data sources about horseshoe crab representations over the last 4 years (scientific texts, field notes, interview transcriptions), I have been able to establish various points of comparison for exploring multiple concepts about horseshoe crabs. Working with my analytic memos written about these concepts, I have been able to establish interrelation-ships between them. "Theory evolves during actual research, and it does this through continuous interplay between analysis and data collection." See Strauss and Corbin, *Basics of Qualitative Research*, 273. Similar to other qualitative research, content analysis can be *exploratory* and *descriptive*, enabling limited insight into why significant relationships or trends occur. The aim is not toward standardization of facts into scientific units but, rather, an appreciation and play with the range of variation of a particular phenomenon. Outliers, representations that do not fall neatly into the collection of the most common themes and concepts, are useful because they enable analysts to capture this range of variation and the dimensions of the concepts.

2 Endotoxins are small bacterially derived hydrophobic molecules that can easily contaminate labware and infect humans and animals.

3 Ryder, *Victims of Science*; and Singer, *Animal Liberation*.

4 Unless otherwise specified, all quotes of Jennifer Mattei are from interviews with the author, 2013–2016.

5 For discussions on invertebrate suffering, see, e.g., Elwood, "Pain and Suffering?"; and Mather, "Animal Suffering."

6 Approximately 95%–99% of the planet's animal species are invertebrates, leading them to be called the "silent majority." See Smithsonian National Zoological Park, "Invertebrate Facts: The Silent Majority."

7 See Battelle, "Simple Eyes." In 1967, the American physiologist Dr. Haldan Keffer Hartline received the Nobel Prize in Physiology or Medicine for optic research utilizing horseshoe crabs. By studying the crabs' optic nerve's electrical impulses, scientists have extrapolated from this research to understanding the integration of

visual information and circadian rhythms. For other species, including humans, see Chabot and Watson, "Daily and Tidal Rhythms."

8 Penn and Brockmann, "Age-Based Stranding and Righting."

9 Botton and Ropes, "Populations of Horseshoe Crabs."

10 Mark Botton, personal communication, 2015; Rebecca Anderson, phone interview, February 4, 2014.

11 Fredericks, *Horseshoe Crab.*

12 Novitsky, "Discovery of Commercialization."

13 Helmreich, *Alien Ocean*, xi.

14 Jegla and Costlow, "Temperature and Salinity Effects"; and Laughlin, "The Effects of Temperature and Salinity."

15 Sixto Portillo, personal communication, 2014.

16 On honeybees dying, see Lisa Jean Moore and Mary Kosut, *Buzz.* On clitorises disappearing, see Lisa Jean Moore and Adele E. Clarke, "Clitoral Conventions." On sperm counts declining, see Lisa Jean Moore, *Sperm Counts.*

17 Barad, *Meeting the Universe Halfway*; Chen, *Animacies*; and Bennett, *Vibrant Matter.*

18 Lisa Jean Moore and Mary Kosut, *Buzz.*

19 Wolfe, *What Is Posthumanism?*, xxv.

20 Haraway, *The Companion Species Manifesto.*

21 "Animals are good to think with": This is how Lévi-Strauss is usually paraphrased and translated from the French, but he is more correctly quoted and translated as saying that animals are "good to think." See Lévi-Strauss, *The Savage Mind.* Also see Lisa Jean Moore, *Sperm Counts*; and Lisa Jean Moore and Mary Kosut, *Buzz.*

22 This celebration, "A Celebration to Honor Dr. Carl N. Shuster Jr. and His Years of Horseshoe Crab Study," was attended by several horseshoe crab experts, and it took place on June 4, 2016, at Limuli Laboratories in Delmont, New Jersey.

23 Berkson and Shuster, "The Horseshoe Crab."

24 Walls, Berkson, and Smith, "The Horseshoe Crab."

25 Levin, Hochstein, and Novitsky, "Clotting Cells."

26 It is important to note that the term *extinct* is often colloquially used to express the idea that populations are so small they cannot be profitably utilized for commerce (i.e., blood harvesting). When used scientifically, the term *extinct* means that the species is gone.

27 For animal-themed ethnographies, see Alger and Alger, *Cat Culture*; Arluke, "Ethnozoology"; DeMello, *Animals and Society*; Myers, "No Longer the Lonely Species"; Sanders, "Understanding Dogs: Caretakers' Attributions"; Taylor, "Never an It"; Kohn, "How Dogs Dream"; Jerolmack, *The Global Pigeon* ; Cherry, *Culture and Activism*; Candea, "I Fell in Love with Carlos the Meerkat"; Haraway, *Primate Visions*; Fitzgerald, "Doing Time"; Davis and Maurstad, *The Meaning of Horses*; Cudworth, *Social Lives with Other Animals*; and Dooren, *Flight Ways.*

28 Haraway, *The Companion Species Manifesto.*

29 Raffles, *Insectopedia.*
30 Kirksey and Helmreich, "The Emergence of Multispecies Ethnography," 545.
31 Lisa Jean Moore and Mary Kosut, *Buzz.*
32 Barad, *Meeting the Universe Halfway.*
33 Mark often raised an eyebrow at my encouraging the girls to go swimming in the Jamaica Bay waters.
34 Kolbert, *The Sixth Extinction.*
35 Ursula Heise, *Imagining Extinction.*
36 Morton, *Hyperobjects.*

CHAPTER 2. ENDANGERED

1 Dries, "Living Fossils"; and Briggs et al., "Silurian Horseshoe Crab."
2 Williams, *The Country and the City.*
3 Norgaard, *Living in Denial.*
4 Malinowski, *Argonauts of the Western Pacific,* 16.
5 Gould, *Time's Arrow, Time's Cycle,* 3.
6 Richard Fortey, as quoted in Trevisick, *Survivors.*
7 Kirby, Smith, and Wilkins, "World's Largest Horseshoe Crab."
8 Briggs et al., "Silurian Horseshoe Crab."
9 Taussig, *The Devil and Commodity Fetishism,* 4.
10 Weber, *The Protestant Ethic,* 181.
11 Fortey, *Horseshoe Crabs and Velvet Worms,* 227.
12 Silverstein, *The Giving Tree.*
13 This experience is similar to that described by Bernadette Bensaude-Vincent and Isabelle Stengers in the first chapter of the *A History of Chemistry.* Chemistry started out in the seventeenth century as "the polymorphous variety of artisanal practices and cultural traditions" practiced by a hodgepodge of alchemists, physicians, metallurgists, and mystics (Bensaude-Vincent and Stengers, *A History of Chemistry,* 33). Through time, with efforts to make chemistry a legitimate discipline and a respected profession, mysticism was abandoned for laboratory science. While it is true that we claim to know more about chemicals, it is also true that we know differently through the ascendancy of science as the dominant explanatory model. What gets lost in our exclusive reliance on science?
14 Darwin, *On the Origin of Species,* chap. 2.
15 Horseshoe crabs have a different type of chitinous material than trilobites making up their shell-like bodies, which is less durable than the material that made up trilobite exoskeletons. Because of this difference, there is a more established fossil record for trilobites than for horseshoe crabs.
16 When two different species are related by similar morphologies and reproductive capacities, I question my own species relationships to my own kin. I often wonder if I am really the same species as members of my own family's genealogic tree. My grandmother was a 4 foot 9 inch eighth-grade-educated Italian woman who lived

her whole life in a housing project in the Bronx with no driver's license. She birthed and raised two daughters and had a knack for making chicken cutlets. I am a 5 foot 11 inch queer commuting professor married to a transgender man. Perhaps it is a technicality—but as I consider it, I haven't reproduced with a member of my own species since I used frozen and processed technosemen and plastic syringes to get pregnant. Is it just that I am a more of a cyborg than my grandmother and my daughters more so than me? When does it click over to a new species?

17 Youatt, *Counting Species.*

18 Hartigan, *Aesop's Anthropology.*

19 Martin, "The Egg and the Sperm."

20 Ingold, "Anthropology beyond Humanity."

21 Kirksey, "Species," 776.

22 Hartigan, *Aesop's Anthropology.*

23 Census of Marine Life, "About the Census."

24 Pooley, "Endangered," 262.

25 Kirksey, "Species," 777.

26 Fortey, *Horseshoe Crabs and Velvet Worms.*

27 Kolbert, *The Sixth Extinction*; and Youatt, *Counting Species.*

28 Kolbert, *The Sixth Extinction.*

29 Smith and Zeder, "The Onset of the Anthropocene," 9.

30 Ibid., 8.

31 Thomas et al., "Extinction Risk from Climate Change."

32 Fortey, as quoted in Trevisick, *Survivors.*

33 Stromberg, "What Is the Anthropocene?"

34 Chakrabarty, "The Climate of History," 221.

35 Ellis, "Ecology in an Anthropogenic Biosphere."

36 Ruddiman and Thomson, "The Case for Human Causes."

37 The environmental studies scholar Stacy Alaimo criticizes the drive toward sustainability studies as something that de-politicizes our critical engagement with the ecologies. Our practices in environmental intervention should not be driven by "render[ing] the world as a resource for human use." See Alaimo, *Exposed*, 177.

38 Yusoff, "Anthropogenesis," 11.

39 Tsing, *The Mushroom at the End of the World*; Haraway, "Anthropocene, Capitalocene"; and Jason Moore, *Capitalism in the Web of Life.*

40 Jason Moore, "Anthropocene or Capitalocene?"

41 Youatt, *Counting Species*, 48.

42 Ibid., 127.

43 International Union of Conservation Naturalists, "About the IUCN."

44 Tsing, *The Mushroom at the End of the World*, 29.

45 Butler, *Precarious Life.*

46 Beyond the human-non human animal nexus, there are other signs that human time is over. We are living in precarity, and disaster capitalism drives profit (see Klein, *The Shock Doctrine*). Even more perversely, climate change itself has been turned into a profitable enterprise through the creation of catastrophic bonds, which are bonds issued by an individual concerned with making profit from potential disasters (see Burnett, "The Bonds of Catastrophe"). Precarity is good for business, as members of our species are working to profit off of our own engineered destruction. The sociologist Jackie Orr's haunting photographic essay about the aftermath of an oil spill in the Gulf Coast suggests humans are still fumbling for ways to describe time. As ecological, political, meteorological disasters happen in quicker succession, piling one upon the other, we can no longer signify time by individual or particular disaster events (i.e., mass extinction events, massive weather changes). We are living in the time of more long-lived precarity; that is, catastrophic time has become ordinary time. Orr writes, "In contrast to the increasingly standardized processing of disaster-events through templates of crisis news and emergency preparedness, the slow catastrophe of repetitious wasting—of ordinary time itself wearing thin and human and non-human worlds bearing depleted signs of exhaustion—seems to have not yet found a language for expression, or public reckoning" (see Orr, "Killing Time").

47 Kwan, Shin, and Cheung, "Preliminary Home Range Study."

48 Akbar John and Rozihan, "Design and Development."

49 Colon and Rowden, "Blurring the Roles," 46.

50 U.S. Fish and Wildlife Service, "Polar Bear (*Ursus maritimus*) Conservation Management Plan, Draft."

51 Clarke and Fujimura, *The Right Tools for the Job.*

52 Beekey and Mattei, "The Mismanagement of *Limulus polyphemus*."

53 D. R. Smith et al., "*Limulus polyphemus*."

54 Puig de la Bellacasa, "Making Time for Soil," 694.

CHAPTER 3. AMPLEXED

1 National Geographic Wild, *Alien Crab.*

2 Chris, *Watching Wildlife.*

3 Candea, "I Fell in Love with Carlos the Meerkat."

4 Barad, "Matter Feels."

5 A phrase Bekoff uses throughout *Minding Animals*; also see Irvine, "A Model of Animal Selfhood."

6 Haraway, "Situated Knowledges."

7 Mooallem, *Wild Ones.*

8 On our own reproduction, see Martin, "The Egg and the Sperm"; on nonhuman animal reproduction, see Chris, *Watching Wildlife.*

9 Lisa Jean Moore, *Sperm Counts.*

10 Botton, Loveland, and Tiwari, "Distribution, Abundance, and Survivorship."

11 Shuster, "Observations."

12 It is important to note that this is true of all organisms living in a nonexpanding population: On average only two offspring survive into the next generation (replacing the parents, hence, a nonincreasing population). However, in the case of many mammals, including humans, the reproduction of such a high ratio of fertilized eggs per live offspring does not occur.

13 Darcy quipped to me, "Side note: Googling *mating scar* without quotation marks is *not* advisable. . . . It leads to a lot of questionable *Lion King*–themed fanfiction."

14 Botton, Tankersley, and Loveland, "Developmental Ecology."

15 Brockmann, "Satellite Male Groups."

16 Lishko, Botchkina, and Kirichok, "Progesterone Activates the Principal Ca2+ Channel."

17 Brockmann, "Mating Behavior."

18 For an explanation of the ecology that lives on the horseshoe crab, see Grant, "Living on Limulus."

19 For example, see Brockmann, "Mating Behavior" and "Satellite Male Groups"; Brockmann, Nguyen, and Potts, "Paternity in Horseshoe Crabs"; and Sheri Johnson and H. Jane Brockmann, "Alternative Reproductive Tactics."

20 See Dickinson and Leonard, "Mate Attendance and Copulatory Behavior."

CHAPTER 4. BLED

1 Lonza, "QC Testing Solutions Notebook."

2 National Geographic Wild, *Alien Crab.*

3 Starr, "Bad Blood."

4 Marx, *Economic and Philosophic Manuscripts* (1844), 327.

5 There are unsubstantiated reports of nascent scientific research suggesting that humans could potentially give some of their own blood product to dogs. See Tudor, "How Humans Can Save Pets."

6 Kirksey et al., "The *Xenopus* Pregnancy Test."

7 Lisa Jean Moore and Mary Kosut, *Buzz.*

8 Manji et al., "Porcine Bioprosthetic Heart Valves."

9 Fitz, *Horseshoe Crabs.*

10 Ron Berzofsky, personal communication, 2015.

11 Also from personal experience, it is very difficult to get a sense of how much fishermen make for any catch.

12 Titmuss, *The Gift Relationship.*

13 Niza, Tung, and Marteau, "Incentivizing Blood Donation."

14 Swanson, *Banking on the Body.*

15 It is important to point out that, even though it is part of the gift economy in the United States, until 1994 U.S. prisons entered into deals with pharmaceutical companies to sell blood plasma from inmates, claiming that the profits could be used to subsidize the costs of incarceration. See Carney, *The Red Market.*

16 Hayes, *Five Quarts.*

17 Bakalar, "The Shelf Life of Donor Blood."

18 AABB, "Blood FAQ."

19 Cohen, Feigenbaum, and Adashi, "Reconsideration of the Lifetime Ban."

20 Levin and Bang, "The Role of Endotoxin."

21 Hartigan, *Aesop's Anthropology*, 62.

22 Frazier, "Blue Bloods."

23 Tom Novitzky, personal communication, 2014–2015.

24 Levy, "Crabs in Space."

25 Downes and Ito, *Compendium of Methods.*

26 U.S. Department of Health and Human Services, "Guidance for Industry."

27 Hurton and Berkson, "Potential Causes of Mortality," 294.

28 Leschen and Correia, "Mortality in Female Horseshoe Crabs."

29 ASMFC manages horseshoe crab populations for bait harvest as well as biomedical harvest: "The horseshoe crab fishery supplies bait for the American eel, conch
(whelk) and, to a lesser degree, catfish (Ictaluridae) fisheries. The American eel
pot fishery prefers egg-laden female horseshoe crabs, while the conch pot fishery
uses both male and female horseshoe crabs. Most fishing effort for horseshoe
crabs is concentrated within the mid-Atlantic coastal waters and adjacent federal
waters. However, Massachusetts supports a significant fishery. The hand, trawl
and dredge fisheries accounted for about 85% of the 2012 reported commercial
horseshoe crab bait landings by gear type. This is consistent with the distribution
of landings by gear since 1998." See ASFMF Horseshoe Crab Stock Assessment
Subcommittee, "2013 Horseshoe Crab Stock Assessment Update."

30 ASMFC, "Horseshoe Crab Biomedical Ad-Hoc Working Group Report [on Best
Practices]."

31 ASMFC, "2015 Annual Report of the Atlantic States Marine Fisheries
Commission."

32 Goodman and Nir, "Poachers Are Elusive Catch."

33 Conley, "Crab-Poach Pinch."

34 As stated above, historically rabbits were used for a pyrogen test, in which they
were injected with a product that could contain contamination and their rectal
temperature was then assessed over several hours. This test, still sometimes used,
is time-consuming and expensive; standard protocols require that three rabbits be
used for each test.

35 U.S. Department of Health and Human Services, "Guidance for Industry."

36 Research & Markets, "Pyrogen Testing Market."

37 Ibid.

38 Akbar John et al., "Effects of Blood Extraction."

39 Lisa Jean Moore and Mary Kosut, *Buzz.*

40 Ihle, "Pyrogene™ rFC Assay."

CHAPTER 5. ENMESHED

1 Psuty et al., "Sediment Budget as a Driver."
2 U.S. Army Corps of Engineers, "Review Plan for Plumb Beach Section, 2014."
3 Forman, "New York City Is Crumbling."
4 Freund and McGuire, *Health, Illness and the Social Body.*
5 Haraway, "Situated Knowledges."
6 Rose, "Site Fidelity."
7 Dooren and Rose, "Storied-Places," 5.
8 New York City Department of Transportation, "New York City Screenline Traffic Flow."
9 Barad, *Meeting the Universe Halfway*, 150.
10 National Aeronautics and Space Administration, "Global Climate Change."
11 Gillis, "Seas Are Rising."
12 Turley et al., "Hot, Sour, and Breathless."
13 Loveland and Botton, "Sea Level Rise in Delaware Bay," 52.
14 This phrase "feeling for the organism" is the historian Evelyn Fox Keller's extraction of the geneticist Barbara McClintock's approach to scientific observation, in which even the smallest, most minute detail of biological processes and entities are endlessly fascinating. McClintock used these skills of keen observation and her own intuition to produce her science of genetics. It is in deep engagement with biological and scientific objects that scientists produce theories about life. See Keller, *A Feeling for the Organism.*
15 See Lisa Jean Moore and Mary Kosut, *Buzz*, esp. the conclusion.
16 Ibid.; and Barad, *Meeting the Universe Halfway.*
17 Kirksey and Helmreich, "The Emergence of Multispecies Ethnography," 545.
18 Glaser and Strauss, *The Discovery of Grounded Theory.*
19 Latour, *Reassembling the Social*, 128.
20 Law, "Technology and Heterogeneous Engineering," 130.
21 Walls, Berkson, and Smith, "The Horseshoe Crab."
22 Rebecca Anderson, personal communication, 2014.
23 Horseshoe crabs are managed under the Interstate Fishery Management Plan for Horseshoe Crabs (1998) and under Addenda I (2000), Addenda II (2001), and Addenda III (2004), which can be found on the ASMFC website at www.asmfc.org or by contacting the ASMFC Habitat Specialist at (202) 289–6400. See ASMFC, "Horseshoe Crab."
24 See, e.g., two New York City–related news stories about horseshoe crab poaching: Evans, "Cops Nab Two"; and Goodman and Nir, "Poachers Are Elusive Catch."
25 Shuster, "Distribution."
26 Jennifer Mattei, personal communication, 2014. See also Mattei et al., "Reproductive Behavior in Horseshoe Crabs."
27 Shuster, "Distribution."

28 Morton, *Hyperobjects*, 133.
29 Stewart, *Ordinary Affects*, 95.
30 J. Johnson, "Mixing Humans and Nonhumans Together," 310.
31 For a detailed explanation of how oxygen gets into sand, see Jackson, Smith, and Nordstrom, "Physical and Chemical Changes."
32 However, if another species were deemed Endangered, such as birds like red knots, which rely on horseshoe crab eggs as food, then environmental regulations would affect beach nourishment.
33 Botton, Loveland, et al., "Horseshoe Crabs (*Limulus polyphemus*) in an Urban Estuary."
34 Stewart, *Ordinary Affects*, 1.
35 See Lisa Jean Moore and Mary Kosut, *Buzz*.
36 Diesel Technology Forum. "What Is Clean Diesel?"
37 Grescoe, "The Truth about 'Clean Diesel.'"
38 Plungis, "Volkswagen Emissions Scandal."
39 Blackwelder et al., "The Volkswagen Scandal"; Oldenkamp, van Zelm, and Huijbregts, "Valuing the Human Health Damage"; and Vaughan, "VW Emissions Cheat."
40 Barrett et al., "Impact of the Volkswagen Emissions Control Defeat Device."
41 Berlant, "Slow Death."
42 Colli, "Why It's So Hard for Europeans to Get Compensation."

CONCLUSION
1 Kafka, *The Metamorphosis*, 7.
2 Bennett, *Vibrant Matter*; and Pine, "Last Change Incorporated."
3 This feeling of not being able to contain the magnificence of everything as interconnected reminds me of Emily Webb's struggle in the play *Our Town* by Thornton Wilder. Emily, who has died in childbirth, comes back to visit the town during a day of her choosing. She picks her twelfth birthday, and after a flood of emotions at seeing her youthful parents, Emily has an epiphany about the inability to truly be present for all sensory experiences. She delivers a monologue to the Stage Manager. It expresses the limits of human understanding, our struggles with perceiving the mundane, and the profoundness of our earthbound lives. "Oh, earth, you're too wonderful for anybody to realize you. Do any human beings ever realize life while they live it?—Every, every minute? I'm ready to go back. I should have listened to you. That's all human beings are! Just blind people" (Act 3).
4 Nagy and Johnson, *Trash Animals*.
5 Russo, "There in the Thicket: An Interview with Jason Pine."
6 Bogost, *Alien Phenomenology*.
7 Dooren, Kirksey, and Munster, "Multispecies Studies," 1.

REFERENCES

AABB. "Blood FAQ." American Association of Blood Banks, 2016. www.aabb.org.

Akbar John, B., K. C. A. Jalal, K. Zaleha, P. Armstrong, and B. Y. Kmaruzzaman. "Effects of Blood Extraction on the Mortality of Malaysian Horseshoe Crabs (*Tachypleus gigas*)." *Marine and Freshwater Behavior and Physiology* 44, no. 5 (2011): 321–327.

Akbar John, B., and M. Rozihan. "Design and Development of Smartphone Application (MyHSC) for Real Time Geolocation Tracking and Sighting of Horseshoe Crab Population." Presented at the Third International Workshop on the Science and Conservation of Horseshoe Crabs, Saebo, Japan, June 17, 2015.

Alaimo, Stacy. *Exposed: Environmental Politics and Pleasures in Posthuman Times*. Minneapolis: University of Minnesota Press, 2016.

Alger, J., and S. Alger. *Cat Culture: The Social World of a Cat Shelter*. Philadelphia: Temple University Press, 2003.

Arluke, Arnold. "Ethnozoology and the Future of Sociology." *International Journal of Sociology and Social Policy* 23, no. 3 (2003): 26–45.

Arluke, Arnold, and Clinton Sanders. *Regarding Animals*. Philadelphia: Temple University Press, 1996.

ASMFC. "2015 Annual Report of the Atlantic States Marine Fisheries Commission." Arlington, VA: Atlantic States Marine Fisheries Commission, 2015.

———. "Horseshoe Crab: Management Plans and FMP Reviews." Atlantic States Marine Fisheries Commission. www.asmfc.org.

———. "Horseshoe Crab Biomedical Ad-Hoc Working Group Report [on Best Practices]." Arlington, VA: Atlantic States Marine Fisheries Commission, October 3, 2011. www.asmfc.org.

ASMFC Horseshoe Crab Stock Assessment Subcommittee. "2013 Horseshoe Crab Stock Assessment Update." Arlington, VA: Atlantic States Marine Fisheries Commission, August 2013. www.asmfc.org.

Bakalar, Nicholas. "The Shelf Life of Donor Blood." "Well" column. *New York Times*, March 12, 2013, New York ed.

Barad, Karen. "Matter Feels, Converses, Suffers, Desires, Yearns and Remembers." Interview in *New Materialism: Interviews and Cartographies*, by Rick Dolphijn and Iris van der Tuin. London: Open Humanities Press, 2012. DOI: http//:dx.doi .org/10.3998/ohp.11515701.0001.001.

———. *Meeting the Universe Halfway: Quantum Physics and the Entanglement of Matter*. Durham, NC: Duke University Press, 2007.

Barrett, Steven, et al. "Impact of the Volkswagen Emissions Control Defeat Device on US Public Health." *Environmental Research Letters* 10 (October 29, 2015): 1–10.

Battelle, Barbara-Anne. "Simple Eyes, Extraocular Photoreceptors and Opsins in the American Horseshoe Crab." *Integrative and Comparative Biology* 56, no. 5 (2016): 809–819.

Beekey, Mark, and Jennifer Mattei. "The Mismanagement of *Limulus polyphemus* in Long Island Sound, U.S.A.: What Are the Characteristics of a Population in Decline?" In *Changing Global Perspectives on Horseshoe Crab Biology, Conservation and Management*, edited by Ruth H. Carmichael, Mark L. Botton, Paul K. S. Shin, and Siu Gin Cheung, 433–461. Geneva: Springer, 2015.

Bekoff, Marc. *Minding Animals: Awareness, Emotions and Heart.* Oxford: Oxford University Press, 2002.

Bennett, Jane. *Vibrant Matter: A Political Ecology of Things.* Durham, NC: Duke University Press, 2010.

Bensaude-Vincent, Bernadette, and Isabelle Stengers. *A History of Chemistry.* Cambridge, MA: Harvard University Press, 1996.

Berkson, J., and Carl Shuster. "The Horseshoe Crab: The Battle for a True Multiple-Use Resource." *Fisheries Management* 24 (1999): 6–10.

Berlant, Lauren. "Slow Death: Sovereignty, Obesity, Lateral Agency." *Critical Inquiry* 33 (Summer 2007): 754–780.

Blackwelder, Britt, Katherine Coleman, Sara Colunga-Santoyo, Jeffrey S. Harrison, and Danielle Wozniak. "The Volkswagen Scandal." Case study. Robins Case Network. Richmond, VA: University of Richmond, Robins School of Business, 2016. www.richmond.edu.

Bogost, Ian. *Alien Phenomenology, or What It's Like to Be a Thing.* Minneapolis: University of Minnesota Press, 2012.

Botton, Mark, Robert E. Loveland, John T. Tanacredi, and Tomio Itow. "Horseshoe Crabs (*Limulus polyphemus*) in an Urban Estuary (Jamaica Bay, New York) and the Potential for Ecological Restoration." *Estuaries and Coasts* 29, no. 5 (2006): 820–830.

Botton, Mark, Robert Loveland, and Athena Tiwari. "Distribution, Abundance, and Survivorship of Young-of-the-Year in a Commercially Exploited Population of Horseshoe Crabs *Limulus polyphemus.*" *Marine Ecology Progress Series* 265 (2003): 175–184.

Botton, Mark, and J. W. Ropes. "Populations of Horseshoe Crabs, *Limulus polyphemus,* on the Northwestern Atlantic Continental Shelf." *Fisheries Bulletin* 85, no. 4 (1987): 805–812.

Botton, Mark, Richard Tankersley, and Robert Loveland. "Developmental Ecology of the American Horseshoe Crab *Limulus polyphemus.*" *Current Zoology* 56, no. 5 (2010): 550–562.

Briggs, D. E., D. J. Siveter, M. D. Sutton, R. J. Garwood, and D. Legg. "Silurian Horseshoe Crab Illuminates the Evolution of Arthropod Limbs." *Proceedings of the National Academy of Sciences of the United States of America* 109, no. 39 (2012): 15702–15705.

Brockmann, H. Jane. "Mating Behavior of Horseshoe Crabs *Limulus polyphemus*." *Behaviour* 114 (1990): 206–220.

———. "Satellite Male Groups in Horseshoe Crabs *Limulus polyphemus*." *Ethology* 102 (1996): 1–21.

Brockmann, H. Jane, C. Nguyen, and W. Potts. "Paternity in Horseshoe Crabs When Spawning in Multiple-Male Groups." *Animal Behavior* 60 (2000): 837–849.

Burnett, D. Graham. "The Bonds of Catastrophe." *Cabinet: A Quarterly of Art and Culture* 57 (Spring 2015): 73–78.

Butler, Judith. *Precarious Life: The Power of Mourning and Violence.* London: Verso Books, 2004.

Candea, Matei. "'I Fell in Love with Carlos the Meerkat': Engagement and Detachment in Human Animal Relations." *American Ethnologist* 37, no. 2 (2010): 241–258.

Carney, Scott. *The Red Market: On the Trail of the World's Organ Brokers, Bone Thieves, Blood Farmers and Child Traffickers.* New York: William Morrow, 2011.

Census of Marine Life. "About the Census," 2010. www.coml.org.

Chabot, Christopher, and Winsor Watson. "Daily and Tidal Rhythms in Intertidal Marine Invertebrates." In *Annual, Lunar and Tidal Clocks: Patterns and Mechanisms of Nature's Enigmatic Rhythms*, edited by Hideharu Numata and Barbara Helm, 41–63. Tokyo: Springer Japan, 2014.

Chakrabarty, Dipesh. "The Climate of History: Four Theses." *Critical Inquiry* 35 (2009): 197–222.

Chen, Mel. *Animacies: Biopolitics, Racial Mattering, and Queer Affect.* Durham, NC: Duke University Press, 2012.

Cherry, Elizabeth. *Culture and Activism: Animal Rights in France and the United States.* New York: Routledge, 2016.

Chris, Cynthia. *Watching Wildlife.* Minneapolis: University of Minnesota Press, 2006.

Clarke, Adele E., and Joan H. Fujimura, eds. *The Right Tools for the Job: At Work in Twentieth -Century Life Sciences.* Princeton, NJ: Princeton University Press, 2014.

Cohen, I. G., J. Feigenbaum, and E. Y. Adashi. "Reconsideration of the Lifetime Ban on Blood Donation by Men Who Have Sex with Men." *JAMA: Journal of the American Medical Association* 312, no. 4 (2014): 337–338.

Colli, Francesca. "Why It's So Hard for Europeans to Get Compensation after Dieselgate." *Conversation*, November 22, 2016. Leuven: University of Leuven, Lirias Repository. http://www.kuleuven.be/english.

Colon, Christina, and John Rowden. "Blurring the Roles of Scientist and Activist through Citizen Science." In *Civic Learning and Teaching*, edited by Ashley Finley, 45–52. Washington, DC: Bringing Theory to Practice, 2014.

Conley, Kirstan. "Crab-Poach Pinch." *New York Post*, May 29, 2013, Metro section. www.nypost.com.

Crutzen, P., and E. Stoermer. "The Anthropocene." *Global Change Newsletter* 41, no. 1 (2000): 17–18.

Cudworth, Erika. *Social Lives with Other Animals.* New York: Palgrave Macmillian, 2011.

Darwin, Charles. *On the Origin of Species by Means of Natural Selection, or the Preservation of Favored Races in the Struggle for Life.* London: John Murray, 1859.

Davis, Dona, and Anita Maurstad, eds. *The Meaning of Horses: Biosocial Encounters.* New York: Routledge, 2015.

DeMello, Margo. *Animals and Society: An Introduction to Human-Animal Studies.* New York: Columbia University Press, 2012.

Dickinson, Janis, and Marty Leonard. "Mate Attendance and Copulatory Behavior in Western Bluebirds: Evidence of Mate Guarding." *Animal Behaviour* 52, no. 5 (1996): 981–992.

Diesel Technology Forum. "What Is Clean Diesel?" 2016. www.dieselforum.org.

Dooren, Thom van. *Flight Ways: Life and Loss at the Edge of Extinction.* New York: Columbia University Press, 2014.

Dooren, Thom van, Eben Kirksey, and Ursula Munster. "Multispecies Studies: Cultivating Arts of Attentiveness." *Environmental Humanities* 8, no. 1 (2016): 1–23.

Dooren, Thom van, and Deborah Bird Rose. "Storied-Places in a Multispecies City." *Humanimalia: A Journal of Human/Animal Interface Studies* 3, no. 2 (Spring 2012): 1–27.

Downes, F. P., and K. Ito. *Compendium of Methods for the Microbiological Examination of Foods.* Washington, DC: American Public Health Association, 2001.

Dries, Amy. "Living Fossils: Conserving and Protecting Horseshoe Crabs." *New York State Conservationist,* June 2015, 17–19.

Ellis, Erle. "Ecology in an Anthropogenic Biosphere." *Ecological Monographs* 85, no. 3 (2015): 287–331.

Elwood, R. W. "Pain and Suffering in Invertebrates?" *Institute for Animal Laboratory Research Journal* 52, no. 2 (2011): 175–184.

Evans, Lauren. "Cops Nab Two in Horseshoe Crab Heist Gone Wrong." *Gothamist,* May 29, 2013. www.gothamist.com.

Fitz, Tom, producer. *Horseshoe Crabs: Prehistoric Paramedics.* Documentary. Juniper, FL: Schoolyard Films, 2012. www.schoolyardfilms.org.

Fitzgerald, Amy J. "Doing Time in a Slaughterhouse: A Critical Review of the Use of Animals and Inmates in Prison Labor Programs." *Journal of Critical Animal Studies* 10, no. 2 (2011): 12–46.

Forman, Adam. "New York City Is Crumbling," *Time,* March 13, 2014. www.time.com.

Fortey, Richard. *Horseshoe Crabs and Velvet Worms: The Story of Animals and Plants That Time Has Left Behind.* New York: Vintage, 2012.

Frazier, Ian. "Blue Bloods." *New Yorker* 90, no. 8 (2014): 52.

Fredericks, Anthony. *Horsehoe Crab: A Biography of a Survivor.* Washington, DC: Ruka Press, 2012.

Freund, Peter, and Meredith McGuire. *Health, Illness and the Social Body: A Critical Sociology.* Upper Saddle River, NJ: Prentice Hall, 1999.

Gillis, Justin. "Seas Are Rising at Fastest Rate in Last 28 Centuries." *New York Times*, February 22, 2016, Science section. www.nytimes.com.

Glaser, Barney, and Anselm Strauss. *The Discovery of Grounded Theory*. Chicago: Aldine, 1967.

Grant, D. "Living on *Limulus*." In Limulus *in the Limelight: A Species 350 Million Years in the Making and in Peril?* edited by John T. Tanacredi, 135–146. New York: Kluwer Academic, 2001.

Goodman, J. David, and Sarah Maslin Nir. "Poachers Are Elusive Catch in City Waters." *New York Times*, July 3, 2013, New York Region section. www.nytimes.com.

Gould, Stephen Jay. *Time's Arrow, Time's Cycle: Myth and Metaphor in the Discovery of Geologic Time*. Cambridge, MA: Harvard University Press, 1987.

Grescoe, Taras. "The Truth about 'Clean Diesel.'" *New York Times*, January 2, 2016, Sunday Review section. www.nytimes.com.

Haraway, Donna. "Anthropocene, Capitalocene, Plantationocene, Chthulucene: Making Kin." *Environmental Humanities* 6 (2015): 159–165.

———. *The Companion Species Manifesto*. Chicago: Prickly Paradigm Press, 2003.

———. *Primate Visions: Gender, Race and Nature in the World of Modern Science*. New York: Routledge, 1989.

———. "Situated Knowledges: The Science Question in Feminism and the Privilege of Partial Perspective." *Feminist Studies* 14, no. 3 (1988): 575–599.

Harding, Sandra. *Whose Science/Whose Knowledge? Thinking From Women's Lives*. Ithaca, NY: Cornell University Press, 1991.

Hartigan, John, Jr. *Aesop's Anthropology: A Multispecies Approach*. Minneapolis: University of Minnesota Press, 2015.

Hartsock, Nancy. "Foucault on Power: A Theory for Women." In *Feminism/Postmodernism*, edited by Linda Nicholson. London: Routledge, 1990.

Hayes, Bill. *Five Quarts: A Personal and Natural History of Blood*. New York: Ballantine, 2005.

Heise, Ursula. *Imagining Extinction: The Cultural Meaning of Endangered Species*. Chicago: University of Chicago Press, 2016.

Helmreich, Stefan. *Alien Ocean: Anthropological Voyages in Microbial Seas*. Berkeley: University of California Press, 2009.

Hill Collins, Patricia. *Black Feminist Thought: Knowledge, Consciousness and the Politics of Empowerment*. New York: Routledge, 1990.

Hurton, Lenka, and Jim Berkson. "Potental Causes of Mortality for Horseshoe Crabs (*Limulus polyphemus*) during the Biomedical Bleeding Process." *Fishery Bulletin* 104, no. 2 (2006): 293–298.

Ihle, Saskia. "Pyrogene™ rFC Assay—a Reliable Animal-Free Alternative to LAL." Lonza webinar, June 2012 (archived). www.lonza.com.

Ingold, Timothy. "Anthropology beyond Humanity." *Soumen Antropologi/Journal of the Finnish Anthropology Society* 38, no. 3 (2013): 15–23.

International Union of Conservation Naturalists. "About the IUCN," 2016. www.iucn.org.

Irvine, Leslie. "A Model of Animal Selfhood: Expanding Interactionist Possibilities." *Symbolic Interaction* 27, no. 1 (2004): 3–21.

Jackson, Nancy, David R. Smith, and Kari Nordstrom. "Physical and Chemical Changes in the Foreshore of an Estuarine Beach: Implications for Viability and Development of Horseshoe Crab *Limulus polyphemus* Eggs," *Marine Ecology Progress Series* 355 (2008): 209–218.

Jegla, T. C., and J. D. Costlow. "Temperature and Salinity Effects on Developmental and Early Posthatch Stages of *Limulus*." In *Physiology and Biology of Horseshoe Crabs: Studies on Normal and Environmentally Stressed Animals*, edited by J. Bonaventura, C. Bonaventura, and S. Tesh, 103–113. New York, 1982.

Jerolmack, Colin. *The Global Pigeon*. Chicago: University of Chicago Press, 2013.

Johnson, J. "Mixing Humans and Nonhumans Together: The Sociology of the Door-Closer." *Social Problems* 35, no. 3 (1988): 298–310.

Johnson, Sheri, and H. Jane Brockmann. "Alternative Reproductive Tactics in Female Horseshoe Crabs." *Behavioral Ecology* 23, no. 5 (2012): 999–1008.

Kafka, Franz. *The Metamorphosis*. New York: Classix Press, 1915.

Keller, Evelyn Fox. *A Feeling for the Organism: The Life and Work of Barbara McClintock*. San Francisco: W. H. Freeman & Co., 1983.

Kirby, Doug, Ken Smith, and Mike Wilkins. "World's Largest Horseshoe Crab." *Roadside American.com*, March 22, 2016. www.roadsideamerica.com.

Kirksey, Eben. "Species: A Praxiographic Study." *Journal of the Royal Anthropological Institute* 21 (2015): 758–780.

Kirksey, Eben, Dehlia Hannah, Charlie Lotterman, and Lisa Jean Moore. "The *Xenopus* Pregnancy Test: A Performative Experiment." *Environmental Humanities* 8, no. 1 (2016): 37–56.

Kirksey, Eben, and Stefan Helmreich. "The Emergence of Multispecies Ethnography." *Cultural Anthropology* 25, no. 4 (2010): 545–576.

Klein, Naomi. *The Shock Doctrine: The Rise of Disaster Capitalism*. New York: Knopf, 2007.

Kohn, Eduardo. "How Dogs Dream: Amazonian Natures and the Politics of Transspecies Engagements." *American Ethnologist* 34, no. 1 (2007): 3–24.

Kolbert, Elizabeth. *The Sixth Extinction: An Unnatural History*. New York: Henry Holt & Co., 2014.

Kwan, Billy Kit Yue, Paul Shin, and Siu Gin Cheung. "Preliminary Home Range Study of Juvenile Chinese Horseshoe Crab *Tachypleus tridentatus* (Xiphosura) Using Passive Tracking Methods." In *Changing Global Perspectives on Horseshoe Crab Biology, Conservation and Management*, edited by Ruth H. Carmichael, Mark L. Botton, Paul K. S. Shin, and Siu Gin Cheung, 149–166. Geneva: Springer, 2015.

Latour, Bruno. *Reassembling the Social: An Introduction to Actor-Network Theory*. Oxford: Oxford University Press, 2007.

Laughlin, Robert. "The Effects of Temperature and Salinity on Larval Growth of the Horseshoe Crab *Limulus polyphemus*." *Biological Bulletin* 164 (1983): 93–103.

Law, John. "Technology and Heterogeneous Engineering: The Case of the Portuguese Expansion." In *The Social Construction of Technological Systems*, edited by Wiebe Bijker, T. Hughes, and Trevor Pinch. Cambridge, MA: MIT Press, 1987.

Leschen, A. S., and S. J. Correia. "Mortality in Female Horseshoe Crabs (*Limulus polyphemus*) from Biomedical Bleeding and Handling: Implications for Fisheries Management." *Marine and Freshwater Behavior and Physiology* 43, no. 2 (2010): 135–147.

Levin, Jack, and Frederick Bang. "The Role of Endotoxin in the Extracellular Coagulation of Limulus Blood." *Bulletin of the Johns Hopkins Hospital* 115 (September 1964): 265–274.

Levin, Jack, H. Hochstein, and T. Novitsky. "Clotting Cells and *Limulus* Amoebocyte Lysate: An Amazing Analytical Tool." In *The American Horseshoe Crab*, edited by Carl Shuster, R. Barlow, and Jane Brockmann, 310–340. Cambridge, MA: Harvard University Press, 2003.

Lévi-Strauss, Claude. *The Savage Mind*. Chicago: University of Chicago Press, 1966.

Levy, Sharon. "Crabs in Space." *New Scientist* 181, no. 2438 (2004): 42–43.

Lishko, P. V., I. L. Botchkina, and Y. Kirichok. "Progesterone Activates the Principal Ca2+ Channel of Human Sperm." *Nature* 471 (2011): 387–391.

Lonza. "QC Testing Solutions Notebook." Walkersville, MD: Lonza, 2014. www.lonza.com.

Loveland, Robert E., and Mark Botton. "Sea Level Rise in Delaware Bay, U.S.A.: Adaptations of Spawning Horseshoe Crabs (*Limulus polyphemus*) to the Glacial Past, and the Rapidly Changing Shoreline of the Bay." In *Changing Global Perspectives on Horseshoe Crab Biology, Conservation and Management*, edited by Ruth H. Carmichael, Mark L. Botton, Paul K. S. Shin, and Siu Gin Cheung, 46–63. Geneva: Springer, 2015.

Malinowski, Bronislaw. *Argonauts of the Western Pacific: An Account of Native Enterprise and Adventure in the Archipelagoes of Melanesian New Guinea*. London: Routledge & Kegan Paul, 1922.

Manji, Rizwan, Alan Menkis, Burcin Ekser, and David Cooper. "Porcine Bioprosthetic Heart Valves: The Next Generation." *American Heart Journal* 164, no. 2 (2012): 177–185.

Martin, Emily. "The Egg and the Sperm: How Science Has Constructed a Romance Based on Stereotypical Male-Female Roles." *Signs* 16, no. 3 (1991): 485–501.

Marx, Karl. *Economic and Philosophic Manuscripts* (1844). In *Early Writings* by Karl Marx, translated by Rodney Livingstone and Gregor Benton. New York: Vintage Books, 1975.

Mather, Jennifer. "Animal Suffering: An Invertebrate Perspective." *Journal of Applied Animal Welfare Science* 4, no. 2 (2001): 151–156.

Mattei, Jennifer, Mark Beekey, Adam Rudman, and Alyssa Woronick. "Reproductive Behavior in Horseshoe Crabs: Does Density Matter?" *Current Zoology* 56, no. 5 (2010): 634–642.

Mooallem, Jon. *Wild Ones: A Sometimes Dismaying, Weirdly Reassuring Story about Looking at People Looking at Animals in America*. New York: Penguin, 2013.

Moore, Jason W. "Anthropocene or Capitalocene? On the Origins of Our Crisis." *World-Ecological Imaginations: Power and Production in the Web of Life*, personal blog, May 13, 2013. https://jasonwmoore.wordpress.com.

———. *Capitalism in the Web of Life: Ecology and the Accumulation of Capital*. New York: Verso Books, 2015.

Moore, Lisa Jean. *Sperm Counts: Overcome by Man's Most Precious Fluid*. New York: New York University Press, 2007.

Moore, Lisa Jean, and Adele E. Clarke. "Clitoral Conventions: Graphic Representations of Female Genital Anatomy, c 1900–1991." *Feminist Studies* 21, no. 2 (1995): 255–301.

Moore, Lisa Jean, and Mary Kosut. *Buzz: Urban Beekeeping and the Power of the Bee*. New York: New York University Press, 2013.

Morton, Timothy. *Hyperobjects: Philosophy and Ecology after the End of the World*. Minneapolis: University of Minnesota Press, 2013.

Myers, O. "No Longer the Lonely Species: A Post-Mead Perspective on Animals and Sociology." *International Journal of Sociology and Social Policy* 23, no. 2 (2003): 46–68.

National Geographic Wild. *Alien Crab*. Film. Washington, DC: National Geographic Wild (Nat Geo Wild) television channel, 2012.

Nagy, Kelsi, and Phillip David Johnson, eds. *Trash Animals: How We Live with Nature's Filthy, Feral, Invasive and Unwanted Species*. Minneapolis: University of Minnesota Press, 2013.

National Aeronautics and Space Administration. "Global Climate Change: Vital Signs of the Planet." Washington, DC: National Aeronautics and Space Administration, 2016. www.nasa.gov.

New York City Department of Transportation. "New York City Screenline Traffic Flow, 2010." New York: New York City Department of Transportation, May 2012. www.nyc.gov.

Niza, Claudia, Burcu Tung, and Theresa Marteau. "Incentivizing Blood Donation: Systematic Review of Meta-analysis to Test Titmuss' Hypotheses." *Health Psychology* 32, no. 9 (2013): 941–949.

Norgaard, Kari Marie. *Living in Denial: Climate Change, Emotions and Everyday Life*. Cambridge, MA: MIT Press, 2011.

Novitsky, Thomas. "Discovery of Commercialization: The Blood of the Horseshoe Crab." *Oceanus* 27 (1991): 13–18.

Oldenkamp, Rik, Rosalie van Zelm, and Mark Huijbregts. "Valuing the Human Health Damage Caused by the Fraud of Volkswagen." *Environmental Pollution* 212 (2016): 121–127.

Orr, Jackie. "Killing Time (Slow Catastrophe)." In special issue "Gender, Justice, and Neoliberal Transformations," ed. Elizabeth Bernstein and Janet R. Jakobsen, *Scholar and Feminist Online* 11, nos. 1–2 (2013). http://sfonline.barnard.edu.

Penn, D. P., and H. Jane Brockmann. "Age-Based Stranding and Righting in Horseshoe Crabs (*Limulus polyphemus*)." *Animal Behavior* 49 (1995): 1531–1539.

Plungis, Jeff. "Volkswagen Emissions Scandal: Forty Years of Greenwashing—the Well-Travelled Road Taken by VW." *Independent*, September 24, 2015, Business section. www.independent.co.uk.

Pine, Jason. "Last Change Incorporated." *Cultural Anthropology* 31, no. 2 (2016): 297–318.

Pooley, Simon. "Endangered: Living Lexicon for the Environmental Humanities." *Environmental Humanities* 7 (2015): 259–263.

Psuty, Norbert P., Andrea Spahn, Tanya M. Silveira, and William Schmelz. "Sediment Budget as a Driver for Sediment Management at Plumb Beach, New York, USA: Vectors of Change and Impacts." *Journal of Coastal Conservation* 18, no. 5 (2014): 515–528.

Puig de la Bellacasa, Maria. "Making Time for Soil: Technoscientific Futurity and the Pace of Care." *Social Studies of Science* 45, no. 5 (2015): 691–716.

Raffles, Hugh. *Insectopedia*. New York: Pantheon, 2010.

Research & Markets. "Pyrogen Testing Market by Product Global Forecast to 2019." Dublin, 2015. www.researchandmarkets.com.

Rose, Deborah Bird. "Site Fidelity." *Deborah Bird Rose*, personal blog, October 20, 2014. http://deborahbirdrose.com.

Ruddiman, W. F., and J. S. Thomson. "The Case for Human Causes of Increased Atmospheric CH_4 over the Last 5000 Years." *Quaternary Science Reviews* 20 (2001): 1769–1777.

Russo, Joseph C. "There in the Thicket: An Interview with Jason Pine." *Cultural Anthropology*, May 17, 2016. www.culanth.org.

Ryder, Richard D. *Victims of Science: The Use of Animals in Research*. London: Davis-Poynter, 1975.

Sanders, Clinton. "Understanding Dogs: Caretakers' Attributions of Mindedness in Canine-Human Relationships." *Journal of Contemporary Ethnography* 22, no. 2 (1993): 205–226.

Shuster, Carl. "Distribution of the American Horseshoe 'Crab', *Limulus polyphemus* (L.)." In *Biomedical Applications of the Horseshoe Crab (Limulidae)*, edited by Elias Cohen, 3–26. New York: Alan R. Liss, 1979.

———. "Observations on the Natural History of the American Horseshoe Crab: *Limulus polyphemus*." Woods Hole, MA: Woods Hole Oceanography Institute, 1950.

Silverstein, Shel. *The Giving Tree*. New York: Harper & Row, 1964.

Singer, Peter. *Animal Liberation*. New York: Harper Collins, 1975.

Smith, Bruce, and Melinda Zeder. "The Onset of the Anthropocene." *Anthropocene* 4 (2013): 8–13.

Smith, D. R., Mark Beekey, H. Jane Brockmann, T. L. King, and J. A. Zaldívar-Rae. "*Limulus polyphemus*." *The IUCN Red List of Threatened Species*, 2016. www.iucnredlist.org.

Smithsonian National Zoological Park. "Invertebrate Facts: The Silent Majority." Washington, DC: Smithsonian, 2016. nationalzoo.si.edu.

Solnit, Rebecca. *Men Explain Things to Me*. Chicago: Haymarket Books, 2015.

Starr, Douglas. "Bad Blood: The 9/11 Blood-Donation Disaster." *New Republic*, July 29, 2002.

Stewart, Kathleen. *Ordinary Affects*. Durham, NC: Duke University Press, 2007.

Strauss, Anselm, and Juliet Corbin. *Basics of Qualitative Research*. Newbury Park: Sage, 1990.

Stromberg, Joseph. "What Is the Anthropocene and Are We In It?" *Smithsonian Magazine*, January 2013. www.smithsonianmag.com.

Swanson, Kara. *Banking on the Body: The Market in Blood, Milk, and Sperm in Modern America*. Cambridge, MA: Harvard University Press, 2014.

Taussig, Michael. *The Devil and Commodity Fetishism in South America*. Chapel Hill, NC: University of North Carolina Press, 1980.

Taylor, Nik. " 'Never an It': Intersubjectivity and The Creation of Animal Personhood in Animal Shelters." *Qualitative Sociological Review* 3, no. 1 (2007): 59–73.

Thomas, C. D., A. Cameron, R. E. Green, M. Bakkenes, L. J. Beaumont, Y. C. Collingham, B. F. N. Erasmus, et al. "Extinction Risk from Climate Change." *Nature* 427 (2004): 145–148.

Titmuss, Richard. *The Gift Relationship: From Human Blood to Social Policy*. London: George Allen & Unwin, 1970.

Trevisick, Shaun, dir. *Survivors: Nature's Indestructible Creatures*. Episode 1: "The Great Dying." Video. London: BBC, 2012.

Tsing, Anna Lowenhaupt. *The Mushroom at the End of the World: On the Possibility of Life in Capitalist Ruins*. Princeton, NJ: Princeton University Press, 2015.

Tudor, Ken. "How Humans Can Save Pets with Blood Transfusions." *PetMD*, December 4, 2014. www.petmd.com.

Turley, C., et al. "Hot, Sour, and Breathless—Ocean under Stress." Washington, DC: Oceana, 2013. www.oceana.org.

U.S. Army Corps of Engineers. "Review Plan for Plumb Beach Section, 2014." Brooklyn, NY: Department of the Army, North Atlantic Division, Corps of Engineers, 2012.

U.S. Department of Health and Human Services. "Guidance for Industry: Pyrogen and Endotoxins Testing." Washington, DC: Food and Drug Administration, Center for Drug Evaluation and Research, Division of Manufacturing and Product Quality, Office of Compliance, June 2012. www.fda.gov.

U.S. Fish and Wildlife Service. "Polar Bear (*Ursus maritimus*) Conservation Management Plan, Draft." Anchorage, AK: U.S. Fish and Wildlife Service, 2015. www.fws.gov.

Vaughan, Adam. "VW Emissions Cheat Estimated to Cause 59 Premature US Deaths." *Guardian*, October 29, 2015, Environment section. www.theguardian.com.

Walls, E. A., A. J. Berkson, and S. A. Smith. "The Horseshoe Crab, *Limulus polyphemus*: 200 Million Years of Existence, 100 Years of Study." *Reviews in Fisheries Science* 10 (2002): 39–73.

Weber, Max. *The Protestant Ethic and the Spirit of Capitalism*, translated by Talcott Parsons. London: Routledge, 1930.

Wilder, Thorton. *Our Town: A Play in Three Acts*. New York: Harper Perennial Modern Classics, 1938.

Williams, Raymond. *The Country and the City*. Oxford: Oxford University Press, 1975.

Wolfe, Cary. *What Is Posthumanism?* Minneapolis: University of Minnesota Press, 2010.

Youatt, Rafi. *Counting Species: Biodiversity in Global Environmental Politics*. Minneapolis: University of Minnesota Press, 2015.

Yusoff, Kathryn. "Anthropogenesis: Origins and Endings in the Anthropocene." *Theory, Culture and Society* 33, no. 2 (2016): 3–28.

INDEX

Actor–Network Theory (ANT), 138–39, 144; defined, 138

agency: entangled, 23, 137; of the nonhuman, 12, 138. *See also* female mate choice

agricultural fertilizer: use of horseshoe crab carapace in, 4, 13, 17, 160; as water contaminant, 135

Alaimo, Stacy, 169n37

Alien Crab (film), 31, 68, 94

American Red Cross, homophobic policies of, 104

amoebocytes, definition of, 105. *See also* blood

amplexus: defined, 76–77; in horseshoe crabs, 3, 9, 26–27; mated pairs in, 79–88; sex roles in, 87. *See also* female mate choice; reproduction; satellite males

Anderson, Rebecca, 7, 114

androcentrism, 74, 76. *See also* reproduction

animal studies. *See* critical animal studies

animals. *See* nonhuman animals

Anthropocene, 47–52; as anthropocentric term, 51; defined, 50; as "hot" term, 51; mass extinction and, 50;

anthropocentrism: and Actor–Network Theory, 144; and anthropomorphism, 157; of classification, 45; and deep time, 34, 37; defined, 21; and empathy, 34; in everyday life, 150; as unethical, 66

anthropogenesis, 51

anthropomorphism: anthropocentrism and, 157; critical, 73, 93; defined, 71; unavoidability of, 157

assemblages, xii

Atlantic States Marine Fisheries Commission (ASMFC), 139; harvesting permits issued by, 114, 172n29, 173n23; uneven regulation by, 116

awl, used in tagging, 62–64, 86, 161

bait. *See* harvesting

Bang, Frederick, 105

Barad, Karen: on becoming, 133, 157; on everyday lives of objects, 139; on intraaction, xii, 12, 23, 137; on objectivity, 71–72; on materiality, 150

beach nourishment: effect on horseshoe crabs, 143–45; and endangered species, 174n32; as hardening the shoreline, 135, 143; for humans' sake, 131; after Hurricane Sandy, 132; as response to rising sea levels, 78, 135

becoming with: affective dimensions of, 35; anthropomorphism of, 93; horseshoe crabs, xii, xiv, 14, 30, 69, 93, 128, 136, 150, 157–58, 160; nonhuman animals, xi, 69, 160; ontological experience of, 22; queen bees, 73; as speculative, xii, xiv; vs. thinking with, 157–58. *See also* enmeshment; entanglement

being with. *See* becoming with

Bellacasa, María Puig de la, 66

Belt Parkway: creation and maintenance of, 131–32; effect of beach nourishment on, 145; effect on horseshoe crabs, 133, 146; effects of global warming on, 128; intraaction with, 138; as major access route, 1, 126, 131; threatened by shoreline erosion, 127
Bennett, Jane, 12
Bensaude-Vincent, Bernadette, 168n13
Berlant, Lauren, 152
Berzofsky, Ron, xv; on horseshoe crab harvesting, 110–11; on bleeding, 112; on synthetic pyrogen testing, 124
Beyoncé, 71
biodiversity, 25; global loss of, 48, 60; as normative category, 53
biomedicine, uses of horseshoe crabs in, xii, 3–4, 8, 13–14, 27–28, 98–114, 147, 159. See also bleeding; blood; harvesting; Limulus amoebocyte lysate (TAL) test; Tachypleus amoebocyte lysate (TAL) test
biopower, 53
Blazejowski, Blazej, 8
bleeding (horseshoe crabs): amount of blood collected in, 112; debates over the ethics of, 99–100; desirability of females in, 113; as "donation," 27, 94, 99–101, 158, 160; as "draining," 100; experience of, 104; implication of general population in, 27–28, 30; long-term effects of, 113–14; mortality rate in, 59, 113; preparation for, 100–101; secrecy around, 119; as "spa day," 101, 158. See also biomedicine; blood; harvesting
blood (horseshoe crabs): amoebocytes in, 8, 27–28, 105; color of, 8, 48, 105; compared with human blood, 104–5; profitability of, 105–6; as source of immunity, 105. See also biomedicine; bleeding

blood donation (humans): author's experience of, 95–98; in a crisis, 97–98; to dogs, 171n5; feeling of connection after, 96–98; as illegal to pay for, 102–3; from incarcerated people, 171n15 (chap. 4); as intraspecies only, 99; as made possible by horseshoe crab blood, 124; regulation of, 103–4; short supply of, 103–4; social significance of, 104; as source of Rhogam, 103
Blum, Mal, 155
Botton, Mark, xv, 9, 18–21, 43, 116, 148, 168n33; on adaptation of horseshoe crabs, 135; as co-chair of the IUCN Horseshoe Crab Specialist Group, 55; on difficulties with horseshoe crab censusing, 59; on LAL testing, 117; on mating scars, 81; on penetrometers, 144; as teaching the author, 136
Brockmann, H. Jane, xv, 10; on bleeding regulations, 121–22; on female mate choice, 84–92; on satellite males, 83; on scientific metaphors, 92; teaching the author to tag horseshoe crabs, 63–64
Brooklyn, New York: author's residence in, xiv–xv, 21; Beltway Parkway in, 132; donating blood in, 94–98; horseshoe crabs in, xiv–xv, 21, 24; Junior's Restaurant in, 43; urban beekeeping in, 150. See also Plumb Beach, New York
Butler, Judith, 56

Callon, Michel, 138
Candea, Matei, 69
Cambrian Period, 31, 41. See also deep time
capitalism: alienation under, 39, 40–42, 66, 98; and autonomy, 152; and biomedicalization, 163; disaster, 170n46; effect on consciousness, 2; informal

economies in, 102; as organization of nature, 52. *See also* Anthropocene; Capitalocene; disenchantment; rational calculation

Capitalocene, 52

carapace: of dead horseshoe crabs, 47, 128; defined, 6; dried out, 94; as ecology, 137, 171n18; as enchanting, 41, 159; fouling organisms on, 19, 24, 85, 137; handling of, 41; making a hole in, 62, 64, 161; mating scar on, 81; size of, 24, 59, 80, 126, 134, 136; as site of sinus, 112; quality of, 19, 85, 126. *See also* agricultural fertilizer; mating scars; molting

Carcinoscorpius rotundicauda (Mangrove horseshoe crab), 8

catastrophe. *See* ecological catastrophe

Cedar Key, Florida, xv, 161; as site of citizen science, 63; as spawning ground, 78–79, 84–92

Census of Marine Life, 45

censusing, 45; difficulty with horseshoe crabs, 58; as tedious, 60; through tagging, 62

Center for Environmental Research and Coastal Oceans Monitoring (CERCOM), 54

Chabot, Christopher, 113–14

Chakrabarty, Dipesh, 50

charismatic megafauna, 26, 56

Charles Rivers Laboratories, 100, 102, 117

chemistry, history of, 168n13

Chen, Mel, 12

child (children): author as, xiv, 3, 33, 158–60; books for, 42, 74–75; and embodied knowledge, 158–59; observing, 33, 37; as responsible for conservation, 57; save the, 152

citizen science, 60–65; among college students, 60; conducted by author, 63–64, 162; in Singapore, 60

Clarke, Adele, 11

climate change: and the Anthropocene, 25, 50; denial of, 35, 38; effect on urban infrastructure, 127; increasing pace of, 60; as profitable, 170n46; and sea-level rise, 135. *See also* extinction; global warming; Hurricane Sandy; sea-level rise; species decline

clitoris, xiii, 11

college students: reactions to horseshoe crabs, 40–41; as citizen scientists, 60

Colon, Christina, xv, 18–21, 148; as citizen science expert, 60; on effect of shoreline erosion on horseshoe crabs, 141

colony collapse disorder, 57

companion species: in animal studies, 21, 165n8; as controlling humans, 40; criteria for, 5; endotoxins lethal for, 27, 106; horseshoe crabs as, 13, 16–17; horseshoe crabs as having, 36; vulnerability shared with, 56, 122

conservation: biodiversity as goal of, 25, 53; vs. biomedical industry, 27–28; concept of species in, 46–77; of horseshoe crabs, 4, 53–66, 78; citizen science and, 60–66; organizations for, 15–16, 25–26, 54–55, 62; *See also* endangerment; horseshoe crab

"Crabby," 38

crabness, 22, 137, 159, 161

creationism, horseshoe crabs as "evidence" for, 37–38

critical animal studies, 21, 40, 71, 129; examples of, 167n27

cultural studies, 11

cut (concept), 70–73; defined, 72; around queen bees, 72–73; around horseshoe crab reproduction, 77, 81, 91; political implications of, 93

cyborgs: author and daughters as, 169n16; humans as, 13, 123

Darwin, Charles, 43

daughters, author's: and anthropocentrism, 24; birth of, 73, 81; as cyborgs, 169n16; and gender norms, 33; at Mercury Lounge, 155–56; as research assistants, xiv–xv, 129–30, 159; as research objects, 24; worried about species decline, 57–58

"death of the subject," xi

deep time, 4, 31–43, 48; affect and, 34–35; anthropocentrism and, 34, 37; defined, 34–35; as difficult to conceive, 33–34, 36, 39; as experienced by horseshoe crabs, 36, 42–43, 135, 159; the fossil record and, 36; and the future, 36–37; humans as a speck in, 67; as increasing human perspective, 66; vs. lived time, 32–33, 39–40; measurement of, 34

Deepwater Horizon oil spill, 170n46

disasters. See ecological catastrophe; Hurricane Sandy

disenchantment: under late capitalism, 40–42; science as, 168n13. See also enchantment; rational calculation

Dooren, Thom van, 131

Earth Day, 68, 117, 152

ecological catastrophe, 67, 141, 160, 170n46; and the Anthropocene, 50; enormity of, 35; urban beaches as image of, 129. See also climate change

eggs (horseshoe crab): 64, 69, 113, 128; burying, 9, 35, 91; censusing of, 142–44; contamination of, 29; clutch of, 82; density of, 24, 93; digging for, 30, 136, 143–44; fertilization of, 82–84, 88, 137; laid through gonopores, 82; life expectancy of, 77; method for collecting, 144; protection of, 114; structure of, 82. See also reproduction

Ellis, Erle, 50

empathy: as anthropocentric, 34, 157; as anthropomorphic, 73, 157; for nonhuman animals, 2, 157; for satellite males, 83, 87; sensorial, 161; for vertebrates vs. invertebrates, 6. See also intraspecies mindfulness

enchantment, 32, 39–42; horseshoe crabs as source of, 41–42; and play, 159–60; restoration of, 67, 159. See also disenchantment

endangerment: categories of, 25–26; criteria for, 58; of horseshoe crabs, 4, 28, 153; of honeybees, 14; human complicity in, 32; implications of the label, 31; as normative category, 65; as reflection of human priorities, 46; workshops about, 24. See also horseshoe crabs, threats to

endotoxins: use of horseshoe crabs in detecting, 4, 27–28; "dangers" of, 106, 108, 118; defined, 106, 166n2. See also Gram-negative bacteria; Limulus amoebocyte lysate (LAL) test; Tachypleus amoebocyte lysate (TAL) test

enmeshment: of agency, 137; as anthropomorphizing, 93; in blood donation, 98; different dimensions of, 69–70; at different scales, 13; of humans and honeybees, 23; of humans and horseshoe crabs, 4, 14, 16; and human precarity, 57; as incomprehensible, 152–53; and intraspecies mindfulness, xiii; the mesh (concept), xiii, 75, 93, 98; as moral horizon, 67; vs. specific etiology, 128. See also entanglement

entanglement, 45, 47; in Actor–Network Theory, 138; as ambivalent, 65; of author and informants, 75; in coming to matter, 4; of humans and horseshoe crabs, xii, 4, 13, 15, 23, 128, 157; of humans and insects, 13, 22; intraaction in, 23; of knowledge and objects, 24; and toxins, 13. *See also* enmeshment

Environmental Protection Agency, 147

epistemology, xi, 22; and authority, xi; and deep time, 33; vs. ontology, xii, 158, 162; somatic, 158; transgressive, 93

ethical responsibility: to avoid anthropocentrism, 66; conservation as, 51, 57; intraspecies mindfulness as, 23

external fertilization, defined, 82. *See also* eggs

extinction: defined, 167n26; fossil record, 49; mass, 2, 25, 32, 47–48; "extinction vortex," 49

"feeling for the organism," 136, 173n14

female mate choice (horseshoe crabs), 83–92; monandry vs. polyandry in, 83, 90; scientific interest in, 86; as reproductive agency, 89; as understudied, 85. *See also* amplexus; reproduction; satellite males

femininity: and epistemic authority, ix–x, xiii; and size, 80

feminist studies, xiii, 162; of science, 44. *See also* new materialisms

Ferullo, Chris, 145

field notes: from Plumb beach, 1, 19–21; from horseshoe crab conservation conference, 15–16; from Cedar Key, Florida, 63–64

fishermen. *See* harvesting

Food and Drug Administration (FDA), 18; blood donation policies, 103–4; as not licensing synthetic pyrogen tests, 124; required tests for injectables, 107

Fortey, Richard, 37, 41, 50

fossil record, 31, 49; and deep time, 36; of horseshoe crabs, 8

Frazier, Ian, 105

Freedom Worship Baptist Church, 37

Gateway National Recreation Area, 129

gender: assumptions about, 70, 75, 159; norms, 33, 71, 74, 163. *See also* androcentrism; female mate choice; femininity; heterosexual imperative; intolerant females; reproduction; satellite males

genetic testing, 44

geologic time. *See* deep time

Geryasio, Darcy, 80

global warming, 2, 4; as ecological crisis, 133; enormity of, 35, 142; everyday experience of, 144; extreme weather due to, 132, 134; as hyperobject, 28, 46, 128, 141–42, 147, 159; pesticides as contributing to, 57; rising sea levels caused by, 134. *See also* climate change; ecological catastrophe; hyperobject; sea-level rise

globalization, 28, 117

god trick (concept), 73

Gould, Stephen Jay, 36

Gram-negative bacteria: defined, 106; types of, 106–7; as resistant to sterilization, 107. *See also Limulus* amoebocyte lysate (LAL) test; *Tachypleus* amoebocyte lysate (TAL) test

greenwashing, 151–52

groin (breakwater), defined, 132

grounded theory, x, 11; defined, 94–95, 166n1

Gulf States Marine Fisheries Commission, 121

habitat (horseshoe crabs), xv, 18, 26, 28; variation in, 133

habitat generalists, 139

Haraway, Donna, 13, 52, 73; on becoming with, 157; on naturecultures, xiv, 165n8

Hart, Mary, xv; on female mate choice, 84–92

Hartline, Haldan Keffer, 166–67n7

Hartsock, Nancy, xi

harvesting (horseshoe crabs): for bait, 4, 17, 139, 172n29; for black market, 18, 140; as informal economy, 102; for pharmaceutical industry, 101; prices, 102, 171n11 (chap. 4); regulation of, 114–17; techniques, 110–11. *See also* bleeding; poaching

Heise, Ursula, 26

Helmreich, Stefan, 8

heterosexual imperative, 68, 74, 91, 93. *See also* reproduction

Hiroshima, atomic bombing of, 16

Holocene, 49–50

honeybees, xiii, 1, 11, 51, 53, 149; as co-producers of knowledge, 69; disease among, 57; as entangled with humans, 13, 47, 57; gendered assumptions about, 70; as indicator species, 3; and intraspecies mindfulness, 23; lifespan of workers, 34; and masculinity, 14; as outliving humans, 56

"Horseshoe Crab" (song), 155–56

horseshoe crabs: as aliens, 8, 31; as ancient survivors, 8, 31, 37, 41, 48–49; anatomy of, 6–10; as babies, 1–2, 20, 159; book gills of, 82; bred in captivity, 9, 26, 110; as commodity species, 106; compared with victims of the atomic bomb, 17; as co-producers in knowledge, 69; diet of, 7; different species of, 8; exploitation of, 15–18, 163; everyday life of, 36, 147, 150; eyes of, 6, 166–67n7; geolocation app for, 58; handled by the author, 1–3, 20–21, 30, 64, 126, 136, 158, 161; human uses of, 3–4; as informants, 30; as juveniles, xv, 19, 29; as not true crabs, 9; as outliving humans, 163; playing with, 3, 129, 158; size by sex, 80; telson of, 3, 6; threats to, 17–18. *See also* agricultural fertilizer; am-plexus; becoming with; biomedicine; bleeding; blood; carapace; censusing; conservation; creationism; deep time; eggs; enchantment; endangerment; endotoxins; female mate choice; fossil record; habitat; habitat generalists; instar; mating scars; molting; reproduction; satellite males; sentinel species; site fidelity; spawning; stabilomorphs; tagging; trash animals; trilobites; trilobite stage; *and generally Horseshoe Crabs: Prehistoric Paramedics* (film)

humanism, 10–12; defined, 10–11; and sociology, 10–11

Hurricane Sandy, 132, 143

hyperobject, definition of, 141. *See also* global warming

"ice age," 50

indicator species. *See* sentinel species

Industrial Revolution: as beginning of the Anthropocene, 50

Ingold, Timothy, 45

instar, 9, 77–78; defined, 77. *See also* trilobite stage

interdependence. *See* entanglement; enmeshment

Intergovernmental Panel on Climate Change, 134

International Union for the Conservation of Nature (IUCN): as author of the Red List, 25–26, 54–55, 146; as organizer of IUCN Horseshoe Crab Specialist Group, 25, 54–55

International Workshop on the Science and Conservation of the Horseshoe Crab, 15–16, 25, 55, 99–100

Interstate Fishery Management Plan for Horseshoe Crabs, 173n23

intolerant females (horseshoe crabs), 90–92, 160; defined, 92; political implication of the term, 91–92. *See also* female mate choice

intraaction: of all things, 152; defined, 23; of humans and crabs, xii–xiii, 16–17, 23, 42; of researcher and object, 133, 137–39; sensorial, 161–62. *See also* intraspecies mindfulness

intraspecies mindfulness: 129, 153, 157; and Actor–Network Theory, 138; defined, 23, 136–37; and enmeshment, xiii. *See also* empathy

invertebrates: as "silent majority," 166n6; suffering of, 6, 166n5; vs. vertebrates, 6

iron cage of rationality, 40

Iwasaki, Yumiko, 43, 48, 53

Jamaica Bay, 129; merits of swimming in, 168n33

Jamaica Bay Institute for Science and Resilience, 60

Japanese Society for the Preservation of the Horseshoe Crab, 16

Keller, Evelyn Fox, 173n14

Kirksey, Eben, 45, 47

Kosut, Mary, xiv, 13, 22–23, 122

Kreamer, Gary, xv

Latour, Bruno, 138

Lévi-Strauss, Claude, 14, 156–57, 167n21

Levin, Jack, 100, 105, 109

Limulus amoebocyte lysate (LAL) test: applications of, 108–9, 119; as destructive test, 109; exaggeration of benefits of, 118–19; as FDA standard, 18, 109; function of, 27, 108–9, 111; invention of, 100, 105; possibility of running out of, 125; profitability of, 105–6; as pyrogen test, 106–7; as replacing animal testing, 109–10; as stressful for horseshoe crabs, 27, 111–12; technique for, 112; xenophobic fears about, 122

Limulus polyphemus (North American horseshoe crab), 8, 79, 84, 111, 135, 158; designation as Vulnerable, 26, 31, 54, 65, 153, 158

Lonza Switzerland, 117, 123

Loveland, Bob, 17–18, 135

mad cow disease (bovine spongiform encephalopathy), 57, 96

magic. *See* enchantment

Malinowski, Branislaw, 36

mansplaining, ix

Marx, Karl, 98

mated pairs (horseshoe crabs). *See* amplexus; female mate choice; mating scars; reproduction; satellite males

materiality, 13, 150; vs. representation, 72, 160

mating scars, 80–81; as a term, 80. *See also* amplexus; reproduction

Mattei, Jennifer, 84, 148; on compassion for invertebrates, 5; on egg contamination, 29; on extinction vortices, 140; as founder of Project *Limulus*, 61; on tagging horseshoe crabs, 62–63

McClintock, Barbara, 173n14

Mercury Lounge, 155

microsociology, x

molting (horseshoe crab), 9, 77–78; carapace in, 43, 77–78

Moore, Jason, 52

Morton, Timothy, 28, 46, 141

Moses, Robert, 131

multispecies ethnography, xii, 24, 71, 122, 159; defined, 22; as new genre, 138

Museum of Natural History, 37

Nagasaki Prefecture, Japan, 4

National Park Service, 129, 132, 147

nature, xiii; as discursive production, 45; vs. culture, 22

naturecultures, xiv

neoliberalism, 129

Neolithic Period, 36

new materialisms, 12–13; feminist, 13

New York City: crumbling infrastructure of, 127; as object of human site fidelity, 131

New York State Environmental Conservation Police, 115–16

nonhuman animals, 5, 14, 45, 56–57, 62, 122, 131; and Actor–Network Theory, 138; fluid exchange with, 99; and humans, xi, xiii, 21, 28, 132, 170n46; and intraspecies mindfulness, 23, 136; and nature, xiii; as others, 30; reproduction of, 68, 74; as symbolic ciphers, 69; testing on, 99, 109–10, 172n34. *See also* critical animal studies; honeybees; horseshoe crabs; queen bees; trash animals

nonhuman objects, 12, 161–62; as actors, 144. *See also* nonhuman animals

Norgaard, Kari Marie, 35

Novitsky, Tom, xv; on "dangers" of endotoxins, 108; on benefits of LAL testing, 118; on underregulation of TAL testing, 121

objectivity: as cultural production, 69; as accountability, 71–72; "phantom objectivity," 40; in science, 90, 92. *See also* positivism

ontology: of matter, 13; in posthumanism, 12; vs. epistemology, xii, 2, 71, 162. *See also* crabness; epistemology

Orr, Jackie, 170n46

oxygen: low levels in from oceans, 135; low levels in sand, 144–45, 174n31

Pangea, 36

penetrometer, 144–45

pharmaceutical industry, xv, 100; as culpable for poor treatment of horseshoe crabs, 101

place-attachments, 131

Plumb Beach, New York, xv, 18–21, 48, 94, 159; citizen science at, 60–61; as ordinary, 149; research projects at, 133; restoration projects at, 132; as spawning ground, 76, 78, 137; as urban beach, 126–53; uses of, 132

poaching (horseshoe crabs), as fertilizer, 17–18, 144–15; as common, 114; news stories about, 115, 173n24

polar bears, 53, 74; as charismatic megafauna, 56; extinction of, 62

politics, of human–nonhuman relations, xiii

Pooley, Simon, 46

positivism, in sociology, 12

posthumanism, definition of, 12–13

precarity: defined, 56; in the experience of time, 66; as ordinary, 170n46; and nonhuman animals, 56–57

primordial soup, 41

Project *Limulus*, 61–62; as successful citizen science project, 63

Pulse Nightclub, 97, 104

pyrogen testing; as growth industry, 119–20; on rabbits, 172n34; with synthetic tests, 123–24. *See also* endotoxins; *Limulus* amoebocyte lysate (LAL) test; *Tachypleus* amoebocyte lysate (TAL) test

Pyrogene, costs of switching to, 123–24

qualitative research, 12, 15, 18, 24; defined, 165–66n1; as immersive, x–xi. *See also* sociology

queen bees: "balling" of, 73; as empowering, 72; human interest in, 71–73; pity for, 73; reproductive labor of, 72–73. *See also* anthropomorphism; empathy; reproduction

queer studies, xiii, 12

rabbits, pyrogen testing on, 109–110, 172n34
Raffles, Hugh, 22
Rankin, Jim, 38
rate of speciation, 44
rational calculation: as disenchanting, 40–42, 66; humanist bias of, 10, 12; as obstacle to understanding, 160, 166
reproduction (sexual) of horseshoe crabs, 68–69, 75, 77; human, 170n8; human fascination with, 72–74; human narratives about, 68–69, 82; gendered assumptions about, 70, 75; life expectancy in, 77, 171n12 (chap. 3); media products about, 68, 74; nonhuman animal, 170n8; role of egg and sperm cells in, 45, 74, 82. *See also* amplexus; female mate choice; heterosexual imperative; intolerant females; mating scars; queen bees; satellite males; spawning
Rhogam, 103
Rockaway Inlet, 129
Rose, Deborah Bird, 131
Ryder, Richard, 5

Sandy Point, Connecticut, 63, 79
Sasebo, Japan, 15, 25, 55
satellite males, 83–88, 137; defined, 83; author's empathy for, 83, 87; human identification with, 87; as reproductively successful, 87–88
"Science Wars," 11
scientists, as informants and objects of study, 75
sea-level rise, 4, 147; affective understanding of, 150; effect on horseshoe crabs, 129, 131, 141; effect on shoreline, 128; extreme weather as a result of, 134; as global, 129; as "hot, sour, and breathless," 135; as intraaction, 137; as rarely thought about, 142; shoreline engi-

neering, 29, 132, 135, 147, 160; shoreline erosion as result of, 3, 29, 127, 129, 141, 147. *See also* beach nourishment; climate change; global warming; Hurricane Sandy
sentinel species (indicator species): defined, 3–4; horseshoe crabs as, 3–4, 18, 29
September 11 attacks, 97
shoreline engineering. *See* sea-level rise
shoreline erosion. *See* sea-level rise
Shuster, Carl N., Jr., xv, 14, 30, 167n21
Singer, Peter, 5
site fidelity: as affective longing, 131; defined, 28–29; in horseshoe crabs, 28–29, 130, 139; in humans, 131. *See also* reproduction; spawning
site tenacity. *See* site fidelity
Slothrust (band), 155
slow death, 152
Smith, Dave, xv; on risk tolerance, 64; on endangerment, 65
sociology: animals in, 4–5; humanism in, 10–11; layers in, 24; positivism in, 12. *See also* qualitative research
South Shore, Long Island, New York, xv
spawning (horseshoe crabs), 26–27, 58, 139; defined, 26; effect of bleeding on, 113; as exciting for humans, 26, 137; high tides during, 6, 8–9; and site fidelity, 28, 79,139; vulnerability during, 47–48. *See also* amplexus; reproduction; site fidelity
species: and biological essentialism, 45–47; controversy in classifying, 46–47; differing definitions of, 44; as discursive production, 45; and kinship, 168–69n16; risk tolerance of, 64; usefulness as a term, 45–47. *See also* conservation; rate of speciation; species being; species decline; speciesism

species being: defined, 98; feeling of, 98, 163
species decline, 25–26, 50; efforts to ameliorate, 52; of horseshoe crabs, 145–148, 153, 158
speciesism, 5, 12, 15, 75, 163; defined, 5
sperm, xiii, 14; count of, x, 11; gendered assumptions about, 70, 74
stabilomorphs, horseshoe crabs as, 8
standpoint theory: xii, 22; defined, 165n4
Stengers, Isabelle, 168n13
Stewart, Kathleen, 142, 149
Strauss, Anselm, 94–95, 166n1
sustainability studies, 169n37
symbolic interactionism, ix, 11
symbolic ciphers, 69

Tachypleus amoebocyte lysate (TAL) test, 27–28; as more unregulated than LAL testing, 120–22
Tachypleus gigas (Malaysian or Indonesian horseshoe crab), 8; in TAL testing, 120
Tachypleus tridentatus (Chinese or Japanese horseshoe crab), 8, 53; in TAL testing, 120
tagging, of horseshoe crabs, xv, 62–63, 85, 162
Taussig, Michael, 40
tenderness, xi–xiii
thinking: with animals, 14, 156–57, 167n21; vs. being, 157
Titmuss, Richard, 102
trash animals, horseshoe crabs as, 159
trilobite stage, 77; defined, 83

trilobites, as relatives of horseshoe crabs, 8, 43–44, 168n15
Tsing, Anna, 52, 56
Tsuchiya, Keiji, 15–17

urban beaches, xv, 1, 4, 24, 53, 126; as dirty, 129–33, 153. See also beach nourishment; sea-level rise
urban beekeeping, x, 52, 150
U.S. Fish and Wildlife Service, 61, 63

vertebrates. See invertebrates
Volkswagen: "clean diesel" claims, 126, 150; scandal and recall, 151–53
vulnerability: empathy through, 73; of horseshoe crabs to predation, 77; of humans, 4, 15, 56, 122, 127; IUCN classification of Limulus as Vulnerable, 26, 31, 54, 65, 153, 158; site fidelity and, 28, 139. See also endangerment; precarity

Weber, Max, 40, 93
Wellbaum, Leah, 155–56, 163
Wells, H. G., 112
Wilder, Thornton, 174n3
Wolfe, Cary, 13
womansplaining, ix
wonder. See enchantment

xenophobia. around LAL testing, 122

Youatt, Rafi, 53
Yusoff, Kathryn, 51

Zika virus, 56

ABOUT THE AUTHOR

Lisa Jean Moore is Professor of Sociology and Women's Studies at Purchase College, State University of New York. Her previous books include *Sperm Counts: Overcome by Man's Most Precious Fluid*; with Monica Casper, *Missing Bodies: The Politics of Visibility*; and, with Mary Kosut, *Buzz: Urban Beekeeping and the Power of the Bee*. She lives in Crown Heights, Brooklyn, with her family.